Praise for *Growing I*

"In *Growing Big Dreams*, Robert Moss skillfi world of the shaman and the dreamer, the wou. minding us that the drought of dreaming characteristic of our ever, may be the cause of our many dysfunctions, he eases us into the twilight zone where synchronicities spring forth and treasures await. With all the allurements of a born storyteller, he urges us to hunt the dreams that are hunting us, to call soul back into our lives. Like a true lover, he sends us twelve gifts to teach us how to manifest our inner power and beauty. Just reading him is a joy, and this book is one more feather in the cap of a master teacher of dreaming."

— **Catherine Shainberg, PhD**, author of
Kabbalah and the Power of Dreaming

"Robert Moss is internationally known for teaching the power of the art of dreaming. In *Growing Big Dreams* he goes far beyond a typical book on the subject. He is a brilliant writer and an incredible storyteller, and you will find magic in this book: You will learn how to consult with your dreams to create your soul's desire, how to travel through time, and aspects of the landscape of dreams that no other author has approached.... This is a remarkable book that's deeply relevant to our times, giving us keys to remembering our soul's purpose and living our bigger story."

— **Sandra Ingerman, MA**, award-winning author of
Walking in Light and *The Book of Ceremony*

"A magnificent gift from a master of dreams. Robert Moss's twelve secrets unpack a world of magic, showing us various ways to enter the healing world of our dreams. After my first reading, I followed the wisdom of *Growing Big Dreams* and was immediately rewarded with guidance from the dream world. I'm already rereading the book and recommending it to my friends and students. This is a book you'll want on your bookshelf to refer to over and over again."

— **HeatherAsh Amara**, author of *The Warrior Heart Practice*

"An essential read for these times when we must reaffirm our dreams as oracles, our stories as valuable, and our imaginations as the fertile ground in which the future of our global collective is already being seeded. Robert Moss writes of our 'dream drought' as a pandemic and shows that where there is struggle and setback, there is also opportunity."

— **Danielle Dulsky**, author of *The Holy Wild* and *Sacred Hags Oracle*

"In *Growing Big Dreams*, Robert Moss shows why Einstein was correct when he famously declared, 'Imagination is more important than knowledge.' This splendid book is one of the clearest guides to unleashing the power of our imagination through our dream life. Our imagination is the gateway to creativity. To open the gate, let dream shaman Robert Moss be your guide."

— **Larry Dossey, MD**, author of *One Mind*

"A fascinating journey into the art of dreaming, *Growing Big Dreams* brings your inner imagineer to life. In this playground of intuition, you can discover new dimensions of yourself, along with the creativity and insight that can lead to real awakening."

— **Kim Chestney**, author of *Radical Intuition*

"Robert Moss's books are full of good-sense reminders that our dreams are the road map for where we are and what vistas await. Frankly, we need this book right now when the whole world seems to be changing....Moss has filled *Growing Big Dreams* with signposts to follow, a GPS of the inner realm, and maps to show us the way toward a possible future self."

— **Normandi Ellis**, author of
Hieroglyphic Words of Power and *Dreams of Isis*

"Robert Moss is the ultimate dream guide for our time, with his deep knowledge of history as well as his incredible shamanic background, not to mention his own extensive travels to the far regions of this world many times over. In his latest work, he brings a complete gift to masterful dreamers as well as those who are new to the path of dreams. We need this book now more than ever."

— **Kelly Sullivan Walden**, bestselling author of *It's All In Your Dreams*

"With the warmth and ease of an experienced magic maker, Robert Moss weaves a spell that binds together stories, myths, synchronicities, and the secret desires of the soul as expressed in dreams. He invites us to explore the power of images and childlike play, grow our own big stories, and manifest our heart's desire. A beautiful book that carries a much-needed vision of bright possibility during these times of global shift."

— **Dr. Clare Johnson**, author of
The Art of Lucid Dreaming and *The Art of Transforming Nightmares*

"Robert Moss has a big, strong voice. He's funny and deeply serious at the same time, erudite about a wide range of dream lore and dream practices. He shows that the way of dreams is a way of growth — how we grow from our dreams, how we grow into them, how we can grow bigger in heart than we've ever imagined — if only we learn to trust what we imagine."

— **Rodger Kamenetz**, author of *The History of Last Night's Dream*

GROWING
BIG
DREAMS

Also by Robert Moss

Active Dreaming

The Boy Who Died and Came Back

Conscious Dreaming

The Dreamer's Book of the Dead

Dream Gates: A Journey into Active Dreaming (audio)

*Dreamgates: Exploring the Worlds of Soul, Imagination,
and Life beyond Death*

Dreaming the Soul Back Home

Dreaming True

Dreamways of the Iroquois

Mysterious Realities

The Secret History of Dreaming

Sidewalk Oracles

*The Three "Only" Things: Tapping the Power of Dreams,
Coincidence, and Imagination*

The Way of the Dreamer (video)

Fiction

The Cycle of the Iroquois

Fire along the Sky

The Firekeeper

The Interpreter

Poetry

Here, Everything Is Dreaming: Poems and Stories

GROWING BIG DREAMS

MANIFESTING YOUR
HEART'S DESIRES
THROUGH TWELVE SECRETS
OF THE IMAGINATION

ROBERT MOSS

New World Library
Novato, California

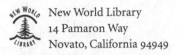 New World Library
14 Pamaron Way
Novato, California 94949

Text design by Tona Pearce Myers

Library of Congress Cataloging-in-Publication Data

Names: Moss, Robert, date, author.
Title: Growing big dreams : manifesting your heart's desires through twelve
  secrets of the imagination / Robert Moss.
Description: Novato, California : New World Library, 2020. | Includes bibli-
  ographical references. | Summary: "*Growing Big Dreams* shows readers how
  to manifest the life they truly desire by utilizing the power of the creative
  imagination. The author describes a wide array of techniques to access
  the creative imagination, including conscious dreaming, visualization,
  summoning spirit guides, cultivating psychic states of consciousness, and
  more."-- Provided by publisher.
Identifiers: LCCN 2020026350 (print) | LCCN 2020026351 (ebook) |
  ISBN 9781608687046 | ISBN 9781608687053 (ebook)
Subjects: LCSH: Dreams. | Parapsychology.
Classification: LCC BF1091 .M7944 2020 (print) | LCC BF1091 (ebook) |
  DDC 154--dc23
LC record available at https://lccn.loc.gov/2020026350
LC ebook record available at https://lccn.loc.gov/2020026351

First printing, September 2020
ISBN 978-1-60868-704-6
Ebook ISBN 978-1-60868-705-3
Printed in Canada on 100% postconsumer-waste recycled paper

 New World Library is proud to be a Gold Certified Environmentally Responsible Publisher. Publisher certification awarded by Green Press Initiative.

10   9   8   7   6   5   4   3   2   1

Contents

Introduction   1

Invocation of the Gatekeeper   13

1. Dreams Show You the Secret Wishes of Your Soul   15

2. Your Great Imagineer Is Your Magical Child   47

3. What Is in Your Way May Be Your Way   69

4. You Have Treasures in the Twilight Zone   91

5. Your Body Believes in Images   109

6. Your Big Story Is Hunting You   131

7. You Are Magnetic   159

8. There Is a World of Imagination, and It Is Entirely Real   185

9. If You Can See Your Destination, You Are Halfway There 215

10. You Can Grow a Dream for Someone
    Who Needs a Dream   229

11. You Don't Have to Drive Used Karma   249

12. The Stronger the Imagination,
    the Less Imaginary the Results   271

Envoi: Notes for the Road   297
Blessing for the Road   301
*Appendix: The Lightning Dreamwork Game
   and the Dream Reentry Technique*   303
Notes   307
Bibliography   319
Resources   331
About the Author   333

Introduction

*The path to heaven doesn't
lie down in flat miles.
It's in the imagination with which
you perceive this world, and the
gestures with which you honor it.*

— MARY OLIVER, "The Swan"

The greatest crisis of our lives is a crisis of imagination. We come to a dead stop because there is a barrier in front of us and we can't imagine a way to get around or over it. Our work space feels like it is walled with cement blocks that are closing in more tightly every day, but we can't imagine where we would go if we quit. We can't breathe in an airless relationship but can't picture how to take off. We look in the mirror, when we dare, and see the age lines, the skin blemishes, maybe the thinning hair, not the beauty that we may carry inside.

We go on repeating to ourselves the tired old stories, strapped onto us by family or past histories of defeat and disappointment. Or we cling to memories of brighter days, or that win on the high school sports field, or that sweet summer romance, or that medal for valor, or that early success that was never repeated. Either way, by nursing grief or guilt or nostalgia, we manage to go through life looking in the rear-view mirror, stuck in the past, never fully available to the present moment.

Or we miss the moment by carrying anxiety about the future,

screening mental scenarios for what could go wrong. We give ourselves a hundred reasons not to take the risk of doing something new, something that would take us beyond the gated communities of the mind into the wilds of creative adventure.

Conscious of it or not, we go around repeating our negative mantras. *I'm too old. I'm not pretty enough. I don't have the money. People always let you down. People don't change. I'm so tired.* You don't think you do this? Pause for a moment. Take off the headphones. Listen to what's playing on your inner soundtrack. It may be a song. *"Am I blue?"*

I confess there are days, between snowstorms in a northeastern winter, when my mood can slump and go the color of the dirty gray ramparts of ice on the curb in my small, gritty city. And more days like these in the shut-up times of the pandemic. I don't want to get out of bed even to walk the dog, who is waiting for me patiently. I may be stirred back to life by a dream or a cheering message from a loved one or hopes of an ocean beach vacation or a foreign adventure. But when I find it is still hard to rise above a low, lethargic mood and dump those negative mantras — *My legs hurt, I'm played out, I can't walk on the ice* — I call in one of the greatest life coaches I know.

I know him from his most famous book. Maybe you do too. His book is titled *Man's Search for Meaning.* His name is Viktor Frankl. He was an existentialist — which is to say, someone who believes that we must be authors of meaning for our own lives — and a successful psychiatrist in Vienna before Nazi Germany swallowed Austria in 1938. He was a Jew and a freethinking intellectual, two reasons for the Nazis to send him to a concentration camp. For several years he was in Auschwitz, the most notorious of the Nazi death camps.

In the camp, every vestige of humanity was taken from him, except what he could sustain in his mind and his heart. He was in constant pain, reduced to a near skeleton with a tattooed number on his arm, liable at any moment to be beaten or killed on the whim of a guard. He was there to be worked to death. He watched those around him shot or pummeled or carted off to the gas chambers every day.

He made an astonishing choice. He decided that, utterly deprived of freedom in the nightmare world around him, he would tend one precious candle of light within. He would exercise the freedom to choose his *attitude*. It sounds preposterous, if you don't know the story of what unfolded. When people tell us we have a bad attitude in ordinary circumstances, we are usually not grateful. The suggestion that we can choose our attitude when the world around us seems cold and bleak or we have suffered a major setback, even heartbreak, sounds cruel. But let's stay with Viktor Frankl.

When the light went out in his world, he managed to light that inner candle of vision. Despite the pain in his body and the screams and groans around him, he made an inner movie, a film of a possible life in a world where the Nazis had been defeated and Hitler was a memory. It was an impossible vision, of course, an escapist fantasy. There was no way he was going to survive Auschwitz.

But he kept working on his inner movie, night after night, as director, scriptwriter, and star. He produced a scene in which he was giving a lecture in a well-filled auditorium. His body had filled out, and he was wearing a good suit. The people in the audience were intelligent and enthusiastic. The theme of his lecture was "The Psychology of the Concentration Camps." In his movie, not only were the death camps a thing of the past; he had retained the sanity and academic objectivity to speak about what went on during the Holocaust from a professional psychiatric perspective.

This exercise in inner vision, conducted under almost unimaginably difficult circumstances, got Viktor Frankl through. One year after the war ended, in a good suit, he gave that lecture as he had seen himself doing in his inner movies.

What do we take away from this?

First, that however tough our situation may seem to be, we always have the freedom to *choose our attitude*, and this can change everything. Let's allow William James to chime in: "The greatest weapon against stress is our ability to choose one thought over another."

Second, that our problems, however bad, are unlikely to be quite as bad as the situation of someone who has been sent to a Nazi death camp. That thought may help us to gain perspective, to stand back from a welter of grief and self-pity and rise to a place where we can start to dream up something better.

Third, that *we can make inner movies*, and if they are good enough it is possible that they will play in the theater of the world.

If we take Viktor Frankl's example to heart, we see that *choosing your attitude* can be an exercise in creative imagination that is much more practical and original than trying to edit your inner soundtrack (though that is worth trying) or telling yourself that you can't afford the energy of a negative thought (you can learn to use the energy of any strong emotion, including grief and rage).

Would you like to make your own life movies, in which you enjoy the satisfaction of your deepest desires? Are you willing to grow a vision of bright possibility so rich and alive that it *wants* to take root in the world?

Then you want to learn to use your imagination. The word *imagination* comes from the Latin *imago*, or image. *Imagination* has been defined as the faculty that clothes the forces at play in the inner world in images so we can perceive and interact with them. *Phantasia*, from which we derive *fantasy*, is the Greek word for imagination. It means "making visible." The act of making visible makes it possible for humans to communicate with beings that are more than human. "Phantasia was the organ by which the divine world spoke to the human mind," Robert Johnson observed in *Inner Work*:

> From my experience I am convinced that it is nearly impossible to produce anything in the imagination that is not an authentic representation of something in the unconscious. The whole function of the imagination is to draw up the

4

material from the unconscious, clothe it in images, and transmit it to the conscious mind. Whatever comes up in the imagination must have been living somewhere in the fabric of the unconscious before it was given an image-form by the imagination.

This book will help you connect with your inner imagineer and become scriptwriter, director, and star of your own life movies, choosing your preferred genre and stepping into a bigger and brave story. Where do you find the material and inspiration for this?

1. Dreams show you the secret wishes of your soul. Let's start with your dreams. Every night, if you make the effort to catch some of what is going on, you will find that your dreams take you beyond what you already know. You have a personal film production company, behind the curtain of the world, that is making dreams exclusively for you. That comedy or horror flick, that romance or action-adventure, may be screened in the night to help you see where you are and how you are or to give you a glimpse of other life possibilities. In other dreams, you get out and about, you socialize, you make visits and receive visitations. And as I write this, in the era of a pandemic, it is both comforting and exciting to wake up to the fact that dreamers can travel without leaving home.

Dreaming, you are a time traveler. You travel to past times, to parallel times, and into the possible future. You scout out challenges and opportunities that lie ahead. Beyond seeing the future, it is possible that, during dreaming, the observer effect noted in physics comes into play and you take part in the selection of events that will manifest from a quantum soup of possibilities.

There is even more going on in your nights. Indigenous wisdom teaches that through dreams we learn the secret wishes of the soul. We are called to follow our hearts' desires, as opposed to the calculations of the ego and other people's agendas and expectations. We are recalled to our deeper life purpose and given sources and resources in a more profound reality that will help us to follow our path with heart.

2. Your great imagineer is your magical child. Don't doubt for a moment that you have the imagination required to grow a vision of manifesting your heart's desires that can carry you beyond the stuck places and the dark, dreary times. Your inner child is a master of dreams and imagination. She knows the magic of making things up. She engages effortlessly in the deep play that generates creative ideas without regard for consequences. Maybe you lost contact with her as you started to grow up and the adult world trod on her dreams. Maybe there was a time when her world seemed so cold and cruel that she wanted to run away, and she may actually have succeeded in running away, to a safe space in Grandma's house or a garden behind the moon. Maybe this is why you have been in a dream drought for so long: when she went away, you lost the beautiful, bright dreamer in you. In chapter 2, you are going to learn how to reclaim that magical child, how to convince her that you are safe and you are fun, so that you can bring her energy and joy and imagination into your current life.

3. What is in your way may be your way. The philosopher emperor Marcus Aurelius came to accept, as a rule for his own life, that the obstacle may be the way. When you find yourself blocked or challenged on your life road, that may be a prompt for you to look for a better way, to develop a needed skill, or to summon the pluck and perseverance to see something through. You'll want to look again at what you feel is blocking or opposing you on your life road. Sometimes a block is a pause button, indicating, *Not right now. Try later.* You may discover that a block has been placed in your way to induce you to find a better way. For every door that won't open or slams shut in your face, look for one that may be opening. For every setback, search for opportunity. Look for a gift in every wound or challenge, though this can be hard and may require hindsight from some distance away.

4. You have treasures in the twilight zone. The best place for you to find creative solutions, become a lucid dreamer with minimal effort, and meet your council of inner advisers is the twilight zone between sleep and awake. The liminal space of hypnagogia, as sleep researchers call it, has been a solution state for innovators in many fields, including science and technology. You can take off from here any night (or day, if you take naps) on lucid dream adventures. When you make it your game to have more fun in the twilight zone, you have an antidote for insomnia: why push yourself to sleep if you don't feel like it and can play wonderful virtual reality games without getting out of bed? You may even find yourself engaged in a type of horizontal meditation that leads to the continuity of consciousness prized by practitioners of the yoga of sleep and dreams. You will also find this an ideal space for making your own life movies, for creative visualization for manifestation and healing.

5. Your body believes in images. Medical science confirms that the body does not seem to distinguish between an imaginal event and a physical event. Imagine yourself racing down a ski slope in a blur of snow, and your body's electrical and chemical systems will respond as if you are out there on the mountain, as was confirmed long ago when sports psychologists wired up Olympic skiers. You are naturally psychosomatic. The thoughts, feelings, and corresponding images you entertain can bring you up or bring you down, sometimes at amazing speed, as they program the fantastic pharmaceutical factory inside your body. So you want to develop your own pharmacy of healing images. Dreams, happy life memories, and stories from mythology and folklore will be vital sources. You also want to call in the help of the animal doctors. Connecting or reconnecting with your spirit animals, which is at the heart of shamanic practice, gives an instant boost to your immune system and helps to clarify the natural path of your energies. You will also discover that in the imaginal realm you can travel to places of healing that are altogether real.

6. Your big story is hunting you. Australian Aborigines say that the big stories are hunting the right people to tell them, like predators stalking prey in the bush. The trick is to put ourselves in a place where the big stories can find us. We do that when we attend to our dreams and the dreamlike play of symbols and synchronicity in the world around us. We want to learn to step out of the tired old stories we have inherited from family, from other people telling us who we are, from personal histories of failure and defeat. When we are seized by the big story, we step beyond limiting definitions and beliefs. As P. L. Travers, the author of *Mary Poppins*, wrote, "Myth, by design, makes it clear that we are meant to be something more than our personal history." Great healing becomes available because we can now draw on the immense energy that is generated by the sense of serving a larger purpose and living a mythic life. The muse, or creative genius, and the intelligences of the world behind the world come to support our life projects, because we are following a deeper call.

7. **You are magnetic.** The world around you is going to reflect the changes you are making or need to make. You know, in your shivers, when synchronicity strikes. You feel the universe just got personal. Something from beyond the curtain wall of your ordinary perception is reaching through to give you the nod or a secret handshake or, alternatively, to pull the rug from under you. Awakening to synchronicity isn't merely about getting messages. It is about growing the poetic consciousness that allows you to taste and touch what rhymes and resonates in the world you inhabit. It is about how the world behind the world reveals itself by fluttering the veils of your consensual reality. Learning to look at the world around you as a living forest of symbols will help you grow your creative imagination as you expand the sensorium of your perception. You'll open to oracles that speak to you through the wind in the trees, through a vanity license plate, through an overheard snatch of conversation, through the exact conjunction between an unsolicited email and something you just said or started. This is a path of natural magic, and when you follow it you find yourself moving beyond self-limitation into a larger life.

8. There is a world of imagination, and it is entirely real. The imaginal realm is where mystics, shamans, and creators of all traditions have always wanted to go. There are schools and palaces and temples and pleasure gardens and places of healing here. Some have outlasted structures on earth. Wise teachers who have left their bodies on earth interact with students and colleagues who are traveling beyond the body, drawn together by mutual affinity. You will be aroused by travelers' reports of what they have experienced and accomplished in the magic library, in the House of Time, and in the scholar city of Anamnesis.

You will build your own creative studio in the imaginal realm and grow your Tree of Vision as a ladder between the three tiers of the shaman's cosmos and a launchpad for expeditions across time and space.

9. If you can see your destination, you are halfway there. Ancient Polynesian navigators were able to guide big voyaging canoes across thousands of miles of ocean without maps or instruments not only by reading wave and wind, birds and stars, but by a practice of conscious dreaming and visualization that produced a strong living vision of the destination. They taught that if you go toward your destination with all your inner senses — taste it, hear it, see it, smell it, feel it on your skin — you draw your destination toward you.

10. You can grow a dream for someone who needs a dream. Guaraní shamans perform soul healing by giving you the right words. When a shaman is talking to you, they say, he or she is giving you soul. Their term *ayvu* means "word soul." This comes alive in you when your heart is touched, and the magic words enter you and change you. We can learn to be soul singers and word doctors for each other. We can learn to grow a dream — a healing image, a soul story, a song that calls back soul — for someone who does not have a dream. You will be invited to learn the arts of dream growing, story swapping, and poetic enchantment for the benefit of others. You'll learn my powerful and original vision transfer technique, which has brought fire and spirit to many. You'll rejoice when you see it working in the life of someone you've been concerned about through the brightness of returning soul shining in their eyes.

11. You don't have to drive used karma. The time is always now. All other times — past, parallel, or future — can be accessed in this moment of now and may be revisioned and revised for the better. You are ready to learn how to reach across time to other versions of yourself and other members of your multidimensional family. You can communicate, mind to mind, with a younger self and provide the counsel or course correction she needs in her own now time. You can do this with personalities in other times whose dramas and relationships are relevant to your current life passages. You can check in with your parallel selves who made different choices and are following different event tracks in the many worlds, and you can share gifts and lessons. You are about to discover that you stand at the center of all times and need not be bound by past or alternate histories, including your résumé life and the demons under your bed.

12. The stronger the imagination, the less imaginary the results. Your world is as rich or poor, as alluring or dull, as you can imagine. You will have learned, by the end of this book, how to grow a vision your body believes and your Greater Self endorses, one so rich and strong it wants to take root in your world. When you move in the energy field of that vision, the world responds to you, because you are magnetic.

Now you generate events and encounters that open new doors, and your days sparkle with a champagne fizz of magic. Your dreams speak louder and brighter, and the extraordinary comes to meet you on any street corner. You have deep certainty that what your heart longs for is already accomplished. This is strange but *right*. The world gives you a thumbs-up. *Right on.*

Find your calling, and that changes everything. When you follow your soul's calling, your gifts are multiplied, because you draw supporting powers from the unseen, starting with your own creative spirit.

Oh, yes, you'll work at this, but you'll work in the spirit of deep play. Your old negative mantras and self-limiting beliefs will fall away like a discarded snakeskin. You'll play with the blocks that once defeated you. When you meet adversity, you'll waste no time in seeking to turn it into opportunity. You will act on the knowledge that the great trick in life is to find what you love and do it and let the world support you.

Imagine that.

Invocation of the Gatekeeper

The Gatekeeper, for me, is one of the most important archetypes that is active in our lives. He or she is that power that opens and closes our doors and roads. The Gatekeeper is personified in many traditions: as the elephant-headed Ganesha in India, as Eshu/Eleggua in West Africa, as Anubis in ancient Egypt, as Hermes or Hecate in ancient Greece. I open all my circles by invoking the Gatekeeper in a universal way.

They say in Spanish, "Tiene que pagar el derecho" — "You have to pay for the right to enter." In many traditions, it is customary to make an offering to the Gatekeeper when embarking on a project or a journey. The offering required of us may simply be to check in and show a little respect. At the start of this journey together, let me offer you the invocation of the Gatekeeper that I make every day:

> May my doors and gates and paths be open
> and the doors and gates and paths of those I love
> and my doors and gates and paths between the worlds.
> And may the doors and gates and paths of any who wish
> to do me or those I love any harm be closed.
> May it be so.

It works.

1

Dreams Show You
the Secret Wishes of Your Soul

Ondinnonk. I first heard this strange word in a dream. It was the kind of dream that starts in that drifty space between sleep and wake. I was lying flat on my back on my bed in the middle of the night when I saw a shape in midair. A double spiral. It reminded me of the spirals on the guardian stone of the Paleolithic temple tomb at Newgrange in Ireland, which I had visited on a recent trip. I felt myself rising from my body to flow through the spirals. Soon I was flying, out above the rooftops of my little city. This was not an exotic experience for me. I have always enjoyed flying in dreams and dreamlike states. Maybe you have too. Sometimes it's like swimming in air; sometimes it's more Superman-style, arms out. This time I was definitely beating wings. The wings of a red-tailed hawk, adjusted to my size. I experimented with flying as a bird, soaring and diving, catching a thermal, swooping down to look at something from an angle I could not have managed in my human body.

I felt myself drawn north, ever north, by a powerful intention. I let myself follow this intention, flying over a primal landscape that seemed to lack modern roads and development. Interstate 87, the Adirondack Northway, running beside Lake Champlain toward Montreal, was notably missing. I was drawn into a cabin in the woods somewhere near Montreal. An indigenous woman with long gray hair received me and spoke to me for what seemed like a long time. Her speech was cadenced and beautiful, like lake water lapping, wave upon wave, but I could not understand any of it. As she spoke, she stroked a beaded belt that hung from her shoulder. The design showed a she wolf with two small human figures, male and female. Romulus and Remus? No, this was a different culture, different people. I would need new eyes and especially new ears to understand.

This was the start of my engagement with a teacher from the First Peoples of the land where I am now living. I have written at length about the origins of this connection in other books. I have come to believe that I received the call because of my relationship, across centuries, with an Irishman whose birthplace I had recently visited. He came to the American colonies and lived among the Mohawk Indians like a tribal king. The *arendiwanen* — woman of power — who called me had tried to influence him in the earlier time they shared. Now she was reaching out to me, as master shamans are known to do, because she needed information from her future for the survival of her people in a time before the American Revolution. She spoke to me holding the credentials of the Mother of the Wolf Clan of the Kanienkehaka, the People of the Stone, known to whites as the Mohawk. Her language was studded with very ancient spiritual vocabulary, some of it from the Huron, her birth people. Her monologues continued over many nights. She never translated, and I was unable to step into one of those bubbles of understanding where everything is clear to you although it is coming from an utterly foreign language or mindset.

If I was going to make sense of these night seminars, which felt vitally important, I was going to have to do some work. Synchronicity brought me new friends from the Confederacy of the Longhouse (in which the Mohawk are Keepers of the Eastern Door), including Native linguists, who helped me decode some of what I was taking down phonetically. They had a hard time with my efforts to say the words I was given out loud. "It's not just your Anglo-Australian accent," they told me. "You are giving us very old words. It's like listening to Shakespeare's English. And there's some Huron in it."

The word *ondinnonk*, as I recorded it, eluded immediate translation. I eventually found it in a report sent by a Jesuit missionary from Huron country to his superiors during the harsh winter of 1647–1648. Father Ragueneau noted that the birth people of the shaman who had called me believed that "in addition to conscious desires…our souls have other desires which are, as it were, both natural and hidden…. They believe that our soul makes these natural desires known to us through dreams, which are its language…. They call this Ondinnonk, a secret desire of the soul expressed by a dream."

I was on the edge of understanding a view of dreaming and healing that may have been shared by all our ancestors. My night seminars continued. The Huron/Mohawk woman of power I came to call Island Woman reminded me that we need to look in dreams for clues to what the soul wants, what the heart yearns for, as opposed to the agendas of the everyday mind and the expectations other people lay on us. She told me, "Dreams that are wishes of the soul (when they are true dreams as well as wishes) can tell you that you need something you didn't know you needed or something you denied wanting because you felt ashamed for wanting it."

She taught me that in her tradition, it is the duty of caring people to gather round a dreamer and help her to read the secret wishes of the soul and take action to honor those wishes. This brings us to the first secret of imagination. To manifest our hearts' desires, we must start by knowing what they are. Our dreams will take us from the surface agendas of the everyday waking mind to the heart of this matter, to what the soul wants.

Dreaming Is Waking Up

Sargon did not lay down to sleep but he lay down to dream.
— "Sargon and Ur-Zababa"

From more than four millennia ago, we find a text confirming that dreaming is not fundamentally about what happens during sleep:

it is about waking up to a deeper reality and a deeper order of importance. Sargon, who was to become famous as a king, was dreaming on assignment. He was employed at the time as cupbearer to Ur-Zababa, the Sumerian king of Kish. Ill and anxious, the ruler of Kish asked Sargon to dream on his behalf. We then read, "Sargon did not lay down to sleep but he lay down to dream." People in his time believed that dreams are a field of interaction with gods and spirits. Sargon dreamed of a goddess, but his dream brought no comfort to his king. He saw the goddess Inanna as a beautiful young woman "high as the heavens and vast as the earth" who drowned Ur-Zababa in a river of blood. Ur-Zababa tried to have the dreamer killed, but he was the one who died, and Sargon took his throne. The people believed, because of his dream, that Sargon was under the aegis of the great goddess.

Across the human odyssey on the planet, most societies have valued dreams and dreamers for three reasons. First, they have understood that dreams give us access to sources of knowledge and wisdom beyond the ordinary mind, whether we call those sources god or goddess, or nature, or the ancestors, or the higher self. Second, it has also been widely understood that dreams show us the future, preparing us for challenges and opportunities that lie ahead. Third, most cultures have recognized that dreaming is related to medicine: dreams diagnose symptoms that may be developing in the body; they can be a source of imagery for self-healing; and they show us the state of our emotional and spiritual health.

Dreaming, from an ancient and indigenous perspective, is about more than what happens during sleep. It is about waking up. In ancient Egypt, where they did a lot of dreaming, the word for "dream," *rswt*, also means "awakening" and is written in hieroglyphs with a determinative in the form of a wide-open eye.

Consider the dream of a successful Wall Street businessman that called him to a different landscape and a different life. He dreamed of a golden key to a barn on a rural property. The dream and his sense of its promise were so powerful that he embarked on a search for that barn in that rolling green landscape. He found it near Austerlitz in upstate New York, twenty minutes' drive from the farm where the indigenous woman of power called me in my own dreams. When the Wall Street trader found that barn, he converted it into an amazing multipurpose space where he hosted one of my first weekend workshops, titled Soul Work. He decided that the barn and all it meant for him was his own central soul work and moved, little by little and then definitively, out of his high-paid, high-stress job on Wall Street to the country.

The Dreams Are Coming Back

In contemporary society, dream drought has been a widespread affliction, almost a pandemic. This is deadly serious, because night dreams are an essential corrective to the delusions of the day. They hold up a mirror to our everyday actions and attitudes and put us in touch with deeper sources of knowing than the everyday mind. If you lose your dreams, you may lose your inner compass. If your dreams are long gone, it may be because you have lost the part of you that is the dreamer.

Traditional Iroquois say bluntly that if we have lost our dreams, it is because we have lost a vital part of our soul. This may have happened early in life through what shamans call soul loss, when our magical child went away because the world seemed too cold and cruel. Helping the dream bereft to recover their dreams may amount to bringing lost souls back to the lives and bodies where they belong. This is something I teach and practice. In my story "Dreamtakers" in *Mysterious Realities,* I describe a shamanic journey to help return dream souls to people who have lost them.

If you are missing your dreams, you don't have to continue this way. There are several ways you can seek to break a dream drought any night you want to give this a try. You can set a juicy intention for the night and be ready to record whatever is with you whenever you wake up. You can resolve to be kind to fragments. The wispiest trace of a dream can be exciting to play with, and as you play with it you may find you are pulling back more of the previously forgotten dream.

If you don't remember a dream when you first wake up, laze in bed for a few minutes and see if something comes back. Wiggle around in the bed. Sometimes returning to the body posture we were in earlier in the night helps to bring back what we were dreaming when our bodies were arranged that way.

If you still don't have a dream, write something down anyway: whatever is in your awareness, including feelings and physical sensations. You are catching the residue of a dream even if the dream itself is gone. As you do this, you are saying to the source of your dreams, "I'm listening. Talk to me."

You may find that though your dreams have flown, you have a sense of clarity and direction that is the legacy of the night. We solve problems in our sleep even when we don't remember the problem-solving process that went on in our dreaming minds.

And recall that you don't need to go to sleep in order to dream. The incidents of everyday life will speak to you like dream symbols if you are willing to pay attention. Keep a lookout for the first unusual or striking thing that enters your field of perception in the course of the day and ask whether it could carry a message. When you make it your game to pay attention to coincidence and symbolic pop-ups in everyday life, you oil the dream gates so they let more through during the night.

Dream recovery may be soul recovery. Call back your dreams, and you may find you are bringing back a beautiful, bright dreamer who left your body and your life when life got too hard. Maybe she has been hiding out in Grandma's cottage or a garden behind the moon. Sometimes the right song will help to bring back that magical child with all the dreams fluttering like fireflies in her hair. I wrote a song in this cause, and you are welcome to try it:

The dreams are coming back.
Slow down and feel their firefly glow.
Stay still and hear the rustle of their wings.
Open like a flower
and let them feed from your heart.
Don't be afraid to remember
that your soul has wings
and you have a place to go flying.
The dreams are coming back.

Dreaming Can Get You Through

Dreaming helps get us through life. It can save us from a fall and even get us to the top. It puts us back in touch with our soul purpose and gives us everyday tools to thrive and survive. I was made vividly aware of this when I did an interview on a public radio station and a series of callers phoned in, eager to share their dreams.

A songwriter described how he wakes in the middle of the night with new songs playing in his mind. Sometimes they are complete, with words and music. Sometimes he has to work on them for a bit. He is in a long tradition of songwriters and composers who have plucked new pieces from their dreams. I was reminded of John Lennon's statement that "the best songs are the ones that come to you in the middle of the night and you have to get up and write them down so you can go back to sleep."

As we discussed diagnostic dreams, the host recalled the case of a man who dreamed a rat was gnawing on his throat. Shaken by the dream, he sought medical assistance, going from one physician to another until his throat cancer was detected and treatment began. He credited that dream with saving his life.

An IT professional recounted a situation in which his office was preparing to install a new system. The day before, his supervisor told him to go home and get some sleep. He took a nap and saw himself in a workaday situation. He saw and recognized the code he would be applying. Suddenly the screen in his dream went fuzzy, and a voice said firmly, "NO. It should be like this." The code changed.

When he went into the office the next day, he found that the code they were working with was wrong. He made the necessary changes, as had been done in the dream. "Good thing you caught that," his supervisor told him. The IT specialist explained to his boss that he had dreamed the correction. "Never heard of anything like that." The supervisor shook his head. "Maybe I should have my analysts do a lot more sleeping."

A woman caller spoke of a recurring dream theme whose full significance became clear to her only at the end of a long relationship. She dreamed again and again that her partner was missing. She couldn't find him or couldn't get through to him on the phone. Sometimes she felt he was hiding from her. By the time of the breakup, she had been compelled to recognize a long pattern of deception; in fundamental ways, her partner had been missing for much of the time they had been together.

We discussed what is going on when a dream theme repeats over and over. I suggested that it's either because we need to get the message or because we need to take action on that message. We may have a notion of what a recurring dream is about, but we can't bring ourselves to do what is necessary — which would be very understandable if we were dreaming our partner was missing. Like a helpful and well-informed friend who is looking out for us, the dream theme will come again and again until we do something about it.

Toward the end of the show, the host asked me to share a "big" dream of my own. How to pick one out of so many? Yet I knew at once which dream I would tell, because earlier in the program — when asked to explain how dreaming can help to move us beyond hatred and war — I had quoted a phrase in the Mohawk Indian language. The phrase is *tohsa sasa nikon'hren*. It literally means, "Do not let your mind fall."

We fall into dark times, in the traditional Mohawk cosmology, when we forget the higher world — the Earth in the Sky — from which we come. Our ability to heal our enmities and grow as a life-form depends on not forgetting a higher source of wisdom and a higher order of reality. Dreaming is the main link between our ordinary minds and that higher spiritual plane, a way of not letting our minds fall.

So I told a watershed dream from my life decades before, in which I entered a space where a circle of people who lived very close to the earth were singing and drumming. I hesitated at the entrance of their longhouse, fearing I was intruding. But they welcomed me into a place they had waiting for me.

At a certain point, I lay by the fire pit, at the center of the circle. One by one, the dream people came to me. They took red-hot coals from the fire and placed them over my ears and my eyes, and on my tongue, and over my heart. They sang in their own language, which I could now understand: "We do this to open your ears, so you may hear clearly. We do this to open your eyes, so you may see clearly. We do this to open your mouth, so you will speak only truth. And we do this" — placing the coal over the heart — "so that henceforth you will speak and act only from the heart."

I was fully lucid in this night vision. When I rose from my bed, I did no analysis. Vitally energized, I jumped in my car and drove to a lake in a state park east of my home. I promised to the lake and the trees and the red-tailed hawk that came knifing through the clouds, "Henceforth I will speak and act only from the heart."

On the darkest days, a dream like this can be a hearth fire and a homing beacon. Charging us with the power of a drama deeper than our ordinary reality, inciting us not to let our minds fall — these may be the biggest ways that dreaming helps us through.

The Many Faces of the Dream Guide

Our authentic spiritual allies and teachers come looking for us in dreams. They put on masks or costumes adapted to our level of understanding. There is an old Greek saying that "the gods love to travel in disguise." The sacred guide may appear in a form that has been shaped by our religious upbringing — or in a form that is wildly shocking to conventional beliefs.

The encounter with the guide may challenge us to brave up, to move decisively beyond the fear and clinging of the little everyday mind, in order to claim our connection with deeper sources of wisdom and true power.

The guide can take many forms, in dreams and on the roads of waking life. Our true spiritual teachers often use shock or humor in their efforts to wake us up to the real nature of things, and they love to play dress-up.

An earnest woman in a church group once asked me whether she could meet her guardian angel in her dreams. "Absolutely," I told her. When I began to explain the process of dream incubation, she interrupted me. "I've done that three times, and each time I asked to meet my guardian angel, I got Garfield the cat."

I asked her to describe to a visiting space alien, "Who is Garfield the cat?" She explained that he's greedy and always looking out for number one. "*Angel* means 'messenger,'" I pointed out to her. Could there be a message in Garfield's approach to life? This earnest woman, who had clearly given a lot of her life to service to others, thought about this. Then she stole a quick look at the buffet and asked, with a mischievous glint in her eyes, "Would it be okay to jump the line and get some chocolate cake while it's still left?" I reassured her that Garfield, as guardian angel, would say, "Absolutely."

The angel can be terrifying as well as funny. Rumi evokes beautifully the terror the Virgin Mary felt when the archangel Gabriel appeared to her in the moment of the Annunciation. In the presence of a supremely greater power, she leaves her body. Whereupon the angel says to her (in paraphrase): "You flee from me from the seen to the unseen, where I am lord and master? What are you thinking of?"

The truth of our dealings with higher sources of knowledge —

and above all the guide of our soul — is that we don't need to go looking for them because they are forever looking for us. After the terrible journey through all the hells of the medieval imagination, when Dante at last finds Beatrice (the guide appearing in the form of a beautiful woman he loved and lost), she complains to her retinue of angels that for many years she reached out to him in dreams, but he would not listen.

It may be that the most important spiritual teacher we can know is no stranger, but our own higher self. As we shall see, the liminal state of consciousness between sleeping and waking is an especially propitious time for conversation with this guide.

When You're Having a Baby in Your Dreams

I am cradling a newborn baby. She is beautiful, and her breath is soooo sweet. I place the baby carefully on a lambskin I have stuffed between books on a high shelf, making a kind of hutch. I arrange things so she can't roll off the shelf.

This was my dream from an afternoon nap. I woke with a sense of joy, tenderness, and wonder. In ordinary reality, it's most unlikely that I'll have another child. It's also most improbable that if entrusted with someone else's baby, I'd think it was appropriate to treat her this way. When I went down to my office after my nap, I found that contracts had arrived for a book I was planning to deliver that spring. This book would be my next literary baby, and the birth announcement came in the dream.

Baby dreams, like dreams on any theme, can be literal or symbolic. Expectant mothers dream of babies before they know they are expecting. During a pregnancy, baby dreams can rehearse both mother and child for the delivery. They can also be part of a process of "getting to know you" during which a new personality introduces itself and checks out the family it will be joining.

It's not unusual for pregnant mothers to dream of giving birth to animals. Indigenous peoples are quick to recognize that such dreams can bring knowledge not only of the character of the incoming soul but of its spiritual connections. A St. Louis television host told me on her show that when she was pregnant, she dreamed of giving birth to a lizard. "It just slid right out." Though startling, the dream was very auspicious. The delivery was smooth and quick. We also discussed qualities of the lizard that might belong to the new child, including the ability to grow back.

Baby dreams can be birth announcements from others in the family — advance word of a coming grandchild, for example. A dream announcing a literal birth may also be one that invites spiritual parenting. The First Peoples of my native Australia say that every soul on the way to birth needs a spiritual parent to help it find its way safely to its home in our world. The spiritual parent — a godparent in a deeper sense than that word has come to mean in English — may or may not be one of the birth parents. The connection between the incoming soul and the spiritual parent will be made in dreams.

As in my dream of the baby on the bookshelf, baby dreams are often about something other than a literal baby. If you dream of having a baby and you are unlikely or unable to give birth in a literal sense, ask yourself: *What new thing am I getting ready to bring through in my life? What will I create?* The creative act is always a process of birthing something new into the world.

A mother dreamed she had grown a huge pregnant belly. Probing gingerly, she found she was carrying twins, but there was something really strange about their anatomies. She was not enthusiastic about bearing twins at her stage in life. When we discussed the dream, I asked her to explain what was strange about the shapes she felt inside her dream self's swollen belly. "It was like they had hard, sharp edges," she said.

I asked her, "Hard and sharp like what?"

She responded, "Like books!" She decided she was pregnant with two books she hoped to write. Several years after the dream, she completed the first of those books and was writing the second.

Baby dreams can be more than birth announcements; they can suggest a care and nurturing plan we need to follow to support an initially vulnerable new life venture. A woman embarking on a new career dreamed she gave birth to a tiny, very fragile baby. She found it hard to hold the baby. It kept slipping from her grasp, so she would find herself struggling to maintain a safe grip or to catch it when it started to fall. This dream seemed to mirror, rather exactly, the challenges of birthing that new career.

Another dreamer was horrified when she let a newborn baby fall because she was overloaded with a huge crate full of stuff she associated with her work situation. Studying the dream, she realized she needed to let go of a job that was interfering with a creative project she wanted to bring through; better to lose the workload than the baby.

A birth announcement in our dreams may be about the beginning of new life in a spiritual sense. I was moved when a friend recently shared a dream in which she received a birth announcement from a deceased relative, announcing that he had been reborn on the Other Side.

Let's not forget that Gabriel, the archangel of the Annunciation — who brings the most celebrated of all advance birth announcements — is also the angel of dreams and the patron of travel on the astral plane.

Waters of Dreams

In drugstore dream dictionaries, we are told that water, as a dream symbol, is about emotions. Well, ye-e-es, it may be, but what you find in your dream waters and what I find may be very different things.

As with any dream, a dream of water may be symbolic, literal, or an experience of a separate reality. I have dreamed, over decades now, of being able to travel to the seafloor without any breathing problems and of encountering a Mother of the Deep and various other characters who seem to embody the elemental powers of the ocean. I have dreamed of sacred healing pools, and delight in mermaid coves, and the kind of inundation that brings fresh, new growth bursting into the world.

I have also noticed that some of our dreams of water may be simultaneously literal and symbolic. We dream of a tsunami or a hurricane, for example, and that occurrence turns out to be both a natural event that is played out in the world and a terrific emotional storm that blows up in our personal lives.

How water moves or fails to move in dreams is a very important source of guidance to me on the state of my body and my creative energy. Clogged pipes and logjams — in physical reality as well as in night dreams — alert me to the need to do some clearing and free up energy that needs to be in flow.

Water transforms, and it goes through its own transformations, from vapor to liquid to solid and back through the sequence. We come from the water, and our bodies are composed mostly of sea-water. Our dreams may open us to the teachings of water: to flow rather than to push, to stream round an obstacle rather than charge it head-on.

The waters of dreams offer entry into a different element, sometimes a different universe. In the deep, we may receive deep healing or encounter sacred powers.

In one of my workshops, a scientist from Virginia shared a wonderful dream in which he plunges deep into the ocean and then up into space, doing the butterfly stroke, repeating the motions until he is circling the planet. We didn't analyze this dream. We dove into it and enjoyed its energy. With the dreamer's permission and the aid of shamanic drumming, our whole circle accompanied him back into his dream in a marvelous adventure in group lucid dreaming. Some of us met creatures of the deep beyond those chronicled in *National Geographic*, interacting with mutual respect. Some joined dolphin pods. I enjoyed skimming the Pacific in waters around my native Australia.

When I think of water and the need for flow in any satisfying and creative life, I remember my favorite statement in the Forty-Two Negative Confessions that were made in the Judgment Halls of Osiris in an ancient Egyptian passage to the afterlife. In the presence of grim assessors, the traveling soul is required to swear that he or she has not committed various crimes and immoral acts. This is the affirmation I love best, as recorded in the so-called Egyptian Book of the Dead, whose literal title is *The Book of Going Forth by Day*: "I have not obstructed water when it should flow."

I want to be able to say that on any day.

You Are a Time Traveler in Your Dreams

Coming events cast a shadow before them. You have felt this some mornings as you emerge from a dream you may or may not remember. The shadow of a mass event can fall like the shadow of a mountain, over many. Most days the shadow is softer and more intimate. As you rub sleep from your eyes, the shadow that falls over you may be cast by your roving dream self, returning to your time with a sun that has not yet risen in your world at its back.

Once you wake up to the fact that you dream the future, you can grow the ability to do something more interesting: to harvest and apply dream information to shape the possible future for the better.

Our dreams are constantly coaching us for challenges and opportunities that lie ahead of us on the roads of life. We see things in our dreams that later happen; this is called precognition. We also see things that may or may not happen, depending on whether we do something with the information. It's possible that we rehearse *everything* that will take place in the future in our dreams, though we forget most of it — until later events catch up with a dream, and we experience that sense of déjà vu.

In dreams, we are time travelers. Released from Newtonian physics and our consensual hallucinations, the dream self travels into past time, future time, and alternate realities. As an *active* dreamer using the skills of shamanic journeying and lucid dreaming, you can travel consciously across time to scout the future for yourself and others and to grow a better future. You may draw confidence from the new physics, which confirms that in the limitless field of nonlocal mind the time is always now. All probable event tracks — past, future, or parallel — are accessible in this moment and may be revised for the better.

Every night, your dream self goes ahead of your waking self, scouting out challenges and opportunities that lie on the roads ahead. This activity is part of our human survival kit. Once you wake up to the fact that you dream events before they happen in regular life, you can graduate to the good stuff, which is changing your possible future for the better and becoming cocreator of your reality.

You are a natural psychic of a high order in your dreams, when you let down your left-brain inhibitions and just do it. You routinely practice precognition, clairvoyance, telepathy. Such powers are sometimes described as examples of ESP. Today scientists are reviving a better term invented by the great Victorian scientist of the unseen, Frederic Myers: *supernormal.* Scientists like Dean Radin maintain that quantum entanglement means supernormal phenomena are inevitable. Laboratory research confirms that supernormal abilities are for real and that the spectrum of possibility extends to retrocausation: reaching back across time to influence events in the past.

Your dreams may also be glimpses of a continuous life your parallel self is leading in a parallel world, in which you made different choices. Physicist Brian Greene speculates that we all have "endless doppelgängers" leading parallel lives in parallel universes. When you develop the skills of Active Dreaming, you can explore this experientially — and learn how to bring gifts and lessons from a parallel world into this one. Through these excursions, you will grow a personal geography of the multiverse and accumulate firsthand data on the reality of parallel worlds.

As a time traveler, you can journey to a younger self in her own now time. As a voice in her mind, you can provide the encouragement and counsel she may need at a time of unbearable pain or challenge. You can be the friend and protector she lacked when her need was great. From this can flow tremendous healing for both of you, you in your present time and her in her own time.

If You Can Dream It, You Can Do It

We have an unfortunate tendency to blow off dreams in which we are living high, romancing with Mr. Right or enjoying a marvelous home or working a job that seems far beyond what we think we can attain in ordinary life. Here's a story from India to encourage you to imagine that you may be able to manifest the secret wishes of your soul, as revealed in a dream, if you are willing to look for a map in the dream and set out on the road that will get you there.

The Sketcher of Pictures

The princess (and all women may be princesses or queens) is dreaming. She dreams of the perfect lover, who satisfies her in every way. The dream streams like silk. It smells like jasmine and honeysuckle.

She opens her eyes and howls with pain and loss, because although her surroundings are opulent, she knows no one like the man of her dreams.

Her father sees that she is very sad and asks what is wrong. When she tells him it has something to do with a dream, the king summons his wise men to listen to the dream and tell her what it means. They gather in a council chamber, ready to give their interpretations.

As the princess recounts her dream, a wild man rushes into the room, his hair a white storm about his shoulders. He is a rishi who lives in the woods and cares nothing for the rules of the court. He grabs a piece of paper, makes a quick sketch, and hands it to the girl.

When she looks at the picture, the princess is stunned. The rishi has captured the very essence of her dream lover.

Abandoning the conclave of dream interpreters, she runs after the wild man from the woods. When she catches up to him, she begs him to tell her the identity of her dream lover. "Who is he? Where can I find him?" Clearly the rishi knows the man of her dreams.

Good teachers don't give you everything all at once. The rishi says only, "The map is in your dream." Then he takes off into the woods.

The princess thinks about it. What does it mean, that a dream contains a map? When she thinks about it some more, she realizes that she was not with her lover among the clouds. She was in a bed in a room in a house in a city in a certain landscape. Though she recognizes none of these places, she has vivid memories of them and feels she would know them again.

So she sets out on a quest. In an Indian village, they may take hours to tell this part. There will be tigers, of course, and bandits, and deserts and snakes and all manner of perils. There will probably be elephants.

But let's catch up with the princess at the moment when her quest is almost over, because there on the horizon, after long travels and many ordeals, she sees the city from her dream. And now she is rushing through those streets to the house from her dream, and up the stairs to the bedroom from her dream, where she finds her lover rising from his dream of her.

It sounds like a fairy story, but there are no fairies in it, nor any of the gods, demons, and others from the rich forests of Hindu mythology. There are only humans and what humans can do when they learn to make maps from their dreams and have the will and stamina to follow them.

Through the perfume of romance, we receive a lesson in practical romanticism. Do the work in dreamwork. Recognize that dreams require action. Learn — why has it taken you so long? — that a dream is a place. Because you have been there, you can go there again. This can bring you, in this physical world, to the place of your dream lover. More often, it will bring you to places in a more spacious universe where you can rejoin the beloved companions of your soul, those who love you across time and space, even when you make each other crazy.

You Can Order Brownies in Your Dreams

That's what the great Scottish writer Robert Louis Stevenson liked to do. He wasn't actually thinking about desserts. Brownies was the name he gave to his dream helpers, a tribe of creative spirits who not only gave him ideas but did half his work for him (so he said) in the night.

> My Brownies, God bless them! who do one-half my work for me while I am fast asleep, and in all human likelihood, do the rest for me as well, when I am wide awake and fondly suppose I do it for myself. My Brownies are somewhat fantastic, like their stories hot and hot, full of passion and the picturesque, alive with animating incident; and they have no prejudice against the supernatural — and have no morals at all.

Stevenson wrote extensively about how his passion for writing interacted with his remarkable dreams and said that from a young age, his dreams were so vivid and moving, they were more entertaining to him personally than any literature. He learned early in his life that he could dream complete stories and could even go back to the same dreams on succeeding nights to give them a different ending. Later he trained himself to remember his dreams and to dream plots for his books.

Stevenson described the central role dreaming and dreamlike states played in his creative process in his 1892 essay "A Chapter on Dreams." During his sickly childhood, he was often oppressed by night terrors and the "night hag." But as he grew older, he found that his dreams often became welcome adventures, in which he would travel to far-off places or engage in costume dramas among the Jacobites.

He often read stories in his dreams, and as he developed the ambition to become a writer, it dawned on him that a clever way to get his material would be to transcribe what he was reading in his sleep. "When he lay down to prepare himself for sleep, he no longer sought amusement, but printable and profitable tales." And his dream producers accommodated him. He noticed they became especially industrious when he was under a tight deadline. When "the bank begins to send letters" his "sleepless Brownies" work overtime, turning out marketable stories.

The case of RLS shows us that dreams can be a creative studio where we don't have to labor alone on what we want to manifest.

It was a single powerful dream visitation that gave novelist Jeffrey Eugenides the creative force to bring through a remarkable book. His novel *Middlesex* is a triumph of creative empathy. It accomplishes what the best novels do, which is to expand our humanity by transporting us inside the lives and perspectives of others. It also shows us how we can do this for ourselves, by using active imagination to enter the lives of ancestors or the body of a person of a different gender, even a gender not commonly recognized.

Eugenides says that it was a dream, simple but shockingly direct and numinous, that gave him the power to finish *Middlesex*. He was living in Berlin at the time, struggling to keep food on the table through a modest fellowship, often sleep deprived because of an infant child, drinking a good deal of German beer in an effort to loosen up.

He was seized by a dream. His entire dream report reads as follows: "An owl, descended out of nowhere, seized me in its talons and blew into my mouth a single breath tasting of blood."

The one-sentence report describes a dream that lasted (he says) all of four or five seconds. Yet he sensed that the owl's visitation "originated not from my mind at all but from a source outside of me." The owl was gigantic "and not particularly realistic." Its plumage reminded him of paintings by Gustav Klimt, with lozenges of color running up and down the wings and over the breast and "a large helmeted ceremonial head."

The owl's eyes were fierce and bright yellow. When the owl dipped its beak to Eugenides's lips, he opened his mouth, unresisting. The owl exhaled one long, forceful breath. With a whoosh, the writer's lungs inflated. This inspiration had a taste: "the mineral, meaty flavor of a predatory diet."

He awakened with the deep knowing that a power had been conveyed to him from a greater source: "the great Owl in the Sky had taken a personal interest in me and my book. The owl had come to give me the power to write."

Dreaming as Epiphany

Early on New Year's Day 2020, I received a call from a woman from one of my dream-sharing circles. Tammie could not wait to tell me her dream from the night.

"I am driving in a forest I don't know," she said. "My car breaks down. I'm worried I am lost in the woods, but a snowy owl flies up to me, and I know it is a guide. The owl takes me to a wise woman who hands me a water drum. She tells me I must play the drum and listen for the waterfall. She also says this is the year when dreams and visions will come back. Don't you think that's a great dream for the new year?"

Well, *yes*. The energy of the dream moved between us. It had all the elements of a *big* dream, the kind that puts you on the threshold of major life events or takes you across that threshold — the marker of an important transition. Her old vehicle breaks down, leaving her in an unknown place. A dream guide materializes in the form of a bird or animal, which would have been recognized and respected by ancestors of many traditions. A wise teacher appears, and her connection with the First Peoples of the land where the dreamer began her excursion is evident from the musical instrument she presents. The water drum is characteristic of the Native American cultures of the Northeast.

Then there is the promise of a coming change, of movement toward the rebirth of a dreaming society, a cause in which the dreamer passionately believes and to which she would like to make a larger contribution than she currently is.

We were able to honor this magical dream immediately, because one of our teachers of Active Dreaming, Nathalie Picard, is Huron/Wendat, from the birth people of the ancient shaman I call Island Woman, and plays the water drum as well as the flute in our retreats. We contacted her. Nathalie immediately offered to have her husband, who is a maker of musical instruments, construct a water drum for Tammie, which she would teach her how to play.

I decided that the turning of the year would be a good time to launch a new experiment to see how the secret wishes of the soul might reveal themselves in the night lives of contemporary dreamers. In many world traditions, it is customary to pay special attention to dreams around the new year. Of course, in older traditions the new year is not marked as January 1, as in the Western calendar. It coincides with a turn in the earth-based wheel of the year, with a festival, perhaps with the death and rebirth of a deity. For Celts, for example, the new year begins in the fall on the night of Samhain, Christianized and then commercialized as Halloween.

However, most of us operate according to a calendar on which the new year starts on the first day of Janus (the two-faced Roman god who gave his name to the month). And it seemed to me that moving into a new decade, the 2020s, gave special juice to the assignment of dreaming in the new year.

In Japan they make a special effort to catch and work with the very first dream of the new year, which they call Hatsuyume. It may come in the night of December 31–January 1, but — since many may be up late partying or suffering the aftereffects — it may instead come in the following day or on the night of January 1–2.

In hopes of a lucky dream to kick off the new year, some Japanese invoke the Shichifukujin, or Seven Lucky Gods, and may place a picture of them under the pillow. These may not be part of our Western belief system, but we have other sources of guidance and blessing available, and it is always appropriate to ask for help and blessing if we do it nicely!

In Japanese tradition, it is very auspicious to dream of three things in Hatsuyume: Mount Fuji, a hawk, or eggplants (aubergines). We don't have to puzzle long over why the highest mountain in Japan or a hawk — the seer of the sky — would be seen as propitious. Aubergine is more mysterious, until we consider the Japanese love of puns and homophones, which come very much into play in reading dreams. The Japanese word for "eggplant" is similar to the word that means "to accomplish" or "to fulfill": both are transliterated as *nasu*.

All this may work fine if you have been raised in Japanese culture. However, I'm not keen on assigning received meanings to personal imagery. And it seems to me that if we are looking to our dreams for guidance for a whole year, we might entertain dreams from more than one or two nights and try to read series as well as individual productions.

I issued an invitation to my students, friends, and followers via my blog and several online forums to make a special effort to catch dreams around the new year. I did not prescribe a time frame; in my mind "around the new year" meant from December 30 until January 6, which is Epiphany in the Christian calendar, the day of "showing forth." I asked my team to submit summary dream reports with just a brief note about feelings and context. I did not insist that participants should set an intention, but I gave some guidance on how to do that if they chose:

If you are ready to dream in the new year, you could set the simple intention:

Show me what the new year will bring.

Or give this a positive spin by couching your request to your dream makers the following way:

Show me the best that life holds for me and those I love in the year ahead.

Be as specific or as general as you like, but ask in a way that excites you and reflects your willingness to receive guidance and enter on new adventures.

I received more than four hundred dream reports from the week leading up to Epiphany, and the contents are precious. They confirm the whole range of gifts that we receive from our night dreams, from course correction to contact with authentic spiritual teachers and reunion with beloved departed relatives. What responders had in common was that they shared a passion for dreaming and were willing to make it a practice, though some had difficulty with dream recall and a few had not yet taken up the essential discipline of keeping a journal. The group included quite a few dreamers who had attended my workshops or taken my online courses, as well as some certified teachers of Active Dreaming. The dreamers were located all over the world map, but mostly in North America, Europe, and Australia. They obviously could not be considered as representative of most people's relationship with dreams in a society where dreaming is not a social priority and many are suffering from a protracted dream drought. However, the dreams themselves can be held to be representative of what is waiting for all of us, if we will only make room for dreams in our lives.

Certain themes emerged and echoed through many reports:

Leaving old stuff behind in order to enter a new year in your life: One dreamer found herself at a threshold. She quivered with excitement, sensing great promise in what lay ahead. As she stepped through the open door, something heavy fell from her shoulders. It looked like a huge overcoat, pockets stuffed with heavy objects she did not want or need to examine. "I didn't know I was carrying all that crap until I dropped it." She felt released, ready for new adventures.

Meeting your animal spirits: It's well-known that when shamans go dreaming, they travel with and sometimes in the form of their power animals. Many dreamers around the new year found themselves spontaneously in this kind of shamanic space in night dreams. Some were challenged: one dreamer ran from a giant bear; another hid from an enormous moose that appeared on her deck, nosing at her window. Some were welcomed and guided — by an exuberant golden retriever running to greet the dreamer on a sandy beach, by a magnificent black stallion, by a soaring eagle or a wise owl. The dreamers readily agreed that all these animal encounters offered invitations to go back inside the dream, in conscious journeys, to brave up to the bear or moose and see if it would now become an ally or to travel further with an animal that was already a friend.

Being introduced or rehearsed for new work: Many of our new year dreamers conducted some kind of job search or were surprised to be working in unexpected ways. One woman dreamed she was keeping bees and decided, on waking, to make that a project in the year ahead. Another dreamed that she was able, in dream life, to spend half her time practicing visual art, which she loves, while actually increasing her income. That gave her an immediate action plan. I dreamed of an invitation from a venerable women's retreat center and made myself ready to respond if it materialized.

Jenny set an intention on New Year's night: "Show me what is ahead in my career." She dreamed she was playing ball on a vintage high school basketball court. An old friend from high school had taken her there. Jenny was reluctant at first, feeling out of shape and reflecting that she had not shot a hoop in many years. However, on the court with her friend she was amazed by how well she played. She laughed and declared, "Wow! I got game!"

She woke feeling deep love for her friend and amazed by how

fit she continued to feel. She noted that in ordinary reality she never played basketball, though her son did. The next day, she found the dream beginning to spill over into physical reality. She had a meeting with a start-up company and was struck by the fact that its offices were in a converted high school complex. The team showed her round the premises. "They open a door and we all walk out onto a vintage basketball court just like my dream. I get goosebumps and tell the team about the dream I had the day before of this basketball court." Should she go to work for this company? It felt like a slam dunk.

Receiving the promise of new creative potential: In a dream around Epiphany, a woman who had just turned sixty was amazed to be told flatly by a physician, "You can still get pregnant." We agreed that — like the dreams of implausible babies discussed earlier — this was a wondrously happy revelation to receive on the day of manifestation, promising fresh, new creative achievements.

Seeing specific glimpses of the future, from personal travel advisories to future news headlines: One mother set the intention "Show me the best possible future for me and my dearest ones." She dreamed that her daughter was playing violin really well in school. A slightly older boy in the school had a fatal illness, and people were worried about when and how to tell him. The dreamer was not satisfied with the poor planning of a teacher responsible for a new class project and told him so.

In waking life, the dreamer's daughter had never taken violin lessons. But when she recounted the dream next morning, her daughter told her she wanted to take violin lessons in the spring. Later, she made discreet inquiries and found that an older boy in school did have the condition identified in the dream. Her action plan included being ready to intercede diplomatically but firmly if she discovered that one of her daughter's teachers was fumbling a class project.

Being shown what needs to be left behind: Some of the least welcome dreams were the most rewarding once they were examined carefully and acted upon. One woman dreamed her ex broke into her apartment and tried to strangle her. This led to practical discussion of how after a breakup we may still need to exorcise our ex by cutting cords of psychic connection and establish effective psychic shields.

Cautions to insist you do what is right for you: I was fascinated by how often the theme of needing to find and follow your own track featured in New Year's dreams. Many dreamers found themselves frustrated by situations in which they were being made to follow other people's itineraries and agendas. Several were aggravated by having to travel on a bus or train, most often with family and friends, that did not go where they wanted to go. When encouraged to compare their behavior and situation in these dreams with waking life, they readily found parallels and decided on action to insist on their own priorities and follow their own paths.

Visits from distant loved ones: In many reports of dreams over the holidays, often friends and family members at a distance were joining the table or inviting the dreamer to take a place at theirs. The dream visits were unimpeded by the detail of physical death. On New Year's Day 2020, one woman dreamed she was with her mother in the kitchen of her new house on the Other Side. She was startled by a chocolate Lab, surely the sweetest dog. Mom told her its name was Happy. The dreamer could not remember a dog like that in her mother's life but was glad she had been given a new friend named Happy.

Sometimes the holiday visitors were ancestors from further back. One woman received a deputation of callers who were vaguely familiar from old family albums and press cuttings. They sat her down with heaps of documents and family papers, giving her specific leads for research, including clues about the life of a grandfather who survived a prisoner of war camp in World War II. They also dangled a pair of precious earrings — emeralds in magnificent settings — in front of her. She was allowed to try them on briefly, then they were reclaimed by her visitors. She was disappointed that she was not allowed to keep the earrings. On waking, she got the message that the earrings were precious because they gave her access to the treasure chest of family memory. They would belong to her only when she was available to *listen up*. After discussing the dream with me, she called her mother to get information about a great-uncle who had survived the Bataan Death March. She also arranged to access National Archives records of other family members going back to the American Civil War. Finally, she resolved to try to reenter her dream, sit down with the departed family members who might want to say more to her, and listen.

Report after report confirmed that dreamers have entirely natural communication with the departed in dreams and states of heightened perception. For many this is direct and life-changing evidence of the reality of the soul and its survival after physical death. The departed appear to us because they have not really left, or because they come visiting, or because in dreaming we enter their realms.

These encounters offer us important opportunities for healing, closure, and the giving or receiving of forgiveness and guidance. The deceased may need help and guidance from us — because they have unfinished business, or are lost, confused, or crippled by guilt, or are unable to detach from old environments and addictions. In such cases, as the poet W. B. Yeats observed, the living may be able to assist the imaginations of the dead.

Everyday Practice: Making Dream Magic

Here are four easy steps to help you bring the energy and magic of dreams into daily life.

1. Make a Date with Your Dreams

Before you go to sleep, write down an intention for your dreams. Make this a *juicy* intention — "I would like to be healed" or "I want to meet my soul mate" or simply "I want to have fun in my dreams and remember." Have pen and paper ready so you can record something whenever you wake up. Write your dream in a journal later, give it a title, and see if you can come up with a personal motto or "bumper sticker" distilling the message or quality of the dream.

2. Share Dreams with a Partner

Regular dream sharing is wonderful fun, builds heart-centered relationships, brings us fresh perspectives on our issues, and helps to nudge us toward taking appropriate action to honor our dreams. You'll want to begin by creating a safe space where you and your partner will give each other undivided attention. Whoever is sharing a dream should tell it as simply and clearly as possible, giving the dream a title. The partner then asks a few simple questions. Start by asking how the dreamer felt when she first woke up — the first feelings are usually an excellent guide to the general character and urgency of the dream. Ask the dreamer whether she recognizes any of the elements in the dream in waking life and whether any parts of the dream might possibly be played out in the future.

You are *not* going to tell each other what your dreams mean. You don't want to steal the dreamer's power or lose the energy of the dream in verbal analysis. You can offer helpful, nonintrusive feedback by saying to each other, "If it were my dream, I would think about such and such." Finally, you'll want to ask the dreamer, "What are you going to do to honor this dream?"

3. Act on Your Dreams

Dreams require action! If we do not do something with our dreams in waking life, we miss out on the magic. Real magic consists of bringing something through from a deeper reality into our physical lives, which is why *active* dreaming is a way of summoning natural magic — but only if we take the necessary action. Keeping a dream journal and sharing dreams on a regular basis are important ways of honoring dreams and the powers that speak through dreams. Here are some more suggestions:

- **Create from a dream.** Turn the dream into a story or poem. Draw from it, paint from it, make it into a comic strip.
- **Take a physical action based on the dream.** Celebrate an element in the dream, such as by wearing the color that was featured in it, traveling to a place from the dream, or making a phone call to an old friend who showed up in it.
- **Use an object or create a dream talisman.** A stone or crystal may be a good place to hold the energy of a dream, so you can return to it at will.
- **Use the dream as a travel advisory.** If the dream appears to contain guidance on a future situation, carry it with you as a personal travel advisory. Summarize the dream information on a cue card or hold it in an image you can *physically* carry.

4. Go Back Inside Your Dreams

Our dreams may offer us gifts of power and healing that we can claim only by going back into the dream space and moving beyond fear or irresolution. We may need to reenter a dream to overcome nightmare terrors, to clarify whether the dream is about a literal or a symbolic car crash, to talk to someone who appeared in a dream, to reclaim our own lost children, to use a personal image as a portal to multidimensional reality — or simply to have more fun!

Dream reentry is one of the core techniques that I teach and practice. If you would like to experiment, start by picking a dream that has some real energy for you. It doesn't matter whether it is a dream from last night or from twenty years ago, as long as it has juice. Get yourself settled in a comfortable, relaxed position in a quiet space and minimize the external light. Focus on a specific scene from your dream. Let it become vivid on your mental screen. See if you can let all your senses become engaged, so you can touch it, smell it, hear it, taste it. Ask yourself what you need to know and what you intend to *do* inside the dream. And let yourself start flowing back into the dream space...

In my Active Dreaming workshops, we use shamanic drumming — a steady beat on a simple frame drum, typically in the range of four to seven beats per second — to help shift consciousness and facilitate travel into the dream space. The steady beat helps to override mental clutter and focus energy and intention on the journey. If you are doing dream reentry at home, you may wish to experiment with a drumming track or soft music (see Resources).

The applications of the dream reentry process for healing are inexhaustible. In this way, for example, we may be able to travel inside the body and help to shift its behaviors in the direction of health. In her wonderful novel for kids of all ages, *A Wind in the Door*, Madeleine L'Engle describes a journey into a world inside one of the mitochondria of a sick boy; when things are brought into balance inside a particle of a cell, the whole body is healed. As we become active dreamers, we can develop the ability to journey in precisely this way. Our dreams will open the ways.

Blue Bird

Sometimes all we need from our dreams is one simple image that brings clarity and direction. In the midst of leading a soul recovery training in France, I set the intention of dreaming on behalf of the group.

In the middle of the night, my upstairs room in an old stone house at the Hameau de l'Étoile was filled with blue light. In the spectrum of blues, I would say that the color was azure. Amazed, I found the source of this light in a great blue bird suspended in midair. The light shone from within it, as if from the heart of a crystal. In that light, I knew that all would be well and that great gifts would come to those who had made the journey to this little village of hope, in the Midi.

The quality of this blue light reminded me of figures who have appeared to me in other visions of the night, especially one I call simply the Blue Lady, who has attended me and prepared me for grand adventures between the worlds. I thought, also, of the blue-skinned deities of Egypt and India. My bird visitor had a crest on its head, bringing an unassertive sense of royalty and grace.

I carried the wonderful energy of this vision with me as I went down for coffee in the refectory in the morning. "Good morning to your waking soul," a member of my training greeted me, with a line from Robbie Burns. I shared my simple dream image by the hearth, and we fanned the ashes from the fire ceremony we had shared the previous night into new life.

2

Your Great Imagineer Is
Your Magical Child

You're going through a dream drought? And you don't notice much magic in the course of your days? Don't worry: you have a world-class dreamer available to you who is no stranger and is ready to help you reopen your dream gates. This is the beautiful child in you who knows the magic of making things up.

To dream strongly and reclaim the practice of imagination, we must look to this master teacher and listen to the children around us. When very young, children know how to go to magic kingdoms without paying for tickets, because they are at home in the imagination and live close to their dreams. When we listen, truly listen, to very young children, we start to remember that the distance between us and the magic kingdoms is no wider than the edge of a sleep mask.

The Peck of the Yellow Chick

As I worked on this chapter, I dreamed I was playing hide-and-seek with a sweet little girl who had magical powers. She could shapeshift into many forms. She chose to turn into a sweet yellow chick. I pretended to be a cat, pawing and mewling, but I stayed in human form. She really did shapeshift into a chick and was able to hide in tiny spaces, like the gap between the inner arm of an easy chair and the cushion. As I reached for her over the arm of the chair, I reminded myself that I must be very careful not to harm this sweet innocent in the course of our game.

I left the dream filled with tenderness and joy. I felt that the yellow chick was in a sense the spirit of endeavor of this chapter, evoking the magical child in all of us. I made a sketch to honor the dream and then decided to try to reenter the dream and talk to the little girl.

I found her at once. She looked about five years old, dressed in a summer frock.

"Who are you?"

Don't be silly. You know who I am.

I realized she was quite correct. I had been dreaming of her over many years. I thought of her as a character in a novel I was writing in an on-again, off-again way. It seemed she had independent life.

"You seem to have plenty of magic."

I am an old soul, as people say where you are. I have taken as many forms as you find in the Celtic shapeshifting poems.

"So why did you become a little yellow chick?"

I didn't want to frighten you.

"Really?"

I want you to see that you don't need to be scared. I let you think you could play the hunter, when I have been hunting you.

I was stunned and in awe. I had thought I was hunting the magical child, when the magical child — one of several — had been hunting me. When I got my breath back, I was filled with a surge of hope.

Through pain and disappointment, through wrenching life choices, by giving up on our brightest dreams, we may have lost our great imagineer. When the world seems too cold and too cruel, our beautiful bright dreamer may go away, leaving a hole in us. This is what shamans call soul loss, and it can leave us bereft of dreams. Yet we may find, when we are ready to go looking for the magical child, that she is already looking for us, which means she can always be found.

What's behind the Green Door

The child in us loves stories, so let's go deeper with a tale from a master storyteller. H. G. Wells, while best known for his science fiction, was a prolific author in many genres. He wrote a beautiful and disturbing parable about soul loss that he titled "The Door in the Wall." Though his tale ends in tragedy, if you look from the right angle, you may find a portal to a place of magic where your magical child is waiting for you, regardless of however many years have passed since she slipped away.

A young boy, wandering the streets of London, comes to a green door in a white wall with a red Virginia creeper. He plucks up the courage to try the door and finds himself in a magical garden. There are panthers who nuzzle him like friendly cats and new friends who play the best games. A wise woman shows him a book that contains living pictures of his life.

Back in the world outside the green door, he is a little boy weeping on a long, gray street in West Kensington at the hour the lamps are lit.

He always longs to return. Strangely, he cannot remember the games he played, only the joy of them. He makes the mistake of confiding in a schoolmate and is mocked and bullied by those with no imagination. We know feedback felons of this type in our own lives, people who have lost their own dreams and encourage us to give up on ours.

As the boy grows into manhood and then an important place in the world, he senses that "some thin tarnish had spread itself over my world." He feels dull and uninspired.

In the space of one year, to his amazement, he sees the green door in the white wall three times, in three different locations. Something extraordinary is going on here. He is being given another chance to go to the magic garden, with the great friendly cats, and the joy of play for its own sake, and the wise one who can show him his larger life. But three times he refuses the invitation. He is a busy man, caught up in grown-up things. He has schedules and appointments to keep. He tries to quell the longing that stirs in him each time he walks past the green door.

So he remains with an aching hole in himself, the place where his child of wonder once lived, until the underworld seizes him, quite literally. They are working on a new line for the London Underground, and he dies when he falls down a construction shaft. We are not told whether he slipped or threw himself down. Did he mistake the black hole for the green door?

We can read this story as a cautionary tale and also as something more.

Imaginal Exercise: Through the Door in the Wall

Picture this: You are walking beside a wall. You come to a door that is painted a bright color. The color is for *you*, and it arouses deep feelings. (For me, the door is usually blue rather than green.) You raise your hand to try the doorknob, and the door opens silently.

You are in a delightful garden, full of flowers and sparkling water, where wild animals — big cats and wolves and bears — greet you and nuzzle you like friendly dogs. You know you are perfectly safe with them. You can communicate with them, mind to mind.

You hear laughter beyond the garden, and you follow it to a delightful place where children are playing games you loved in childhood. There are tea parties, of course, and hopscotch and dancing and puppet shows. You notice that the games take the players on amazing flights of imagination. The boy marshaling toy soldiers is generating and shaping a whole world. You hover close to the child switching lines on a model railroad, and you are rushing with him or her along many tracks, taking you across the landscapes of your childhood. You sit with the girl who is reading *The Velveteen Rabbit* to her friend, and as she adds scenes and brings stuffed toys alive, you know her imagination — and yours — can make dreams real.

You know some of these children very well. They are you, before the tarnish of grown-up things masked the brightness of your first world.

And there is the wise woman, of course, to show you the book of your larger life and remind you that you are in this world to play games you may have forgotten.

You come back through the door to the place where you parked your body, knowing you can find that magic garden again.

Bringing a Child from the Well of Memory

In her dream, Sonya comes to the edge of a deep well. She is horrified to discover that a beautiful but very sad young girl is drowning in the depths of the well. She wants to help. To do this, she must lower herself into the well. She loses her grip and falls. Now she is underwater. Her lungs are filling with water, her senses are swirling, and she knows that she, too, is drowning.

She remembers her intent to rescue the girl. As the will to do this revives in her, she discovers something amazing. She can breathe underwater. She swims to the drowning girl, grabs her, and carries her to the top.

She was eager to tell me the dream.

"First feelings after waking?" I asked the first question I ask of any dream.

"Relief."

"Is there anything in the dream you recognize in the rest of your life?"

"The sadness. I have often felt I am drowning in sadness."

"What do you most want to know about this dream?"

"I want to know about the well. Why is this happening inside a well?"

"If it were my dream," I said, "I would think of the well of memory and of emotions. This well takes me deep into life memories and emotions that are powerful enough to drown me if I fail to set very clear intentions in taking the plunge. The well is also a portal, a doorway. In my dream of your dream, the young person who is drowning in the well is my own younger self. This dream has given me a way to reach to her, to connect with her and help both of us to move beyond that overwhelming grief and sadness. I feel that I can use this connection to support my younger self in her own time. I also feel that the connection between us will allow me to bring the vital energy, joy, and imagination of my younger self into my present life."

The dreamer was nodding vigorously. Her face had been creased with worry or anticipation earlier; now a lovely smile flowered in her features.

"Such a dream requires action," I went on. "I would do two essential things to honor the dream and to use the doorway that has opened between me and my younger self. First, whenever I find myself thinking about sad things that may have happened early in life, I would consciously project thoughts of encouragement to my younger self in her own time. For example, I can tell her, 'You'll survive. You'll make it through. I promise you this.' I believe that you really can reach your younger self in this way, folding time. In doing it, though, you must remember not to succumb to the raw emotions of that earlier time. Your mission is to be the rescuer, as you were in your dream."

More eager nods and smiles.

"Next, if this were my dream, I would want to be sure to do things in my present life that my younger self would enjoy. Eat something she likes. Play a game she enjoys. Go to a place she loves. I would want to encourage the child part of me to see that I am fun and I am safe, so that we can enjoy a creative life together in the present time."

The dreamer eagerly agreed to follow both these suggested plans. As her features continued to soften and brighten, I felt sure that she had drawn her beautiful girl self back into her energy field. This sense was confirmed by the light of spirit in her eyes.

I noted that in English there is another meaning for the word *well*, as in "wellness."

Any night and day, we may go fishing for soul in the dream well.

Opening the Curtain for a Younger Self

We see from Sonya's story how a new dream can provide a portal to a younger self. Sometimes an old dream, one from most of a lifetime ago, can perform the same function. This is very important to recognize when you, or someone you are called to help, has been suffering a protracted dream drought, as in the case of the French woman I'll call Aimée.

She was in the group I was leading for a residential retreat in a restored stone village near Montpellier in southern France. Our day started at the breakfast table with coffee — which the French often took in those huge bowls you must raise with two hands — and baguettes and fruit. And with dreams. We asked one another each morning, "What did you dream?" or "What story have you brought to the table?" When I told my dream of the blue bird, that radiant blue light seemed to shimmer over the long refectory table.

Aimée, however, was not illuminated or amused. When I asked what was troubling her, she all but spat at me. She rattled off her accomplishments in many fields of mindfulness. She was a shamanic practitioner, a meditator, she did yoga and qigong. "But I don't dream. And you people come to the table every morning with dreams like you've come with eggs from the henhouse. I don't think I belong here."

She spoke with trembling emotion. I stepped as carefully as I could when I asked her, "Will you tell me the last dream you remember?"

She hesitated before she said, "It was thirty years ago. I was nine years old. I dreamed that someone was offering me my favorite chocolate. I love chocolate, but all I could see was the hand, at the end of an arm coming from behind a curtain, and my parents had taught me never to accept candy from strangers. So I woke myself up screaming, 'Maman! Papa!'"

"What did they do?"

"They came running. But when they heard it was just a dream, they told me to be quiet and go back to sleep. So I prayed to Jesus and Mary and all the saints. No more dreams."

She was clearly a good Catholic girl, because her prayers were answered. For thirty years, she had not remembered a single dream from the night. And here she was, scared and lonely as well as angry, in a circle of dreamers.

"If I were you," I suggested, "I would try to go back inside that dream and open the curtain and see what is going on."

"It's too late," she insisted.

"Not if the dream still has energy for you." It was obvious that it did. She had paled and her trembling had increased. "And you know about shamanic journeying, so I think you can do this."

We discussed what the journey would require. I asked her to pull up the childhood dream on her mental screen and let it become vivid. She would set an intention — "Show me who is behind the curtain" — and would travel back inside the dream with the aid of my drumming, with the purpose of drawing back the curtain and solving the mystery.

She was not very happy about this plan. The old dream still frightened her. "Will you come with me?" she asked.

"Sure. And you can ask two other people to join us. We'll be your family inside the dream."

While other small teams followed the roads of other dreams, our team watched over Aimée during the journey with the drum, and we saw some of what transpired. Back inside the dream scene, now vividly alive, Aimée pulled back the curtain. She was amazed to find a being of angelic beauty and radiance. When the features resolved, she recognized the face of a man she had loved as a second father. He was her father's best friend, he owned a toy shop where he let her play after hours, and it was all good. She called him uncle.

"It was you!" she shouted at him, sobbing with joy as they embraced. "Why did you hide yourself?"

"Ah, *chérie*, you have forgotten. When I was killed in that car crash, my face was mutilated. I wanted to call on you and give you something sweet, but I did not yet know how to change my looks, so I hid behind the curtain."

We did no analysis. Aimée came up with a simple action plan to honor her encounter. She would take flowers to Uncle Guibert's burial place as soon as possible. And she would drop her prohibition on dreams.

We did not have to wait long for the follow-up. Aimée was the first to arrive at the breakfast table the next day, and she was stamping her foot with impatience. "I've been waiting to tell you my dreams!" The person who had recalled no dreams in three decades now delivered eight dream reports, one after another, rushing along like the cars of a high-speed train. As she spoke, we sensed the dance of fireflies or dragonflies of returning soul all around her.

Riding Unicorns and Other Magic from Childhood

Do you remember dreams or dreamlike experiences from early childhood? A dream from back then may open a time tunnel through which you can travel to a younger self and reclaim your magical child. You may even find that you can play mentor and cheerleader to a younger self in a time of vulnerability or difficult transition.

Very young children don't put dreams in the same boxes as grown-ups, so it's okay if you're unsure whether to call that memory from early childhood a dream or something else.

Aimée's story illustrates the powerful long-term effects that an early dream memory — and perhaps the responses of others to it — may have had in the unfolding of a life. Some of us were fortunate to have family or friends who would listen and tend to our childhood dreams. Others had to keep their dreams secret. Some were damaged by adults who tried to beat their dreams out of them, quite literally.

Robin's family, like so many, did not make room for dreams. She was taught that they were "only" dreams and no one wanted to hear them. The childhood dreams that lingered in memory were mostly "bad" dreams, of being chased by scary monsters and then woken up by a frustrated parent. If she dared to mention things that scared her in the night, she ended up feeling ashamed and silly for being afraid.

When she learned, as an adult, to share dreams with a friend or a circle of dreamers using the Lightning Dreamwork method I developed, Robin realized that her childhood was also rich in "good" dream memories. "It's just that no one ever asked and I had never taken the time to tap into them. I laughed out loud when those memories came back to me. I felt I was truly recapturing part of my lost little girl me."

She delighted in the now vivid recollection of a "good" dream in which she found herself again and again through her childhood. "I had a white shimmery unicorn friend who would fly through beautiful skies, with me on its back. We went to many lush places, with gardens and breathtaking views. I have a sense that there was a whole other world filled with magical beings that I once knew."

I suggested that she might want to go back inside the unicorn dreams and fly again. "Oh, yes! I would like to play with my dream unicorn and explore dream vistas with it. Consider that an action plan."

Lots of adults remember scary dreams from childhood — of running away from witches or giants or horrible monsters. It seems natural that as kids we would feel menaced in dreams by things that appear much bigger than us, because the adult world outside is also very big in proportion to us; we are small and vulnerable.

I want to clap my hands every time an adult remembers that, in childhood dreams, she wasn't necessarily small and fragile, but had magic powers and the ability to face and deal with monsters on their own ground. Lots of people remember, when encouraged, that as kids they could fly in their dreams.

"I loved flying over the lilac hedge I walked beside on my walk to school," Carol recalled. "It was spring, and the hedge was very long, and the lilacs were in full bloom. The color and the scent were wonderful. I flew by swimming through the air. Now I am going to see if I can fly again."

Shirley learned at age four what many adults still need to learn: the best cure for nightmares is to face the challenge on its own ground. At that age, she has red Shirley Temple curls and a frilly pink dress, in the dream as very often in regular life. She is running around a medieval castle, all cold gray stone and dark passageways, and she can't find her way out. She is being chased by a witch — black dress, pointy black hat, warts on her nose and all. The witch chases her round the castle. She is scared the witch wants to eat her and crunch her bones.

"Then it occurs to me that I'm not really afraid of the witch, and I could just turn around and chase her back! I run into the castle kitchen and pick up a bread knife, then it's my turn to chase the witch round and round the castle. Much to my surprise, she runs away from me.

"Eventually I corner her in a passageway and cut her up into little pieces. Instead of being all gooey on the inside, they're perfectly symmetrical squares of what looks like lightly browned ground meat. When she's all chopped up into little pieces, I eat her up."

Understandably, four-year-old Shirley was quite pleased with herself for being brave enough to chase the witch and also a little surprised that the witch's insides looked like Wendy's hamburger patties and there was no blood.

Many years later, Shirley considers herself a "good witch," though she does not wear a pointy hat. She suspects that "I've been a witch for my entire life but was forced to suppress that side of myself when I was very young. I believe now that the dream was simply giving me a hint of where my life would go and telling me I didn't have to be afraid, that the witch was a part of me."

When asked to pull up a dream or memory from early childhood Chelsea found herself back at an empty fairground where her grandpa used to take her to practice riding her bike during summer vacations.

"I begin to walk around on the dusty gravel path. I see my younger self in the distance riding my old pink-and-white banana-seat bicycle. I walk up behind her and place my hands next to hers and hold on to the handlebars to help stabilize the bike as she keeps pedaling, faster and faster.

"I run alongside her grasping the handlebars. Then she scoots up on the seat, and I jump on the back and begin pedaling us even faster. She throws up her arms and smiles at the golden sky as the wind wildly blows over her face and through her hair.

"Dust from the gravel path is rising up all around us. I can sense the warm feeling of love and protection from my grandpa behind us, watching. I acknowledge this feeling of warmth and love. I bask in the loving presence of my grandpa. It's like soaking up sunlight.

"I suddenly find myself back at my grandparents' house. Now I am at the scene of an accident I suffered when I was very young. It is all playing out in front of me again. I walk toward the hill where it happened. As I come to the edge of the hill, the scene freezes. I do the only thing that comes to mind: I embrace my younger self and wrap my arms around her and surround us with an energy bubble of love and protection, with warm feelings I felt while riding my bike with my grandpa.

"I focus all of my energy and surround my grandpa, my dad, and the two me's in the bubble. I focus out the message and intent of love, protection, forgiveness, strength, and intuition. I try to convey the message to all that I have already acknowledged and accepted all that is about to happen and that I only have forgiveness and love for them all."

She felt sure she was *there*, with her child self and her family in their own time. When she came back from her journey, she could still feel the warmth and sense of love. She explained that when she was five she was badly hurt on that hill, riding that banana-seat bicycle, in a collision with a riding lawn mower driven by her stepfather. "I can remember vividly my grandpa running down the hill and taking off his long-sleeve flannel and immediately wrapping it around my hand before me being able to see the damage done."

After she revisited the scene, she felt confident that her journey had helped her child self and others involved, a healing across time. "I believe this benefited all of us in some way. And that maybe I was able to bring a part of that little golden girl home with me."

In the Arms of Great Mother Bear

To reclaim your magical child, you may need to become the shaman of your own soul.

I have never met a human who has not suffered from what shamans call soul loss. Through pain or grief or abuse, part of us goes away. This happens not only because of trauma but because of tough life choices: part of us chose to stay with a certain partner or job, another part wanted to leave and took off. Dream drought, as noted, is a common symptom of soul loss. You are missing your dreams because you are missing a beautiful, bright dreamer in your psyche. She may have gone away when you were very young and she was scared or hurt or lost someone she loved. She may be sheltering in a place of refuge or a Land of Lost Girls. Without her, you may be missing not only your dreams but vital energy and imagination, including the power to make things up.

How do you bring her home? Let's go shamanic for a while and talk about your connection, or lack of connection, with your animal spirits. Many indigenous peoples believe that we are less than whole if we do not have a working relationship with one or more spiritual allies that take the form of animals or birds. I think they are quite correct. I know this for sure: when it comes to bringing home our magical child, there are no better helpers than the animal spirits. Your child self who may be hiding out in a land of Lost Boys or Lost Girls may not trust your adult self, may not believe that you are safe and can be fun. However, she may be more than willing to trust Tiger or Horse or Bear. (I'll use capitals when I am speaking of the animal powers, not simply the animals we know in the physical world.)

At the start of my workshops, we often sing a shamanic song that calls the Medicine Bear into the circle as healer and protector.

Don't cry little one
Don't cry little one
The Bear is coming to dance for you
The Bear is coming to dance for you

For me, Great Mother Bear is the primary form of the ally we are calling. However, as we sing in the Bear we are also calling in all the power animals, with their many gifts. You are welcome to borrow this song and make it your own. You may notice that as you sing, some of your child selves come out to play right away.

A physician in Alaska dreamed that her two grandmothers, one Athabaskan Indian, the other Euro-American, paid her a visit in the same dream. They told her, "Go to Robert Moss. You need to meet the Bear. Until you meet the Bear, you will only be a doctor, not yet a healer."

At the time, the doctor had never heard of me. But she made a search and immediately pulled up the details of a workshop I was leading in Oregon a few weeks later. The title of this program was Dancing with the Bear: Reclaiming the Arts of Dream Healing. The physician did not hesitate. She booked a plane ticket, flew down the coast, drove in a rental car out to a small center near Bend, and was soon singing an indigenous song to call in the healing power of the Bear. On our first morning together, we journeyed together down into the cave of the Bear to receive its gifts.

After the drumming, the physician from Alaska came back with tears of joy in her eyes. She told us, "I now know what is required for me to be a true healer as well as a physician. When my patients come to me, they will get the best that modern medicine has to offer. At the same time, they will receive the healing power of the Bear because that is all around me." Later she confided that when she worked with patients in her office, she felt bear paws over her hands, gently guiding her in diagnosis and healing. And that when she had to accompany a patient to an operating room, she would get everyone present — nurses, orderlies, even the occasional radiologist — to sing the song I had given her to call the Bear.

I want to invite you to embark on a three-part journey to open a place of vision that will never fail you, to enlist Great Mother Bear as your ally in soul healing, and to travel across time to reclaim your magical child and possibly play mentor and cheerleader for a younger self in her own time.

Journey to Grow Your Tree of Vision

Find a quiet place where you can minimize noise and distraction. Sit or stand with the soles of your feet flat on the ground. Picture yourself reaching down through the soles of your feet, with your awareness, down through the foundations of the building, into the deep earth. You are going deep and spreading wide, as the roots of a tree go deep and spread wide.

Breathe in, and as you inhale, feel earth energy rising up into your body. Let the earth energy rise up through your trunk. With each breath, you are stronger, more centered, and more grounded in the earth. Breathe in and let the earth energy rise up to the crown of you. Then let it release and stream down around you like a soft mist, returning to its source.

Let the cycle renew. Breathe in and let the earth energy rise up through your energy body, through your trunk, to the crown of you...and flow down around you like a soft rain.

You are becoming like a tree, rooted in earth, breathing for the world.

Like a tree, you are hungry for light. You reach for light, and it streams down, shining, down from your crown, streaming through every fiber and particle of you.

How like a tree you are, rooted in earth, drinking the light.

Let your body help you find the tree you resemble. A tree that you know, a tree that knows you. Feel your arms becoming branches, your fingers twigs. See how the roots of your tree go down into the earth. Look around in all directions. Feel what it's like when the seasons change, or a strong wind blows, or birds come and go from your branches.

If you have found your tree and can hold it in your inner senses, you have found a portal to the many worlds of the shamans, a place to rendezvous with your spiritual allies, a place of vision that will never fail you — and a passage to your magical child.

Journey to the Cave of Mama Bear

You are now preparing to use your Tree of Vision to make a second journey, like the one the doctor from Alaska made. You are invited to go down into the cave of Mama Bear to receive her guidance and blessing and protection.

This will require deeper relaxation and stronger focus. In the workshops, we use shamanic drumming to fuel and focus the journey. You may want to use a recording of shamanic drumming (see

Resources). Or you may simply want to travel with a song, as shamans often do. You can use the Bear song I gave you.

You place your body in a comfortable, relaxed position, lying down or seated. You want to make the space as dark as possible (sleep shades are useful) and to close your eyes; it is easier to see with inner light in the absence of external light.

You find yourself entering a landscape, approaching your special tree. It may look like a place you know, but your journey will take you far beyond memory. You will find that any tree can be the One Tree, a ladder between worlds.

You are looking at how the roots of your tree go down into the earth. A portal will open among those roots. It may appear to you as the mouth of a tunnel, or a cave, or a rabbit hole, or a fox earth, or an elvish door.

You are going through this portal into a warm breathing space. You may find you are among a whole family of animals. Eventually you find yourself in the welcoming embrace of Great Mother Bear. She holds you and enfolds you, and you feel the milk of her goodness streaming through you. You have found an ally your child self can trust and a medicine friend and protector for all the passages of your life.

Journey to Your Child Self

No need to rush the next part, unless your magical child has been calling you urgently, in your dreams and perhaps in the dreamlike play of synchronicity around you. It may be that this third journey will send you straight into a dream or memory that has been with you all your life, though it may have lain in hiding until now.

Again, you need to relax, get your body in a comfortable position, minimize distractions, and check within to see whether anything is holding you back from a new adventure. As you breathe out, release anything that prevents you from being fully present. As you breathe in, draw in a sense of expanding possibility. If you find your inner skeptic tends to rise up and block you when you try to do inner work, ask him to wait outside while you make the journey. Tell him, "I'll get back to you. First the adventure, later the discussion."

You are again with your tree, and you know Mama Bear is with you. You feel the warmth of her protection all around you.

You are going up into the high branches of the tree. Your child self, who may have always wanted a tree house or been lucky enough to have had one, is already engaged.

From up in the high branches, you look out over the road or river of your life leading up to this present moment. You can see many looks away, like a bird. Maybe you find you have a bird ally on your shoulder who will lend you its vision and its power of flight. Maybe the magical child in you who always knew she could fly is reaching out to guide you.

You are seeking to travel into an early time in your life and engage with a younger self and exchange gifts. She may be going through tough times and need you to step in, mind to mind, as a voice of counsel or encouragement she is lacking. At the very least, you can promise, with absolute truth, "You will make it. You will survive."

Maybe the one you are seeking is the wise child, the one who can lend you vital energy and imagination and remind you what really matters, the one who loves to do what she loves for its own sake, without snagging herself in calculations and consequences.

You are probably going to hug each other. When you do that, you may feel the great arms of Mama Bear wrapped around both of you, holding you together so you won't go missing from each other again.

Everyday Practice: Treat Your Child Self

As you come back, make a little drawing or jot down two or three things that are with you. Keep your sense of that child close. What does she want? What is her pleasure? What does she most need?

Identify and write down three things your younger self would really enjoy in your life right now.

When I was a child, all my boy Roberts loved to draw and paint. I still feel them come close whenever I pick up pencils and colors. One of my boy Roberts loved eating fresh blackberries, picked from thorniest bushes in the deepest places. He'd come back bleeding but with delight, his face smeared with all the blackberries he'd eaten while filling the bucket he'd bring home to his mother, who would make him ice cream with big chunks of blackberry. When I pick blackberries or add fresh blackberries to ice cream from the freezer, I bring some of that boy energy into my body.

Maybe your child self likes to get down on the floor and draw with crayons. Maybe she loves to have tea parties with dolls or teddy bears. Why not have one today, tomorrow? Sit down with your child self and have a tea party together. Go to the ice cream shop, go to the library or the Egyptian room at the museum or the vinyl store or the magic shop. Buy art supplies, read — and write! — a story for the child, dance and skip through the woods, drink the rain in your open mouth. Ride unicorns.

On Not Putting Away Childish Things

"The reluctance to put away childish things may be a requirement of genius." The quotation, from author and journalist Rebecca Pepper Sinkler, is a neat backhand swipe at Paul's injunction (in Corinthians 11:13) about the need for a man to "put away childish things."

C. S. Lewis played with Paul's famous Bible phrase a slightly different way while conveying a message similar to Sinkler's:

> To be concerned about being grown up, to admire the grown up because it is grown up, to blush at the suspicion of being childish; these things are the marks of childhood and adolescence. And in childhood and adolescence they are, in

moderation, healthy symptoms. Young things ought to want to grow. But to carry on into middle life or even into early manhood this concern about being adult is a mark of really arrested development. When I was ten, I read fairy tales in secret and would have been ashamed if I had been found doing so. Now that I am fifty I read them openly. When I became a man I put away childish things, including the fear of childishness and the desire to be very grown up.

Albert Einstein provides a stellar example of the genius of not putting away childish things. Asked how he came up with the theory of relativity, Einstein said: "A normal adult never stops to think about problems of time and space. These are things which he has thought about as a child. But my intellectual development was retarded, as a result of which I began to wonder about space and time only when I grew up."

Famed psychic Eileen Garrett explained her gift as the ability to "go to the child-me" and her "initial knowing" in order to see and understand phenomena beyond the physical. She developed this while practicing "passivity-consciousness" as she lay in bed at twilight.

When she was very young, my daughter Sophie had adventures in a magical land, where she met a special friend. I loved hearing about these travels and encouraged her to make drawings and spin further stories from them.

As I reported in my book *Active Dreaming*, one day Sophie sat down beside me and asked with great earnestness, "Daddy, would you like to know how I get to the magic kingdom?"

"I'd love to."

"Sometimes I take the Sun Gate. Sometimes I take the Moon Gate. Sometimes I take the Tree Gate. Sometimes I take the Rainbow Bridge. And *sometimes* I just punch a hole in the world."

I've never heard anyone say it better. To live the larger life, we need to *punch a hole in the world*. This is what dreaming — when sleeping or waking or hyperawake — is really all about. On our roads to adulthood, we sometimes forget how to do it, just as older children in The Chronicles of Narnia cease to be able to see Aslan as they approach adolescence and become more and more burdened by the reality definitions of the grown-ups around them.

Listening to young children requires us to pay attention; to *attend*, in its root meaning in the Latin, is to stretch ourselves, which requires us to expand our vocabulary of understanding. We owe nothing less to the magical child within us and the young children we may be privileged to know in the world around us. When we do this, we discover that they can be our very best teachers on the secrets of dreaming and imagination.

Homeplay: Six Impossible Things before Breakfast

Do you remember the scene in *Through the Looking-Glass* when Alice laughs at all the nonsense around her and says to the White Queen, "There's no use trying, one can't believe impossible things"?

"I daresay you haven't had much practice," the Queen responds. "When I was your age, I always did it for half-an-hour a day. Why, sometimes I've believed as many as six impossible things before breakfast."

I like the White Queen's practice, and I bet the child in you likes it too. To keep her entertained and give your imagination a gentle workout, try jotting down your responses to the next question: If you gave yourself permission to believe six impossible things before breakfast, what would they be?

When I first tried this out myself (I always road test my own exercises) I made the following list — before breakfast, of course:

- I can make myself inconceivably small and travel inside the body and bring healing — or travel through the nucleus of an atom into another universe.
- I can travel across time and repair the past or improve the future.

- I can talk to animals.
- I can be a superhero for others.
- I can meet and bring together my parallel selves.
- I can travel to my home star.

I have been delighted by what others have produced when they took on the assignment. Christina's list made me clap my hands, and I know my boy Roberts joined in:

- I am galloping on Boreas while standing on my head, drinking the yummiest tea and having my feet massaged by clouds.
- I feel the hum of a rainbow rising through my feet as I walk across it.
- I have taught my cat to knead bread instead of my lap.
- I am traveling inside of a raindrop around the world.
- I am looking at the universe from the inside of a black hole.
- I discover that nothing on my list is impossible with the help of the wonderful thing we call imagination.

Very young children don't need anyone else to set such assignments. A wonderful young Romanian girl I know named Smaranda announced to her mother at bedtime, when she was not yet four years old, "Mama, I will dream a baby deer with mama deer and father deer. And you will dream the moon in the sky. Yes? Good night!!" Now *that* is setting some good intentions for dream manifestation!

3

What Is in Your Way
May Be Your Way

For every setback, look for opportunity. That is a provocative statement, hard to accept when you feel betrayed or shamed or in the depths of grief or loss. When you have lost your job, or your partner has walked out on you, or you have made the worst mistake of your life, how can you accept the idea that by what you fall, you can rise? When you feel crushed by a global pandemic that has put a hold on your life and may have cost you your health or your livelihood or your ability to breathe fresh air outside without a face mask, what gift can you find in the situation?

You have nothing to lose by proceeding *as if*, despite appearance, there may be a gift in the loss. You can try saying to yourself, "Okay. That went down the tube. That door closed. Wait a minute. If that door closed, where's the door that might be opening?"

J.K. Rowling, who suffered rejection again and again before she found a publisher willing to take on *Harry Potter*, put it this way in her 2013 commencement speech at Harvard: "It is impossible to live without failing at something, unless you live so cautiously that you might as well not have lived at all — in which case, you fail by default.... The knowledge that you have emerged wiser and stronger from setbacks means that you are, ever after, secure in your ability to survive. You will never truly know yourself, or the strength of your relationships, until both have been tested by adversity."

You may want to consider the cases of people who have been savagely beaten down by life only to rise again, showing us that there can be a tremendous gift in a wound. I think of Harriet Tubman, the most famous conductor of the Underground Railroad, who helped hundreds of fugitive slaves to escape to freedom in the North in the years before the American Civil War. At about age eleven, she was nearly killed when she was hit in the forehead by a two-pound lead weight hurled by an angry overseer. She carried the scar for the rest of her life. One of the effects of the wound was that she developed a form of narcolepsy that required her to take short and sudden "sleeps" in the middle of any kind of activity. It was during those "sleeps" that she saw visions showing her the roads and river fords and safe houses to which she was able to guide escaping slaves, avoiding the slave owners' posses.

On a path of transformation, you come to a point where you break down or you break through. Sometimes the breakdown is a condition for the breakthrough. At twenty-five, British climber Joe Simpson was climbing the west face of Siula Grande, a mountain in the Peruvian Andes. Near the top, he fell and broke his leg, and his partner had to leave him on the mountainside. He came very close to death. Reflecting on how his life would have unfolded had he *not* had a close encounter with death on the mountain, he wrote in *Touching the Void*, "I would have gone on to climb harder and harder routes taking greater risks every time. Given the toll of friends over the years I'm not confident I would be alive today. In those days I was a penniless, narrow-minded, anarchic, abrasive and ambitious mountaineer. The accident opened up a whole new world for me. Without it I would never have discovered hidden talents for writing and public speaking."

A fair amount of Chronos time may be required to appreciate what Ralph Waldo Emerson called "the compensations of calamity." He wrote that such compensations become apparent "after long intervals of time. A fever, a mutilation, a cruel disappointment, a loss of wealth, a loss of friends, seems at the moment unpaid loss, and unpayable. But the sure years reveal the remedial force that underlies all facts."

One Calamity Is Better
Than a Thousand Counsels

"Bir müsibet bin nasihatten iyidir" — or "One calamity is better than a thousand counsels." I learned this Turkish proverb during my travels in Anatolia. It seems to me to be an excellent maxim for life.

We derive the English word *calamity* from the Latin *calamitas*, meaning "damage, loss, failure, disaster, adversity, misfortune."

Faced with a calamity, we are out of the realm of words and abstract concepts, down in the chop and rawness of physical events. Ordinary time stops, and ordinary calculations fly out the window. We may need to move at light speed or, alternatively, be content to subsist for a while in a state of suspended animation. We can't go by the clock or the manual, the way we did before. This can give us a curious and salutary sense of permission even when we suspect we are being punished: permission to stand outside and above the regular round of appointments and duties and requirements.

It's been said that illness is the Western form of meditation. Calamity may be a universal gateway to transformation, if we are able to recognize the educational opportunity, seize it, and use it to break through rather than break down.

Upending Perception

I derived the title of this chapter from the meditations of the philosopher emperor Marcus Aurelius. He did not record his thoughts for publication or posterity; he wrote them as memos for himself and did not call them *Meditations*, a title bestowed by a much later editor. If you have seen him portrayed by Richard Harris in the movie

Gladiator, you know that (even allowing for scripting hyperbole) Marcus did not live the life of a mere armchair philosopher and was not fortunate in the character of his family or the state of his beleaguered empire.

Nonetheless, in the midst of the fray, writing to establish and maintain a witness perspective on the broiling events around him, he formulated two principles that seem to me to be essential rules of life. The first is that *our lives are dyed in the colors of our imaginations.*

The second goes like this: "Our actions may be impeded...but there can be no impeding our intentions or their dispositions. Because we can accommodate and adapt. The mind adapts and converts to its purposes the obstacle to our acting." In summary: "The impediment to action advances action. What stands in the way becomes the way."

What a magnificent invitation to upend our reflexive response to adversity and seek the opportunity in the obstacle and the gift in the challenge!

It's not about telling yourself that it's all good. It's about *making* it good.

The obstacle in itself is less important than how we see it and respond to it. We have the power to choose our attitude and adjust our perception. At the other end of the social spectrum from the emperor, another Stoic philosopher, the former slave Epictetus, counseled that when presented with an obstacle we need to step back and take a cool, hard look: "Don't let the force of an impression when it first hits you knock you off your feet. Say to it: Hold on for a moment, let me see who you are and what you represent. Let me put you to the test."

This may not be easy when you're caught in the storm of grief or rage or bitter disappointment that comes in the face of a letdown, a wound, a loss, a shaming, or a betrayal. We may have to struggle to rise to a witness perspective and see the larger picture. This gets easier when we adopt the practice of looking back on our lives to see if something good came out of a bad situation.

The Challenge and the Gift

There is a gift in every challenge. The gift of my long boyhood illnesses was to make me very much at home in the worlds of dreaming and imagination. When I was pronounced clinically dead in a Melbourne hospital during an emergency appendectomy at age nine, I seemed to spend a whole life among a different people in a different world, and I came back with clear memories. I was able to enter, at will, what might be called a state of lucid dreaming and to travel in dreaming across time and space. I have known from early childhood that the dream world is a real world and not just a matter of routine processing or personal psychology.

I was born in a conservative era in a military family, and though my family members were supportive, they had no model for understanding my dreams and visions. The first confirmation I received was from an Aboriginal boy who was quite matter-of-fact about traveling to spirit realms, seeing the future, and interacting with the ancestors in dreams. Something of Aboriginal tradition may have reached me by osmosis. Aborigines say that our personal dreams may take us to the Dreamtime, also called the All-at-Once, where we move outside time and can encounter the ancestors.

As I grew to manhood and made my way in the world, I was usually careful about sharing my dreams with anyone beyond close friends, but they guided me at a crucial life turning. I kept a journal, and I would say, looking back, that the worst trouble I got into came from not listening to my night dreams, which are so often a corrective to the delusions and miscalculations of the day. At midlife, I went through a crisis that I came to recognize as a crisis of spiritual emergence. The big dreams and visions of this period, described in *The Boy Who Died and Came Back*, led me to change my life radically and follow the path of a dream teacher, for which there was no career track in our society. I now see that those wretched boyhood years of isolation and illness — twelve bouts of double pneumonia in eight years — had set me on this course and put me through a profound apprenticeship.

I invited participants in one of my retreats to reflect on a time of challenge in their lives that they think, in hindsight, may have brought a significant gift. This inspired deep self-searching and a rich array of experiences large and small illustrating the notion that the obstacle may be the way. Each short narrative is an example of how we can turn a setback into a skill set or a life lesson and how we can always exercise the power to *choose the story* we make out of it. Here is a sampling of what they shared.

Lisa: An Unwanted Move

My challenge: I was living in New Jersey, and my father had just been hired by the University of British Columbia as a professor. I had just tried out for the New Jersey all-star team of girls' softball, made the team, and was going to play shortstop. I was an excellent softball player. The day after I made the team, my father said we were going to move to Canada. I was totally heartbroken.

We moved to Vancouver, and I felt completely out of place. I was an American living in Canada. My accent was different, my clothing choices were different, and I did not feel like I fit into this new landscape. This was the ripe age of thirteen. A coming of age time for a young girl.

The gift: I got on a new team in Canada playing softball and many other sports. I joined a hiking club and learned to live in a land of beauty. British Columbia is nothing like New Jersey. I learned how to connect with people, even though I felt like I might be very different and not fit in.

Monica: "Say 'Bullshit,' Mama"

My challenge: I was in a very difficult marriage in which I experienced a lot of verbal abuse, panic attacks, and exhaustion. One night I asked my husband to come home early so I could get some sleep, since our three-year-old was still up. He came home drunk and yelling and swearing. I told him not to do that in front of our son. He kept on and looked at my son and told him, "You need to get that your mom talks bullshit all the time." He told him, "Say 'Bullshit,' Mama." My son was confused but did what he was told. I saw those little toddler eyes goggling in confusion as he repeated, "Bullshit, Mama." My heart broke. And something snapped within. *I would not let this happen ever again.*

The next day I asked for a separation. I found all the paperwork I needed and served him divorce papers one month later. Through the years that followed, there were bitter fights over money. I continued to do what I needed to do and demanded the money for child support. I refused the story of others that as a single mom, I would be broke.

The gift: I came out stronger. I stood up for myself. I learned to trust again. And I made more money as a single mom than I had when married. Yes, I worked more, but I was happier.

My big gift in all this is I grew as a person. I saw how I contributed to things and also learned that I never have to be treated that way again. I have a wonderful son who has a lovely girlfriend. She has a young daughter. My son treats his girlfriend and her daughter with respect, love, care and is always there for them. I'm one proud mama.

Katerina: Touched by an Angel

Katerina, who is Greek Australian, began her story by quoting what her mother said whenever she went to her with a problem in childhood: "Káthe empódio kai kaló. (From every obstacle comes good.)"

My challenge: I am seven years old and have just been diagnosed with pneumonia. My mother begs the doctor to keep me home and promises she'll take better care of me than the nurses in the hospital. In the meantime our city, Hobart, is ablaze in a tragic bushfire, which destroys many homes and takes the lives of many people.

I'm home very sick and certainly not allowed to go outside into the noxious smoke, although the red sky looks so pretty. Most of the time my mother won't let me out of bed! I can do nothing.

The gift: I fall into a deep slumber that lasts three days. During this sleep I experience arriving in a beautiful, colorful flower garden. I thought I could talk to the flowers and the little fish in the pond. I'm still focused on the fish when I sense a presence beside me. I feel a gentle touch on my shoulder. I look up, and my vision is filled with awe and radiance.

The angel tells me, "Katerina, be happy, you may stay here as long as you need." After the third day I come out of the sleep and feel revived.

This was my first experience of healing with the angels. It came out of illness and isolation, and it has guided my approach to healing, as beneficiary and practitioner, all of my life.

Kirsten: Home Alone

My challenge: My mother abandoned my family and me when I was four years old. This cast a shadow over all my childhood and my early adult life. I felt unworthy, never good enough, riddled with self-doubt. When I was pregnant with my first child, my greatest concern was whether I had the capability of being a good mother to this new life I carried. I knew I would never leave her. I also had no idea whether I could ever be the mother she deserved. I had no model for this role.

The gift: In my early forties a series of events in my life pulled me into a state of deep inquiry. I explored and pulled apart every aspect of mothering I could imagine. I went deep, rescued my inner child, and emerged with the knowing that with an open heart I could mother all things in ways I had longed for. I began to believe in myself, challenge old patterns of conditioning, and express my true self in the world.

Everyone around me noticed the change, and the greatest gift to me was the acknowledgment from my children and their words, "You know, Mum, you're a lot different now, but we like the new you. We can feel your happiness, and that makes us happy too." I can see the ripple effect of my own healing and that I have extended this into all aspects of my life. I know I have given my children something special through my own journey: permission to stand in their truth, to know who they are, and to express themselves freely in this world from the heart.

Jennie: Lost Teacher

My challenge: I was dropped by a spiritual teacher I had been with for twenty-five years. No calls being returned or emails or texts. No invites to spend time together or even have coffee. Nothing. I was very hurt, like a little child. I felt lost and abandoned. Then the anger set in! I raged on until I was exhausted.

The gift: What emerged for me is so much better. I can forgive the teacher who deserted me because, whatever the intention may have been, I feel like a bear cub pushed out of the den to make her own way on her own feet. What I feel now is sweet freedom! I have my new life, and I am ready to explore it with the passion I have always longed for. This would not have happened if I had not been pushed out of a warm and familiar place.

Choosing Our Stories

To grow big dreams, we must learn to step out of the tired old stories woven from past failures and family histories and limited perception and step into bigger and braver stories. And we want to approach every day as the chance to choose a new story or create one. "For every night there is a story, and for every day," wrote Aelius Aristides, an ancient orator who had the ear of emperors and wrote one of the first dream journals on record.

This is vitally important when it comes to weathering the bad stuff and turning adversity into an education. Before the coronavirus pandemic, I spent half my days traveling round the world leading workshops, and I ran into plenty of bumps along the way: flight delays, missed connections, unscheduled overnight stays at airport hotels. My survival strategy was to look for new stories on every trip. I would often ask the stranger next to me in an airplane seat, "What is your story?"

This produced some amazing responses. An off-duty senior flight attendant responded with a story that is itself a model of how to handle a negative situation. "I was purser on a flight, and two of our junior flight attendants approached me at the same time from opposite ends of the plane. One was upset because a passenger in first class was drunk and had been bawling her out. The other showed me a baby pacifier she had found on the floor.

"Juggling the two situations, I decided to take a risk. I walked up to first class, to the unruly passenger, and held out the pacifier in my hand. I said to him, 'I hear you've been throwing a tantrum because you've been missing this.'

"His color changed from red to purple, and I thought, *Shit. I just lost my job.*

"Then he started laughing. He said, 'Okay, you got me. I'll try to behave.'"

I have noticed that the best stories are generated when something goes wrong. When you are off schedule, when you have missed your connection or your itinerary has been switched, a trickster energy comes into play. If you can avoid demonstrating type A personality disorder and stop worrying about something you can't fix, you may find yourself enjoying an amazing chance encounter that will give you a fresh new story for your day.

Here's a story about how the pain and difficulty of getting to a certain destination produced marvelous rewards for a whole group.

Getting Up the Mountain

Many years ago, up on a mountain in the New York Adirondacks, I was leading a very important gathering where I planned to take people on a journey through what I call the Dante Gate. In Dante's *Divine Comedy*, Purgatory is a mountain. You get to climb it only after passing through a gate where you must knock on your heart. I had prepared a journey for a group of advanced dreamers who had been gathering on this mountain for many years in which we would climb the three terrible steps to the Dante Gate: one, a mirror in which you see your true self, in all its facets; another, a black and broken step through which you must look into your own darkness; and the third, a blood-red step where you must choose how you will make a sacrifice. The steep ascent of the mountain lies ahead for the soul pilgrim who proceeds to open his heart. If you make it all the way, you will meet the radiant beloved of your soul. Dante found that being in the form of Beatrice, the beautiful young woman he had loved but could never have.

I put a lot of work into preparing the script for this journey, incorporating stanzas in Dante's terza rima that I intended to read in the medieval Italian original, however poor my accent. I was excited to be crafting a wildly shamanic group journey from a text that is at the heart of Western literature and philosophy.

There was a slight problem that weekend. Our members were supposed to gather for dinner on Friday at the mountain lodge. However, it had started snowing hard the previous day. By the time the first of our party left the county road beside the Hudson River, near its headwaters, to follow the twisting backcountry road up the mountain, two feet of fresh snow had fallen in twenty-four hours. Few of our participants had much experience of driving in snow. They were mostly city people, some from far south, without four-wheel drive or snow tires. Some were driving airport rentals. All of us were greeted by a sign that read "End of Town Maintenance" several miles ahead of the lodge. Beyond it, there was no sign that a plow had been through since the snow began.

Several of our cars got stuck in the snowdrifts. People from the lodge came with a tractor and a big pickup truck and hauled us out, one by one, while working to open the road with a plow. Amazingly, everyone in our group made it to the lodge in time for the gathering.

The warmth of our little community as we shared dinner and then gathered in front of a roaring fire in the log house that was our meeting space was extraordinary. We felt more deeply bonded than ever, after all the adventures we had shared on this mountain over many years. And we were excited. The effort and edginess of our ascent were perfect preparation for the journey of ascension we proceeded to make.

I told the story of Dante's journey up the mountain of Purgatorio, with the dead Latin poet Virgil at his side. I cried as the spirit of Casella, who set some of Dante's poems to music, called to him, "Ma tu perche vai? (Why are you traveling?)"

And I recited the traveler's response:

Per tornar altra volta
La dov'io son, fo lo questo viaggio.
(*So I may return again*
To where I am, is why I journey.)

I asked our thirty dreamers to get comfortable on their blankets or mats on the floor, to blow away anything holding them back, and to prepare to follow Dante's steps up the mountain to the point where Virgil says farewell, announcing, "Per ch'io te sovra te corono e mitrio. (Therefore I crown and mitre you over yourself.)"

The journey was not an exercise in medievalism, though it might have been fascinating to enter fully into the world of Dante's imagination. I downplayed the religious elements in his story. Our purpose in borrowing some features of his mythic geography was to make our personal journeys to encounter a radiant guide — the higher self — that would appear to us in a form adjusted to what we could perceive and receive.

For all those who took part, the journey was a remarkable success, bringing deep soul experiences. It was fueled not only by shamanic drumming and by the circle energy of an intentional community meeting at a very special place but by the difficulties we had shared in getting up there. The arduousness of the journey fed the ardor of the gathering, an example of how what is in your way may become your way.

In Praise of Blocks

The blocks we encounter on our roads — whether they are in ourselves, in our circumstances, or in both — may be teachers and helpers, as well as part of life's cycles. A block can drive us to discover a new direction, spur us to develop new skills and courage and stamina, or lead us to look again at what really matters in life. We may find that obstacles we encounter on our life paths can save us from compounding mistakes, make us take a longer view of our issues, and encourage us to shift direction and notice better options. We may even come to recognize that a hidden hand places some of these obstacles in our way. If we can make the necessary attitude adjustments, we may find, like Marcus Aurelius, that "what stands in the way becomes the way."

I come not to bury blocks, but to praise them. I am talking about the speed bumps we encounter on the roads of life. Sometimes they look like solid brick walls or mountains set in our way. Sometimes we feel we have come to a door that won't open, however hard we pound or however many keys we try.

I once had exactly that sense, of coming to a door in my life that would not open. I believed that everything I most wanted lay behind that door. But I simply could not get through. Frustrated, exhausted by trying, I slumped into an easy chair one afternoon and suddenly had a spontaneous vision of my situation. I saw myself beating until my knuckles were bloody on a great oak door banded with iron. Yep, that's how it was.

A little movie clip began to unfold in my consciousness. It was the kind of dream movie where you are not only the observer but can step right into the action. Slipping into the situation of my second self, I felt a kind of prickling at the back of my neck. I turned — now fully inside the vision — to see an elegant trickster-ish figure beckoning to me from some distance to my right. He was standing in the middle of an archway. Behind him was a scene of great beauty, with a lovely house on a hill above orchards heavy with fruit and flowering trees in full blossom. I knew, in that instant, that everything I was seeking lay through this archway.

As I moved toward it and then through it, I turned to try to understand the whole story. I noticed two things. While with one hand, the Gatekeeper was beckoning me toward the archway of opportunity, with the other hand he was holding the door that had refused me firmly shut. Behind that door was something like a jail cell, a place of confinement. I had been wasting my energies in a vain attempt to put myself into the wrong place.

I carried guidance from this vision, with its dramatic and objective perspective, into my life immediately. I abandoned work on a certain project and ended a certain professional relationship. I soon found myself, in a creative sense, in that wonderful place of the flowering trees.

I learned from this experience something I believe to be relevant to all of us at particular times of challenge in life. When you feel hopelessly blocked, check whether the block is actually a signal to choose a better way forward. Behind that seemingly insuperable block may be a Gatekeeper who is opposing your progress on the path your everyday mind has chosen in order to get you to turn around and find a better way.

This is only one of the ways in which our blocks may be our friends. We may be on the right path, but that path may include challenges that are necessary tests, requiring us to develop the courage and the skills to go forward. As Dion Fortune once put it, the block may be a "thrust-block," like that used by sprinters at the start of a race.

At every major threshold in our life journeys, we are likely to encounter some form of the Dweller on the Threshold, a power that challenges us to brave up and rise to a new level. Faced with such a challenge — and the inner resistance that comes with it — we have a choice. We can break down or break through. I am in favor of breaking through. Practice will teach us when that requires moving forward, despite the block, and when we need to shift direction and go around the block.

Playing with Blocks

Obstacles on the road of life take different forms. They might have different origins and require different treatments. Blocks may encourage you to develop the skills and the readiness to go a certain distance. Blocks can arouse you to nurture the constancy and determination required to do something important. They can be part of your training regime, your life workout. As in my story of the door that would not open, an obstacle may be placed on your path by the Gatekeeper to make you consider a different way.

When you can see your blocks and give shape to them, you can find a way to release or transmute them. And you'll never go wrong if you act in the knowledge that what you want to do with your blocks is to *play with them*.

In one of my workshops, a woman said that she felt tightness in her throat; something was making it hard for her to speak. I asked her to describe the tightness. Did it feel like something was stuck in her throat, or rather as if something was constricting it? She raised a hand to her neck. "It feels like a collar that's too tight."

"That's interesting. You mean like a dog collar?"

"No, no."

"Like a choke collar?"

"No, nothing as brutal as that."

"Well, what does it feel like?"

"It feels like a collar that is buttoned too tight."

"Okay, what kind of collar?"

"Oh, it's a sort of stand-up, high, lacy collar, the kind that old women wore a long time ago."

"What else do you see when you visualize the old-fashioned stand-up woman's collar?"

"I see my great-grandmother. I remember her photograph. I remember her from early childhood."

"Tell me about it."

"She was the one in my Irish family who was always very matriarchal, very dominant, with great absolute control over the subsequent generations of female members of the family. But she was the matriarch who insisted the role of the women was never to stand up to the men, never to speak back to the men, however drunk, however inconsiderate they were. 'You will never challenge the men.' She was the one who used her own authority to silence the women so that they did not protest, did not speak up about what the men in their lives were doing."

"Wow. Now, if that family legacy, that stiff, old-fashioned lace collar, is around your neck, it wouldn't be surprising if you found it hard to speak your truth. What do you want to do with that legacy now?"

She seized the moment. With her hands, she made the motions of ripping off the old lace collar that had prevented her from claiming her voice. She said, with ringing assurance, "My life will be different now. I will say what needs to be said. I will speak truth that has been silenced. And I will speak for all the women of my lineage, going back through the generations."

Another time, I asked participants in one of my classes to scan themselves and notice where they felt pressure or blockage in their bodies. I continued: "Can you see or sense the shape of that block? Does this stir any life memories? What do you need to do about that block?"

The first person to speak up in that class had again felt a block at the throat center. So many people — especially women — feel a blockage that prevents them from claiming their voice. I have come to understand why the Buddhists say that fear of public speaking is one of the six great fears that humans harbor.

A woman in that class told us she could see and feel the hilt of a sword stuck in her throat.

"What do you want to do about that?"

"I need to reach in and pull it out."

She wanted to do this right away. She clasped the imagined sword hilt in her hands and drew it out, pulling slowly and strongly. She said she felt powerful. I asked her to touch her throat to see if there was a wound and, if so, what was needed for healing. She felt the skin closing, smooth and supple, over an old wound caused by men in her life.

She felt she was still holding the sword.

"Do you know what you want to do with it?"

"Not yet."

"Well, that's for you to decide. The Haudenosaunee, or Iroquois, talk about burying your weapons under the roots of the white pine of peace. Something like that might become part of your further meditation, but you did the big thing. You pulled the sword out. If it's my life, I want to celebrate by telling the world something I want to say right now. Do you know what that is?"

"Yes. *I can do it!*"

A woman who had been challenged by lung cancer went to the site of the disease in her body and saw herself sitting below a huge rock. "What's left?" she asked, knowing that she was close to being completely cured. "What more do I need to do?"

She noticed a beautiful tree above the rock wall and knew instinctively that this was the place where she needed to be. However, the climb looked daunting without ropes and harness. She stayed in the scene, and as it became more and more vivid, a boulder shifted when she brushed it with her foot. She pushed it aside without difficulty and found the mouth of a cave. It was dark and wet inside, but she knew she would find her way. As she moved into its depths, the cave floor sloped upward, and she realized she was in a space held within the roots of the great tree as if within a huge and gentle fist. She knew she had found a place of healing and all that was required of her was to come here often — and to spend time with trees in nature, breathing in the green world.

A man in that class felt something weighing on his head. What came with this was a clear vision of his mother with a huge block of ice on her head that was not melting. He realized he was looking at a dramatic image of something that had prevented his mother from showing love and maternal affection to him for as long as he could remember. He was seeing his mother's block as well as his own.

He was not sure how to work with this imagery, so he simply asked for help. Immediately a dragon entered the scene and blew fire on the ice.

I am all in favor of dragons, but this treatment seemed a little too harsh for Mom, and the viewer conceded that he had not actually seen the ice melting and that he felt the fire-breathing dragon might embody some of his own anger. We agreed, after discussion, that the way to proceed might be with a gentler image, one of the sun shining on the ice and letting it melt in an easy, natural way. The viewer agreed to try this and reported later that when he saw the ice melting away from his mother's head, he felt a heavy burden lifting and releasing from his own head.

Exercise: Play with Your Blocks

One of the challenges to clearing the negative images is that frequently we are oblivious to the hold they have over us. Like dust mites or bacteria, they may feed and proliferate far below our conscious perception. They may come swarming through us in a moment of panic, of nausea, of gut-wrenching fear. They often have their origin in past trauma, guilt, or shame. The incidents that gave them a hold over us may be deeply hidden or repressed, locked behind doors we do not want to open.

A paralyzing fear or a numbing block can hardly be called an image at all. Yet there is an image within the fear or the block that is waiting to be discovered, and when that image is brought to consciousness and reworked, vital healing and forward momentum become possible.

We are talking about clearing our personal history. We don't have a "clear history" button in the brain, like the function you can click on the toolbar of your computer. But we can run a self-scan to bring the hidden saboteurs out of the shadows.

Scanning and clearing can be a simple process, one that can sometimes be done on your own. Get yourself in a relaxed, comfortable position in a private space where you can't be easily interrupted or distracted by outside noise. Follow the flow of your breathing. Reflect on places in your life where you have felt blocked or stuck. Go to the place in your body where you feel that block, a tension or fear. Let your body give you an image from that space. Maybe the image relates to a certain time and place in your life story, an issue from the past you still need to resolve.

Use your imagination to see how to deal with that image. Is it something you can reshape? Do you need to go around, or over, or under? Is it actually a necessary roadblock — like my door that would not open — that has been preventing you from going further down a path that is not right for you?

A woman who said she often felt "knotted up" with anxiety did this exercise. The picture that came to her was of a horribly tangled and knotted ball of string. When she visualized herself gently untangling and smoothing out the string, she felt a wonderful sense of inner release. The frayed and knotted string became a strong rope. Soon she was able to picture herself using the rope to climb a steep slope — a spontaneous image of another specific challenge in her life — which would have been beyond her resources and abilities before.

Sometimes the block can be released by an inner or outer ritual involving water. Many societies have practiced rituals for consigning negative or unwanted energies — including the energy of "bad" dreams — to water. In ancient Mesopotamia, it was a common practice to try to transfer such energies to a figure made quickly and roughly from clay. While the blessing of a guardian entity was invoked, the clay sculpture would then be broken up over a river, and the current would be allowed to carry away whatever had been released.

We can do an everyday version of such rituals, with or without the clay. In place of explicit prayer, I like to sing an old song by that great composer Anonymous that is all about getting into the flow. It has many uses, including setting up the cleansing and liberating power of water to take from you whatever has been holding you back. As I sing them and offer them to my groups, the words go like this:

The river is flowing
Flowing and growing
The river is flowing
Down to the sea.
Earth Mother carry me
Your child I will always be

Earth Mother carry me
Down to the sea.

You might want to sing this under the shower, as did one man who found constriction in his throat area. He saw the blockage as caused by two pairs of hands — of people he had known in the past — and then a third pair he recognized as his own. Shocked by the realization that in some sense he had been cutting off his own voice, he let the flow of the water loosen the grip of those six hands. He reported that he felt energized for the rest of the day. He also turned everyday handwashing into a mindful practice. When he washed his hands, he reminded himself that he was freeing his voice.

A woman let herself float down the river in her mind as she sang the song. She found a large, rectangular, solid block behind her heart center that she associated with both physical and emotional issues. River otters came to help her. They worked on the block, breaking it into little fragments that floated away with the current. She felt delicious waves of relaxation and a deep sense of ease, peace, and community.

Time and Madeleine L'Engle

I have lost and found myself many times in the wonderful worlds created by Madeleine L'Engle. Her literary biography confirms some of the lessons of this chapter. Having failed to find her audience as a writer while her family struggled with its finances, she decided to stop writing on her fortieth birthday, in 1958. But she had kept a journal since she was eight, and the habit was impossible to erase. She went on a long camping trip and conceived, on the road, the idea for the book *A Wrinkle in Time*. She shopped it around to publishers and was rejected more than thirty times before this extraordinary sci-fi fantasy novel was acquired by Farrar, Straus and Giroux; it was published in 1962.

In her story we see how the obstacle may prove to be the way, in two senses: it can prompt you to try a different way, and then it can stimulate you to develop the grit and persistence to win once you are on the right path. Through it all, you must journal, journal, journal. I don't know how anyone can become a writer — or lead an examined life — without keeping a journal.

It's All Raw Material

I can't close this chapter without a reminder that for a creative mind, and perhaps especially the mind of a creative writer, *all* experience is raw material. Think of how Stephen King welcomes the nightmares that give him ideas for his bestselling horror stories.

Jorge Luis Borges said it beautifully: "A writer — and, I believe, generally all persons — must think that whatever happens to him or her is a resource. All things have been given to us for a purpose, and an artist must feel this more intensely. All that happens to us, including our humiliations, our misfortunes, our embarrassments, all is given to us as raw material, as clay, so that we may shape our art."

4

You Have Treasures
in the Twilight Zone

Tinker Bell says to Peter Pan in a movie version of J. M. Barrie's story, "You know that place between sleep and awake, the place where you can still remember dreaming? That's where I'll always love you.... That's where I'll be waiting."

I have been following these fairy directions for a very long time. If you can train yourself to maintain relaxed attention in this in-between state, you will notice that you are building a creative studio, a private movie theater that is open at any hour, and a departure lounge for lucid dream adventures. These are only some of the gifts that are waiting for you in the place between sleep and awake.

When you lie down to sleep or rest, what do you see behind closed eyelids? If you are really tired or have been partying hard, your inner lights may go out right away. However, it's likely you'll see and sense a few things, like flashes or light or color or voices that are not in the next room. If you can manage to be drowsy and somewhat attentive at the same time, your impressions may grow. You see geometric patterns or the weave of some fabric. Pictures like children's drawings or cartoons whiz by, too fast and flimsy for you to catch anything much.

Now there are faces and figures, vivid and alive. It doesn't feel like you're looking at them inside your head. It's more like they are in front of you and around you. Who are all these strangers? You may find yourself shifting from your witness perspective and moving among a crowd. Nobody seems to see you. But wait. *Someone is looking at you.* The moment of eye contact may startle you out of your excursion. Maybe another time you could risk an encounter with that stranger.

The longer you can maintain a state of relaxed attention, or attentive relaxation, in this border state, the more is likely to happen. You'll enter different landscapes, some wildly beautiful, some otherworldly. You may sense you are moving at increasing speed until you are flying.

You may step into a drama, a romance, or an adventure that may mystify you to begin with because it does not correspond to anything familiar to you.

There's no doubt you are walking on the wild side. Nothing is fixed. An elephant turns into a tuba. A fish leaps in a pool and becomes the pupil of an enormous eye. An octopus turns into a solar disk with multiple arms, like the Aten of ancient Egypt. You watch a tiger chasing a girl, then you become the girl *and* the tiger, and the tiger is on her, and it's all good, though when you go to the bathroom you check in the mirror to see whether there is blood around your mouth.

Maybe those flighty figures who come and go in your mind are the Hypnagogicks I dreamed about: "They run lightly, playfully, up and down steps and over stoops along my street. They are flying as much as running. They seem light as zephyrs. They are the size of nine-year-old children. I know they are called Hypnagogicks."

Researchers have given us names for the twilight zone of consciousness and its various neighborhoods. The French scholar and physician Albert Maury, writing in 1848, invented the word *hypnagogic* to describe "hallucinations" around the onset of sleep by putting together the Greek words *hypnos*, meaning "sleep," and *agōgos*, which means "bringing, leading, drawing forth." However, Maury himself observed that hypnagogic experiences do not necessarily lead to sleep. Half a century after Maury, British psychic researcher and poet Frederic Myers came up with the bookend term *hypno-pompic* (*pompos* meaning "guide") for experiences on leaving sleep. He defined hynopompic images as "pictures consisting generally in the persistence of some dream-image into the first moments of waking." In the scholarly literature, *hypnagogia* is widely used as a blanket term for all experiences in the liminal spaces before sleep, after sleep, and during breaks in the sleep cycle when the body is still dormant in bed.

These terms fail the beauty test, which Henri Poincaré, the great French mathematician who spent a lot of time in twilight states, considered the best criterion for the accuracy of a formula. The Italian language gives us *dormigveglia* ("sleep-wake"), which looks and sounds lovely. So does its French counterpart, *dorveille*, which was in common usage in the era of the troubadours but has slipped out of the modern vocabulary. (I am trying to change that through the dream teachers I have been training in France. We ask one another at breakfast, "As-tu dorveillé bien?")

We can call this a half-dream state. It is certainly a liminal or threshold state of consciousness (we derive "liminal" from the Latin *limen*, a threshold). But perhaps we can be content, for now, to call it the twilight zone, or (with Tinker Bell) the place between sleep and awake or, quite simply, HG.

The researchers who produce charts showing what goes on in the sleeping brain can't give us useful correlations for HG. Brain waves measured by EEG are all over the place, though there is some evidence that the most creative and attentive minds at play in this zone shift the patterns to beta in problem solving or to theta in deep lucid dreaming.

Though HG experiences are most often visual, the other inner senses come into play. We hear things: our name being called, a strange gust of conversation, a doorbell, an animal cry, and — when we are prepared and lucky — communication worth hearing from a reliable contact. We smell or taste something that is not in our physical environment, maybe the perfume of a lover far away or the taste of the dessert she is eating. These examples suggest that our supernormal abilities, including telepathy and clairsentience, wake up when we are drowsing around sleep.

We are going to catalog the many treasures of the twilight zone. Let's notice that doing well in this treasure hunt requires what excellence in any field demands: practice, practice, practice. To become a master of this zone requires, ironically, your willingness to let go of the desire for mastery, to abandon the need for control, to loosen your ego boundaries, and to be open and available to what presents itself when your eyes are closed. You want to be willing to be surprised, open to new experience, ready to go with the flow and to postpone analysis. This soft mastery also requires you to learn to rest on the cusp of sleep without nodding off completely, at least not before you have experienced fascinating things and registered them.

If you are new to this area, you may be dizzied or frustrated for some time by how fast HG images come and go in the first minutes after you close your eyes. William James, the great American philosopher and psychologist, estimated that he received a thousand images in every ten minutes he spent in the zone, and I am sure this was no exaggeration.

Treasures of the Twilight Zone
Your Cure for Insomnia

Awake in the middle of the night? Don't fret that you can't get back to sleep. Snuggle around in bed, try different body postures, and be open to images that arise in your mind. Eventually you will drift into sleep, but before that you may have a liminal dream adventure or a brilliant new idea. In general, if you don't feel like sleeping, don't medicate or otherwise force yourself into sleep. Try to juggle your schedule so you can take a nap later, when you are ready for it.

In those "sleepless" hours, find something fun and creative to do — especially in the twilight zone!

I don't suffer from insomnia because if I don't feel like sleeping, I don't try to go to sleep. I confess that I am a lifelong biphasic sleeper. My habits would be recognized and approved by most of our ancestors, cross-culturally. For hundreds of thousands of years, humans thought that what the pushers of sleep meds promise — an uninterrupted night of seven or eight hours' sleep — was an unnatural and undesirable thing. Experiments by a team led by Dr. Thomas Wehr at the National Institute of Mental Health have supplied compelling evidence of how our technology has ripped us from our natural cycle. Deprived of artificial lighting for several weeks, the typical subject evolved the following pattern: lying awake in bed for an hour or two, then four hours of sleep, then two to three hours of "non-anxious wakefulness" followed by a second sleep before waking for the day's activities.

One of the most exciting findings in this study involved the endocrinology of the night watch. The interval between first sleep and second sleep is characterized by elevated levels of prolactin, a pituitary hormone best known for helping hens to brood contentedly above their eggs for long periods. Wehr concluded that the night watch can produce benign states of altered consciousness not unlike meditation.

The Power to See What's in Your Mind

The images that arise spontaneously in the twilight state may start with flashes and colors and light, with geometric patterns, and move through a parade of faces and glimpses of various landscapes. At some point you will start to observe that you are being given images of what is in your mind starting from your personal subconscious and ranging to the plenitude of what Carl Jung called the collective unconscious. You will begin to discern what the Viennese psychoanalyst Herbert Silberer named "autosymbolic phenomena." In other words, symbols arise that show you in images rather than words what is with you and what is in you, what you are thinking and feeling and experiencing in a deeper way than in everyday consciousness. This is a source of self-knowledge from which you will come to understand your personal symbols.

Monitor this, and you will grow your symbolic vocabulary and your ability to adopt a witness perspective in your life passages. You will also become quite familiar with what Jung called the shadow side of the psyche and will be able to bring awareness to and resolve aspects of yourself and your life circumstances that you suppressed or denied.

An Easy Way to Revisit Your Dreams

The best way to understand a dream is to get your head back inside it, gather more information, and examine what is actually going on. As a practice, dream reentry has many other virtues. Going back inside a dream to confront a fear or challenge and to dream the dream onward to resolution is the sovereign remedy for "bad" dreams and nightmares. You may want to reenter a dream to talk to someone in the dreamscape, or to enjoy more of a romance or adventure, or to develop personal doorways to the multiverse. The twilight zone is the prime time spot for the practice of dream reentry, if you arrange your life so you have time after sleep to linger in bed, connect with the threads of the dream, and then make it your game to pick up those threads and gently pull yourself back into that other world.

The Practice of Horizontal Meditation

On your back or your side (you'll want to experiment with different body positions), in the twilight state you are ready to practice a simple form of horizontal meditation that can carry you through shifting states to the yogic pinnacle of continuity of consciousness. You can make it your intention to simply observe the rise and fall of images in the half-dream state, maintaining detachment and a witness perspective. Or you can set an intention, called in yoga nidra a *sankalpa*, and then choose, when a corresponding image arises, to breathe energy into it and merge with it or travel through it.

A Place for Healing

The twilight state has long been recognized as a place of encounter with healing powers that may come invoked or uninvoked. In the ancient practice of dream healing in the temples of Asklepios (Aesculapius to the Romans), the healing encounter was invoked, and participants made careful preparations, including ritual cleaning and the gathering of dreams of invitation. It is clear from the testimonies that the actual encounter with the sacred guide and healer usually took place not in sleep dreams but in vivid experiences in the half-dream state of hypnagogia in which the sacred healer might take the form of an animal or serpent.

There is no more gripping account of the *experience* of meeting the healing god in the twilight state than in Aelius Aristides's *Sacred Tales*:

> I seemed almost to touch him. Halfway between sleep and waking, I perceived that he was there in person; one was between sleep and waking. I wanted to open one's eyes but I was anxious that he might leave. I listened and heard things, sometimes as in a dream, sometimes as in waking vision. My hair stood on end, and I wept tears of joy, and the weight of knowledge was no burden.... Only if you have been through it can you know and understand.

When the ancients sought healing in the twilight zone, they often did this with prayer and ritual. They might approach the sacred night by singing a song to call the sacred healer: "Healer of all, come blessed one." In the twilight zone one night, in urgent need of healing, I sang those words. As I stretched my body out on the bed, I saw an enormous snake. It was gray blue. It looked at least twenty feet long. I saw the dark slits of its pupils quite close to me in a head larger than my own. I did not feel fear, but there was a strong sense of the uncanny, the presence of a transpersonal other. I felt this could be the Asklepian serpent, a power mastered for healing.

I decided to trust my visitor. I let the snake enter my energy body. I felt it moving through all my energy centers, from the root chakra all the way up. Slight pressure at the heart, a little tightness at the throat. There was a probing motion at my third eye, as if the snake wanted to open or enlarge my vision center. The movement looped down and back and then repeated. I felt blessed, renewed, and restored.

Your Portal to God Space

The twilight zone is a portal for contact with inner and transpersonal guides. In the third century, the philosopher and mystery initiate Iamblichus recommended attending to "god-sent experiences" in the "condition between sleeping and waking." He counseled paying particular attention to what comes in the hypnopompic state, "when sleep is leaving us, and we are beginning to awake when voices are heard by us, and sometimes bright and tranquil light shines forth."

I frequently have inner dialogues in this state with sources of knowledge I have come to trust. This is a time when I can often receive streams of counsel and information from extraordinary teachers. In *Dreamgates*, I record some of my conversations with the intelligence I decided to call G2. He carried the vocabulary and knowledge of a great Western mystery order. I felt he was a transpersonal figure, though in no way alien to me. Many others have come to me in this liminal state. The most important of these inner guides is certainly no stranger; he is a self who observes and operates on a level of reality above the one I inhabit while living on this earth in a physical body.

Barbara Hand Clow says she knows that communication from another dimension is about to begin when holographic light forms, sometimes of great complexity and brilliance, appear in her inner space. Sometimes contact begins with a light that grows in size and brilliance until it seems the sun is shining in the room.

Your Creative Studio for Problem Solving and Innovation

The most compelling character in Ruth Ozeki's novel *A Tale for the Time Being* stepped out of the twilight zone. The book is a marvelous read, suggesting not only that we are time travelers in dreams but that what we do in dreams can change ordinary reality. In a Q&A for her publisher, Ozeki talks about how she first heard the voice of Nao (hear "Now"), a young Japanese schoolgirl, in that liminal space between sleep and awake:

> The fact is, I did wake up one day with the words and voice of a young girl named Nao in my head, and like my fictional Ruth, I could not stop thinking about her until I discovered her fate. You can look at the novel as a parable about the process of writing fiction. What happens when a character appears and calls the novelist into being? This is magic — the very ordinary magic of writing fiction.

In the history of creative breakthroughs in every field, including science and technology, the twilight zone has been a solution state. In this liminal space your cognitive brain and your intuition can play together nicely. You connect things that you would never normally think of putting together. Visual thinking supplants verbal analysis and takes the mind to places logic and reason cannot reach.

A Launchpad for Lucid Dreaming

The easiest way to become a lucid dreamer is to start out lucid and stay that way. Once you are at home in the twilight zone, you will find that you are given whole menus for lucid dreaming. As scenes form and re-form, you can choose to enter one and embark on an adventure. Or you can call up an image or memory of a certain locale — in ordinary reality or in the imaginal realm — and travel to that place.

I'm in the twilight zone, watching a parade of faces, wondering who these people are, and nobody is looking at me. Are these dead people? Are these strangers I might meet in the street tomorrow? Who are they? Now I'm gliding through crowds. It's interesting. I'm not sure what's going on. Suddenly, I'm on a bridge and I think, *Oh, I'm on the Bosporus. I'm on the bridge between Europe and Asia in Istanbul.* There's a woman in a long white veil. I can see only her dark eyes. I know she is ravishingly beautiful, but I can't see her form. She looks at me with fierce intensity and asks, "Are you Turkish? Or Romanian?" I'm so startled I fall out of the scene. But I am able to reenter it right away, and it becomes a lucid dream adventure. It is made clear to me that I am in contact with a certain Sufi order based in Turkey.

Your Own School of Seership

In twilight states, your natural intuition and psychic abilities come fully alive. You can make it your game to scan your psychic field with your inner sensors and see who and what is there. You may find that some psychospiritual house cleaning is required. You may also find that you have astral visitors, invited or uninvited. You may perceive holographic memories of the place where you are living or staying. You may also have glimpses of people and places you will encounter in coming days.

Andreas Mavromatis cites impressive evidence that "hypnagogia is significantly conducive to paranormal events," including precognition, which is commonly referred to in parapsychology as *psi phenomena.* "Psi states and hypnagogia...are related in their respective psychophysical induction and phenomenology....Hypnagogia is indeed conducive in the production of psi states, and, vice versa, the deliberate/experimental induction of psi states tends to render the latter hypnagogic."

Knowledge of the Subtle Bodies

In the twilight zone it becomes easy to practice shifting consciousness beyond the physical body. You may start by imagining that you can roam the physical space around you while your body is dormant, with eyes closed, inspecting objects from different angles and then turning to contemplate the body in the bed. You can initiate experiments in journeying further beyond the physical body, and little by little you can expand your understanding and experience of multiple vehicles of energy and consciousness.

The journey often begins at a certain threshold, a gap between the worlds, in a twilight of the mind. I may find myself floating upward. I roll over, and as I do so I feel something loosing itself from my physical body. Lights flash at the top of my head, and I am being drawn up into a cone of light, like a pyramid with an opening at the top. There are days when, flat on my back under a tree, I fall upward into the bowl of the sky, like Rumi. There are nights when I feel I am about to blast off like a rocket or be blown from the mouth of a cannon, through circles of red within black. Or I feel myself shedding the body like a snakeskin, dropping it like an old overcoat.

Your Personal Yoga of Manifestation

Your imagination becomes most vividly alive when your body is dormant. If you can maintain a state of relaxed attention on the cusp of sleep, this is an excellent time to set an intention for manifestation.

The intention should be charged with deep desire. You may give it form as a verbal statement or personal mantra. The French hypnotherapist Émile Coué recommended practicing autosuggestion in this state, for example by repeating his affirmation "Day by day, in every way, I am getting better and better." You may also picture a tangible, satisfying scene in which you are enjoying the fulfillment of a life goal.

Your Inner Playground

In the twilight zone you can grow your ability not only to enjoy the Sensurround movies you'll find playing in the Dream Cinema but to make yourself director, screenwriter, and star of your inner productions. I find it delightful simply to lie back and watch images rise and fall and to play with what they give me. Here's an example from my journal for December 23, 2019:

> As soon as I lay my head on the pillow and let my eyelids fall
> I see the pupil of a giant eye. A blue iris with many fine radiating threads of silver and gold and soft green forms around
> it. I now see that the eye is in the sky, floating among fluffy
> clouds. I feel a strong invitation and travel through the pupil
> to exciting scenes in many faraway places. Soon I am leading
> a group in Brittany, near the sea. I walk with a woman friend
> during a break across wetlands. The smell of the sea and of
> seaweed is strong.

Many things might be going on here. I might have been given a glimpse of a possible future situation, a workshop in Brittany that I had scheduled but that was later put in doubt by the pandemic. The eye in the sky seemed like a portal to further adventures. It also aroused my inner artist; I felt compelled to paint it. Above all, I relished how my inner senses came vividly alive in an enjoyable spontaneous outing, while my body was dormant. When it comes to hypnagogia, the play is truly the thing.

Homeplay: Games to Play on the Threshold

Count Your Breaths

No, this is not like counting sheep in order to fall asleep. It's a relaxed way to discover what images arise spontaneously in your mind when you close your eyes and shut out external distractions and the relative attraction they have for you. Just breathe normally and count each in breath. Notice when images arise and start to pull you away from your count. This may happen almost at once. You may find that you can sustain the count while successive images push for your attention. Chances are that by the time you have counted to fifty, you will have let yourself go with one of the images and will have lost the numbers, which is fine. The count doesn't matter, except as a way for you to gauge the relative intensity — the distracting or seductive power — of the images that want to play with you.

Which Side Are You On?

I notice that when I lie on my left side, my dreams and hypnagogic impressions are very social and busy, often starting with a parade of faces. When I lie on my right side, my dreams are more likely to be far voyages to other orders of reality, often with mythic content and far memory of other life experiences. Inner guides — the kind you learn to trust — like me to lie on my back for conversation.

If you experiment in this way, you may find something quite different. On a night when you are in the mood, try changing your body posture in bed and see whether this changes your inner life. And don't forget, as you leave sleep in the morning, to allow yourself to linger in your final posture and see whether dreams you dreamed in that position come back or come alive.

Lie In and Dream On

Try to avoid jumping out of bed as soon as you wake up or the alarm goes off. A period of slow reentry into the daylight world is prime time for hypnopompic experiences. You may find you are still inside a dream or something new is dawning.

Lazing in bed in the half-dream state after sleep, I find myself traveling. I am drawn to a primitive village in Northern Europe, a long time ago. The people know me. Since I don't know them, I check to see what body I am in. I find I have slipped into the guise of a younger man with a hawklike profile, wearing a long robe and a floppy, broad-brimmed hat. I have slipped into a body and a life in another time and place. I am still in contact with my regular, present-time body, which is lying dormant on the bed, but my inner senses are fully engaged in the Northern scene. I plunge into an ancestral drama.

If not much comes in the way of visual images, pay attention to your thoughts and feelings. You may find you have a sense of orientation and direction, even a solution for an issue of the kind we discussed in chapter 1.

Imaginal Exercise: Visit Your Dream Cinema

From the place between sleep and awake, you can travel to a marvelous imaginal locale where you can screen and even produce your own movies, in any genre. Let's call it the Dream Cinema. How do you get there? Through memory and desire.

Start by calling up some life memories of a theater where you had fun and were excited by drama or romance, comedy or adventure. Let that theater become vividly alive in your mind. You may find you are borrowing elements from different movie houses — that place where you watched matinees in childhood, a shiny new multiplex, that funky art cinema with great popcorn.

Put yourself at the entrance to your cinema. Look at the marquee. You may see titles of films you could watch on a regular screen. But pretty soon you'll notice titles that are both fresh and familiar, because they are all about you. They may be titles of dreams that went missing, or that you remember from long ago, or that are being screened for you right now.

You step through the door. Look carefully at the person staffing the ticket booth. This is the Gatekeeper for this adventure, and Gatekeepers have an important function: to make sure that we pay the price of admission and also that we are prepared for what lies ahead. You might say, "I am here for the dream I need to dream." Or "I am here for the story I need for my life right now." Or simply "I'm here for some fun and relaxation."

The ticket person may ask you to put something down. You might be surprised to find what kind of baggage you have been carrying, despite all the work on yourself you've done.

You'll be allowed to go into a screening room. Pick up popcorn or snacks on the way if you like. You'll settle into a comfortable seat. It seems you are alone in the theater, though this could change. Pictures come up on the screen, very much like the rush of patterns and images you see when you first close your eyes in bed. However, quite soon you are looking at clips or trailers, and then what may be the main feature fills the screen.

It's your dream movie that is playing. You can stay in your seat, or you can go through the screen and join the adventure, as actor or observer. You can become the star and the scriptwriter and the director. You may find that this is marvelous practice for producing a life movie that can play in the regular world.

I never tire of leading a journey to the Dream Cinema in my classes or of making private visits, generally in the middle of the night, between sleeps.

Throwing Popcorn at the Screen

Let me share an amusing variant on the script I just gave you. One of my frequent flyers — a teacher of Active Dreaming — told me she found herself stuck in a frustrating, repetitive life story. She decided to go to the Dream Cinema and look for a better story. She told me that I — that is to say, Dream Robert — turned up and proposed that we should pick up some hot buttered popcorn. We carried our popcorn to cushy seats in the theater. The film that came on the screen, to my friend's disgust, was a reprise of the sad old story she had been living.

In the Dream Cinema, we both started throwing popcorn at the screen. Whooping with joy, she cried out, "That's enough with the old life movie that does not sustain me or fulfill my deep desires. Let's have the new one." This worked like a charm. A new story started being enacted on the big screen, giving her confidence and clues about how to manifest that in regular life.

You can borrow this scene if you like and make it your own. When you find a sad old story keeps playing in your life and your mind, picture it playing on the big screen and throw popcorn until it breaks up and stops commanding that space. Your magical child will love this! You'll clear the way to screen fresh things, in your mind and in your life.

Practice: So-Wild

I want to offer you a plan for receiving guidance and embarking on adventures in the twilight zone. It is one that suits our busy modern lives.

When we first fall into bed, our most immediate need is to rest and restore the body. We may be overburdening ourselves and failing to satisfy that need when we set ourselves goals and objectives at the onset of sleep. It is fine to let the first cycle be "industrial sleep," allowing ourselves simply to restore and regenerate the body.

Of course, you may have a rush of HG imagery followed by sleep dreams, and you want to be open to such spontaneous gifts. But you don't want to turn the dream adventure into another chore.

In my experience, prime time for setting or resetting an intention for the night and embarking on liminal or lucid dream excursions is right after the first cycle of sleep. Sleep patterns vary, but chances are you will awaken — and know you are awake — three or four hours after going to sleep. Maybe you need to go to the bathroom or have a glass of water. Fine, do it. Maybe you have dreams, or at any rate elements of dreams, from the first sleep cycle. Jot them down. Titles or key words may be enough.

Maybe you want to putter around for an hour or two before going back to bed. That's okay, too, as long as you leave yourself time for more nocturnal adventures before you need to go out on the business of the day.

Now: settle back in bed. This is the time to set, or reaffirm, an intention for guidance or healing or adventure.

If you have a dream with some juice from your first sleep cycle, you can make it your intention to reenter that dream, explore the dream space, and carry on with the adventure you were having before.

You may find you are in a space where communication with an inner guide is possible.

Or you can simply lay yourself open to the images that will rise and fall between awake and sleep. Chances are that one of these will catch your attention and grow into a living scene that you can enter, the start of lucid dreaming.

Here's an acronym for this simple approach:

S = sleep
O = open to experience
W = wake
I = intend
L = lucid
D = dreaming

SO-WILD, and it works!

5

Your Body Believes in Images

An image carries a physical charge: it sends electrical sparks through the body and it releases a stream of chemicals. Our best medical science confirms that the body does not seem to distinguish between a physical event and a strong thought or memory of an event. This means we have immense power to make ourselves strong and well or sick and depressed, according to the thoughts and images we choose to give our attention to.

Something you need to know: *any* image that belongs to you can be worked in the direction of wholeness and healing.

We hear talk of "imaginary diseases." What we need to understand is that there are diseases of the imagination, symptoms that arise because we have allowed our imaginations to become corrupted. We are all psychosomatic. How we use or abuse our imaginations can bring us up or drive us down.

The body and the deeper self understand the nature of what ails us and seek to convey this understanding — and means of healing — to us through images. When our imagination is dormant or corrupted, the purpose of physical symptoms may be to shake us up so we can receive the imagery that will bring wholeness and healing. A Jungian perspective is that a symptom represents something from your internal state that seeks to become conscious. What does not manage to access consciousness as an image — or does, only to be ignored — may then manifest as a symptom.

We can go to the parts of the body where we are experiencing the symptoms and let images arise. We can work with spontaneous imagery that comes to us in dreams and in other ways. We can embark on imaginal journeys to places of healing — to an inner temple or to the blue lake of healing, a magical locale that will be opened to you in this chapter. We can gift each other with healing images through the technique of vision transfer and word doctoring, as explained in chapter 10. The purpose of the symptoms may be to stir us to awaken to the images that can bring wholeness.

Science Agrees:
Your Body Believes What You Believe

Let's start with a little science. Dr. Harold G. Koenig, professor of medicine at Duke University, reviewed six hundred studies of the impact of spirituality and religion on health. He found that spiritual beliefs have a positive impact on the functioning of the immune and endocrine systems. Patients with a spiritual orientation have significantly higher white blood cell counts and experience significantly lower infection rates than the norm. They also produce notably lower levels of adrenal stress chemicals like cortisol.

Advances in hard scientific research, especially in the fast-expanding field of psychoneuroimmunology (PNI), supply overwhelming evidence that the body believes in images and that our thoughts and feelings can make us sick or make us well. It's interesting to note that long before it had a name, research in the PNI field was guided by dreaming. The first person to isolate and identify a neurotransmitter was Otto Loewi, and he saw how to perform the necessary experiment in a dream. He got out of bed, cut open a frog, and applied vagal juice to its heart, as he had done in the dream;

the relaxant in the vagal stuff was identified as the neurotransmitter acetylcholine.

The research suggests that there is no mind-body separation. According to molecular biologist Candace Pert, there is a "psychosomatic communications network" that operates not only in the brain but in all parts of the body. Our conscious or unconscious thoughts and feelings are constantly affecting our health by sending directives to a pharmaceutical factory inside the body. Our mind is in every cell of our bodies.

Physician Larry Dossey, a leader in mind-body medicine since the 1980s, told me that "the body responds to mental input as if it were physically real. Images create bodily changes, just as if the experience were really happening. For example, if you imagine yourself lying on a beach in the sun, you become relaxed, your peripheral blood vessels dilate, and your hands become warm, as in the real thing."

Brain scans show that when we imagine an event, our thoughts light up the same areas of the brain that are triggered during the actual event. Pioneer work in this area was done by sports psychologists. Skiers were wired up to EMG monitors (which record electrical impulses sent to the muscles) while they mentally rehearsed their downhill runs. It was discovered that their brains sent the same instructions to their bodies whether they were thinking about a jump or actually doing it.

Sports psychology is now based on the premise that the body-mind does not know the difference between an actual event and an imagined one. Mental rehearsal, called covert conditioning in sports, centers on seeing yourself making your moves play by play, in minute detail. This is much more than vague, warm-and-fuzzy "positive thinking." You imagine a flawless performance, and you see yourself make the moves ahead of time.

Our feelings even determine whether our bodies are open or closed to a viral housebreaker. Viruses use the same receptors as neuropeptides to enter a cell, and depending on how much of the natural peptide for a particular receptor is around and available to bind, the virus that fits that receptor will have an easier or harder time getting into the cell. For example, the reovirus, held to be a cause of the common cold, uses the receptor for norepinephrine, a feel-good natural chemical, to enter the cell. If you're happy, it would seem, the cold virus can't get in.

Stress is responsible for 60 to 90 percent of visits to doctors, according to Harvard medicine professor Herbert Benson, founder of the Mind/Body Medical Institute at Massachusetts General Hospital. Stress is the body's chemical response to a situation we *think* is threatening. When we perceive a threat, our sympathetic nervous system releases stress hormones like cortisol, raising heart rate and blood pressure, getting us ready — like our Stone Age ancestors — for fight or flight, even though neither option may be possible or appropriate in our contemporary lives.

Stress distracts the cytokines — chemical messengers that alert immune agents to a problem — and sends them charging wildly through the bloodstream. When they are misdirected, they produce something you don't want: a prolonged inflammatory response that far exceeds what is needed to deal with infection.

It's no surprise to most of us that stress can bring us down and undermine our health. If we have a better grasp of how unconscious emotional energies bring us down, it may be easier for us to move to the understanding that by choosing to express or redirect those energies, we can help make ourselves well.

In Latin, *placebo* means "I shall please." In health care, the term "placebo effect" is used to describe an improvement in health due to the patient's belief that they are receiving treatment when in fact they are not. A placebo might be a sugar pill or the pretense that a patient has received surgery or an IV treatment that was actually not administered. Not that long ago, some American hospital dispensaries contained bottles of sugar and starch pills labeled "Obecalp" — "placebo" spelled backwards.

As ancient healers well understood, the role of personality, drama, and ritual in promoting the placebo effect is huge. From the moment a pilgrim entered an Asklepian temple, he or she was given constant encouragement to believe that healing was available and to abandon old mental habits and self-defeating attitudes. In a society where we find authority in white coats and medical degrees, the placebo effect is strong in patients who meet face-to-face with practitioners.

Build Your Imaginal Apothecary Shop

We are often unaware of our shifting thoughts and feelings. We may be wholly unaware of memories and images, held in the body, that bring us down. The decision to bring unrecognized thoughts and feelings into consciousness is an essential step toward self-healing. Starting from here, we can develop the practice of investing our attention in images that make us well.

We can make it our choice, for example, to increase blood flow to a certain body part, giving it the strength to flush out toxins and the nutrients required to heal. The celebrated journalist and peace activist Norman Cousins got over a broken elbow and back on the tennis court in record time because he spent twenty minutes a day focusing on his intention to increase blood flow through the injured joint, after his doctor explained that elbow injuries often healed slowly because of poor blood supply. He was then able to recover from a crippling connective tissue disease with the aid of focused intention and what he called "laughter therapy." Any image that belongs to you can be a source of power and healing, even the scary stuff you would rather keep in a locked box. The trick is to learn how to develop your personal imagery so it can help you to get well and stay well. Your body is waiting for you to get good at this.

The secret may be to learn to stay with an image, even when it terrifies you, and find the courage to go through the portal of that image and confront the challenge it represents on its own ground. Let me give an example of how that worked for an artist I was privileged to assist.

The Gifts of Spider Woman

A well-known artist asked for my help. We sat on a sofa in front of the double doors of her art studio. The doors were closed and locked. She said, "Robert, I can't go into my studio. It's that bad."

I said, "What's the matter?"

"Well, I've had a series of dreams in which I'm being attacked by a spider," she responded. "I don't like spiders. The spider in my dream is larger than any realistic size — the size of my shoe, last time I saw it."

In the most recent version of the dream, the spider was jumping at her inside her studio. She tried to kill it with a book, which turned out to be a dream journal. But she failed and fled the dream version of her studio. She was now so terrified of the dream antagonist that she would not go into the physical space.

I risked being thrown out of the house by saying to her, "Great dream. Why not go back inside it, face the spider, and see what needs to be done?"

She started sobbing so hard the tears puddled at our feet. I said, "Well, I'll take your hand, and I'll come with you. But you need to do the work. If this were my dream, I would know I need to confront this antagonist and see what's going on and what needs to be done with it."

She was not happy. But she agreed to try. No drumming, nothing except the energy of her fear and the proximity of the dream location and the need to get this sorted out.

It became cinematic. Perhaps you can picture this: We rise from the sofa in our second bodies. We step through the doors to the studio. The spider is waiting inside. It grows until it is almost human size. It's anatomically correct. I don't like the way it looks, but it's not my spider, so I have no fear. The artist is terrified, but she stands her ground. I'm just there as friend and protector. She is the one who is here for this encounter.

After what seems like an agonizingly long time, the spider shape-shifts. It becomes a beautiful woman, perhaps a form of Spider Woman, a Navajo form of the goddess. Spider Woman says to the dreamer, "Because you found your courage, I'm going to give you two gifts. I give you the gift to shapeshift the energy web of your body so you don't need to get the disease again, and I give you the power to shapeshift the web of your creative life so you will enter the most creative period of your career as an artist."

Both promises were fulfilled. Though she did not mention this until after the dream reentry, the artist had an appointment for a biopsy. She had been in remission from cancer, but the doctors were worried that the disease had returned. When she went to the doctor, she discovered she was cancer-free, and she remained cancer-free for many years. She also entered a new creative period in her life. She took up new media. She arranged one-woman exhibitions in world capitals. The promises of Spider Woman were fulfilled.

Let's say it again: the things that scare us in our dreams are not on our case, they're on our side. The story of Spider Woman is a stellar example of what is possible when we brave up to a dream challenge and deal with it on its own ground.

The relevance of dreaming to imaginal healing is immense. It is our spontaneous dreams, including the ones we didn't ask for and may not want, that give us fresh and personal images for our condition. They show us ourselves in ways that are authentic and timely. They show us what is wrong with us in ways that help us get well.

Diagnostic descriptions may baffle us. They may merely mention the name of the first patient identified with that syndrome or the first doctor to look at it. Or they might be difficult versions of neo-Latin or neo-Greek that are very hard to comprehend. Dreams, on the other hand, give us kinesthetic, plastic, fluid, living cinematic images that allow us to recognize and work with what is going on in our bodies and our lives.

Dreams place what is wrong with us or could go wrong with us in a larger context of meaning. They show us how the symptoms that we have or could develop are related to how we approach life and how we approach soul.

Dreams also give us a path of direct encounter with the inner healer, a sacred guide. The sacred healer can take surprising, even shocking, forms, as in the case of the spider that became Spider Woman and the helper that appeared to me on a night when I was desperately ill.

The Bull and the Barbican

After rushing from Hawaii to frozen upstate New York and then further east to Frankfurt, failing to weather vertiginous shifts in temperature and time zones, I had arrived in Barcelona with major symptoms of oncoming cold or flu. In the middle of the night, I was hunched over the sink in my hotel bathroom, my chest screaming with pain when I coughed, and a slosh of stuff I didn't want to look at heaving from me to the drain. *I don't get colds or flu,* I had told myself for years. This was moving very quickly to something worse, bronchitis and possibly pneumonia. I recalled, without cheer, how fast that had happened when I was a boy, when I had suffered life-threatening bouts of double pneumonia twelve times over eight years.

I need to find a doctor. Or at least see if a local pharmacy will sell me some powerful antibiotics without the formality of a prescription. Back to bed, my chest aching, I found that at least I could breathe a little through the nose.

I lay on my back, finding some slight comfort in the surprising quiet of Eixample (the section of Barcelona famous for Antoni

Gaudí's architecture), hoping for at least a little rest. I was gripped by the sense that my condition was really serious and could soon be very much worse. And I am not a hypochondriac — rather, the extreme opposite. *Okay. Try your own stuff. Start by asking for help. And ask the right way.*

It took me some thinking before I got the words of my petition right. Speaking to the Universal Healer, I said, "I ask for the health my body requires to serve the purposes of the soul." *Wait, let's be more specific.* "I ask for the health my body requires to serve my purposes as teacher, creator, writer, healer, and father." From somewhere in the depths, I sensed approval.

Then a power rushed into me, entering me from behind, around the kidneys. Its wild rush and its potency reminded me of a bull. I recalled my encounter, walking the city that morning, with the thinking bull of the Rambla de Catalunya. I felt this huge, bull-like energy spreading all through me and expanding my energy field and my sense of my physical size and strength.

I now felt another stream of energy, rising like a great serpent from the earth, up through the soles of my feet and through all my energy centers. And yet another stream, a tremendous flood of light washing down through my crown to join the others in dynamic, confluent movement.

Now a strong vision arose spontaneously, showing me how my body had been invaded and how its defenders were now moving with decisiveness to trap and destroy the invaders. The scene resembled the barbican of a medieval castle. The barbican was the space between an outer and an inner gate, in front of the main castle walls. It was designed as a death trap for attackers who managed to break through the outer gate. Once invaders got inside the barbican, the defenders could seal the outer gate, leaving the inner gate closed, and then massacre the intruding force by firing arrows at them. Hurling down stones and pouring boiling oil over the invaders were also popular defense stratagems.

I watched with delight as the defenders of my immune system dealt with my body's invaders. Now I could see the brilliance of allowing them through the outer gate and into the death trap. I watched the mass execution of the germs directed by a lord wearing the silver antlers of a stag on his helmet. As the attack faltered and the grisly germ warriors died, I saw a giant of my cause wearing the horns of a bull, wading among my body's enemies, finishing them off with his great ax.

I leaped from the bed, absolutely certain that my battle had been won. I went to the bathroom and coughed. No pain. The phlegm that came out was now brown, not green or yellow. I was expelling the corpses of the illness army. I felt vastly restored.

When I returned to bed and looked again into the imaginal space of the battle, I was delighted to see that the defense forces were now scouring out the space of the barbican. Finally the bull knight summoned women in long white dresses to finish the cleaning, checking that no marks appeared on their fine white linen.

At sunrise, I was in excellent condition, ready for whatever the day might bring. I went out and about happily that morning and traveled on to my next workshop full of bright energy.

What can you take from my story? For starters, the need to recognize that we have inner as well as outer resources and can invoke greater powers for healing. It is very important to set our intentions wisely. If we are going to engage the active support of those greater powers, we must do more than ask for a quick fix or recycle some hand-me-down stuff. It is important to trust in the vital reality of the imagination and to work with the spontaneous images that come to us. And to recognize that the most propitious time for adventures in imaginal healing may come in the twilight zone between sleep and awake.

As I described, I was hacking and retching in the grip of a violent infection whose symptoms resembled those of the coronavirus that manifested eight years later. After I sought help from greater powers, an amazing imaginal battle unfolded quite spontaneously in which I saw the infection contained in a holding area and destroyed there by my body's defenders. Come morning, my body was completely healed.

Years later, in 2020, the medieval character of the scene may have special relevance given the structure of the new virus. When we look at the spikes of the virus, we cannot help but see they are so reminiscent of a medieval war mace.

The key takeaways from my experience can be summed up this way:

1. Remember to ask for help from greater powers.
2. Be ready to work with animal spirits and mythic allies.
3. Imagine that if an illness has entered your body, it can be confined in a holding space and defeated there without gaining access to all of your body.

Hummingbird Medicine

I will offer a simple heart-centered meditation that may find a place in your pharmacy of healing images. Let me introduce it with one of my favorite stories about why people come to my workshops. I was leading a workshop titled Dreaming a Life with Heart up in the old California Gold Rush country near Placerville, once notorious as Hangtown. My facilitator had chosen to put a photo of a hummingbird on the flyer, associated with a quote from me about hummingbird medicine.

When I asked participants in that workshop to introduce themselves, an older couple could hardly wait their turn. "I picked your flyer up at a local market," the man told us. "I was interested because I had open heart surgery last month. I wanted to talk to my wife about coming to the workshop. When I got home I noticed there was a hummingbird inside the car. Definitely a sign. I closed the door fast, wanting to show her the bird. When she came out of the house and I opened the car door, two hummingbirds flew out. They brought us here."

It is said that the hummingbird has the strongest heart of any warm-blooded creature on the planet. It needs that to hover in mid-air, its body still in the midst of constant beating motion. We could all do with that strength of heart and ability to stay calm and centered in the midst of chaos and confusion. Here's how we can invoke the hummingbird medicine.

Imaginal Exercise: Bring Hummingbird into Your Heart

Sit with your eyes closed, following the flow of your breath.

Place your hand on your physical heart. Feel how it is. Does it need something from you? Perhaps you are feeling some gratitude toward this magnificent organ for keeping you going as long as you have been on your life journey.

You become aware that there is something whirring and shimmering in midair right in front of you. Perhaps you can hear the hum of its beating wings.

It is a little hummingbird. Its color is a color from your imagination — emerald or crimson, sapphire or gold, or something less flashy. You marvel at how it can hover in midair, its body seemingly still while its wings beat so fast they are all but invisible.

You would love to have this strength of heart and this ability to stay centered.

You lift your hand from your heart, and your heart begins to open like a flower. Your flower. Your heart opens like a rose…or a hyacinth…or a lotus…

And the hummingbird comes to drink from your heart as it drinks from the heart of a flower. This feels so good.

You can hold the hummingbird medicine in your heart. You gently place your hand over your heart again and feel the petals closing over the hummingbird that now lives inside you. You will carry this medicine in life. Your heart will be stronger, and your life will be heart centered.

The Blue Lake of Healing

I am going to invite you to make a journey to a real place of profound healing potential deep in the realm of the animal powers. You go there only by invitation. I received my invitation many years ago, while camping among ancient poplars in the Great Smoky Mountains, and it had a price.

There is a blue lake of healing on top of a mountain. You must earn the right to go there, by tracking a wounded animal through the woods, following it up steeper and steeper trails, forging ahead even when mountain mist swallows your sight. The animal is connected to you. The places where it is wounded reflect your own condition.

At the top of the mountain, you are amazed to find a shining blue lake. As you watch, the animal staggers to the lake and falls in. It is gone for so long that you fear it has died. Have you come here for death?

At last, you see a stir in the waters. The animal surfaces on the far side of the lake. As it takes off, you see it is whole and healed.

It is your turn to enter the waters of the healing lake. You may go far deeper than your familiar world. How far you go will depend on your courage and imagination.

Are you ready for this?

Imaginal Exercise: Journey to the Blue Lake of Healing

You are outside in a place in nature. You may be walking in light woods. The weather and temperature are exactly what you need them to be. You're walking on a gentle slope. You can smell the air, the freshness. You hear the birds. You're enjoying yourself.

Now, you notice something surprising: spots of bright color on the trail. What's that? Is it paint? Is that a fallen leaf? No, it's too bright. You bend down. You look closely. You're shocked to find that what you're looking at is a spot of fresh blood.

You're anxious and concerned. Something is bleeding on this trail. You want to know what it is. You might be scared, but your curiosity is stronger than your fear. You are hurrying now, and you're going up the hill. The slope is getting steeper. Ahead of you, you see an animal or bird that is clearly wounded and is the source of the blood on the trail. You might be very surprised when you see what animal or bird this is. Its story is connected to you. What is it?

You have no idea how you can possibly help, but you would like to help if you can. Now, a mountain mist is coming down, deep and heavy, and suddenly you can't see anything except the mist. You've lost track of everything, all sense of direction. The only directions you know are up and down. You're pushing uphill, and the going is a bit harder. You're going up through the fog.

The fog clears, and you're at the top of the mountain. To your amazement, you are facing a lake of the most perfect blue, almost electric blue, the deepest, most beautiful blue lake. You catch sight of the wounded animal or bird. It's on the edge of the water, and it folds or flops down, and it's gone. It's gone, and your heart sinks because clearly the animal or bird has drowned. But wait. You see movement on the far side of the lake, and the animal or bird is coming up, and it seems to be fine. It runs off. It flies off. It slithers off. It appears to be healed.

Something tells you, in that kind of deep voice that you know you can trust, that this is a place of healing and that if you're ready, you too can experience what just happened. You yourself can take the plunge into the blue lake of healing. You can go as deep as you need to go, and you can come back healed and revived. You don't know exactly what this will mean. It might mean that you are cleansed from an old energy attachment, something of the old life. Some of the symptoms and stories that have held you back are going to be scrubbed from you. It might mean that deep in the depths of the blue lake you will find a source of healing that is waiting for you. It might mean that going down through the blue depths, you'll come into another world, and that is where you'll find your deepest healing.

The rest is for you to discover during the journey. You can put on a recording of shamanic drumming or nature sounds. If your intention and your practice are strong enough, you may be able to go all the way with those and the flow of your breath.

Find yourself on the trail again, following the spots of blood, identifying the animal or bird. See where it is wounded. This is important: it speaks of the condition of your body and your life. Go up through the mist. Watch the animal go into the lake and come out healed. Then, with hope and with reverence, enter the blue lake of healing yourself. Go as deep as you need to go and then come back, bringing back gifts and discoveries.

When you return, stretch out. Get something down, some notes, some drawings. What animal did you find on the trail? Did you see where it is wounded? How does that relate to your body and your situation in life? Did you enter the blue lake of healing? What did you find? How are you going to honor this?

I have led the journey to the blue lake of healing for many groups all over the world map. I will not forget what happened when I invited a circle of dreamers gathered in a villa in the Carpathian Mountains on the border of Transylvania to make the journey. The group expedition was fueled and focused by shamanic drumming. After I sounded the recall, I asked everyone in the group to write a brief account of their experience, no longer than would fit on one side of one of the index cards we proceeded to hand out. When we collected the cards, we had a remarkable group log of our expedition into imaginal healing. I will offer a sampling of reports, mostly translated from Romanian, to help grow your sense of possibility.

From the Blue Lake of Healing: Travel Reports

"A wounded deer was completely healed as she entered the blue lake in the mountains. In the middle of the lake there was a crystal, and from there healing was being sent for Mother Earth and for all the living creatures on earth. I was healing people and animals, and through healing a part of the light was being sent, so that they themselves became filled with more light."

"The aura of your heart will soften the hearts of those around you. It will transform them into clay that you will mold until it becomes liquid. It must be left ripening in the dark until it becomes light."

"Healing comes from the depth. You can heal yourself there, where you did not think that you could even live! The diamond tunnel with rays of divine light helps you heal yourself."

"The mountain goat was hurt in many places, and still she had the power to reach the lake. The drums and the fire were calling me, recognizing me as one of their people. I was asked why I needed healing. I said, 'Because I want to make art with colors.' Again, I was asked why. I said, 'Because in this way I can travel.' I brought colors to my heart and my body."

"A giant eagle went before me. I became one with her and felt her pain. As I came out of the water my body was translucent. I was light, I was love. I saw my dear ones — I sent love to them, and they sent love to me. Together, we created an immense sphere of light and love and sent it to float above the lake, the country, the planet. Then I transformed into a tree."

"I followed a big stag, wounded in the chest, on the left. He was limping, but still I could not reach him. I arrived at the lake just in time to see him going into water. I ran to the lake, and I saw him getting out on the other side, healed, running toward the forest. I dove into the water, which on the inside looked like an immense lagoon, with light in every corner. There were nymphs and gods at the bottom of the lagoon. My chest hurt on the left side. I felt the energy healing me. When I got out of the water I noticed I had a big scar on the left side of my chest, where my heart was healed."

"Heart wounded, I realized I came here to die. I let myself fall in the blue lake. Sweet fall, like floating. Beings, translucent tall beings, put this golden, shiny, small energy ball inside my heart center, and it started spinning. Golden light revived me, and I started breathing the blue, good water. Breathing like the first breath in my life. Came back from the journey with a new song in my head: 'It is a new life, it is a new dawn.'"

"The stag was bleeding from the eyes, and his back right leg was injured. When he came out of the blue lake, he was healed — and he had dropped his antlers. As he moved away, the antlers grew again, larger than before and golden."

"I met the bear. He was weak, wounded, and tired. At the blue lake he dived below, and then he came out all shining. His fur, once gray and without light, was now shining in the moonlight. After my healing I was given a white and silver dress that looked like the fur of the bear waiting for me on the shore. I climbed onto his back, and we went into the forest, where a shaman woman taught me a dance and an incantation for cleansing: 'I release to the fire, water, earth, and wind what does not belong to me and is a burden for me.'"

Vindecarea exista in fiecare dintre noi. Crede. (Healing exists inside each and every one of us. Believe.)

The Twelve Lights

I want to introduce a new experiment in imaginal healing called Twelve Lights. It was inspired by a conversation with Bonnie Horrigan. Bonnie was one of those who labored mightily to bring ancient ways of shamanic healing and dreaming into our health care system and our contemporary lives. This involved working with souls as well as bodies, developing personal imagery for healing, and asking spirit to be present in any procedure. She was cofounder and former publisher of *Alternative Therapies in Health and Medicine*, a breakthrough medical journal examining alternative and cross-cultural healing practices and the relationship of the human spirit to health and healing.

"I want to tell you my personal experience of dream healing," she said on my *Way of the Dreamer* radio show. "I was in hospital with a serious liver condition. It was really touch and go. Night after night, I would ask for help and guidance, saying, 'Show me the way.'

"At last my wish was answered. A spirit guide I recognized — a female presence who had appeared to me twice before — came to me in a dream. She scanned my body, seeking to understand what had gone wrong. She frowned and told me, 'You only have three lights. People are supposed to have twelve, but nine of your lights have gone out.' She said she was going to reignite the nine lights that had gone out, and that is exactly what she did.

"I woke with absolute confidence that my healing was begun and that I would come out of this fine. And I did."

Bonnie had never heard of "twelve lights in the body" before, nor had I. Clearly road testing was required! I started with a group experiment with thirty dreamers who joined me for a gathering on a mountain in the New York Adirondacks.

I described Bonnie's beautiful experience. I suggested we should approach the journey without limiting ourselves to any received energy paradigms. While we might find that the twelve lights were related to the chakras, or the sephirot on the Kabbalistic Tree of Life, or the energy meridians, we did not want to travel with any maps that might limit our ability to see beyond them.

We shared very rich experiences. Here is a sampling of the travel reports that our journeyers brought back.

The Twelve Lights: Travel Reports

"The lights were swirling, never still, moving around the body."

"I saw clearly how, when lights go out, holes open in your energy body and you are vulnerable to illness."

"I saw a brownish, dim light that seemed to be guttering out. A guide appeared to me and said, 'You don't need to fix that yourself.' She placed her hand over the dim light, and it flared up, strong and bright. My guide then took me back to my infancy, to a time when I was close to death because of a congenital heart defect. I saw her working to turn up my lights. I heard her say that I would survive because my lights are strong."

"I journeyed inside my body, in search of the lights, and was surprised to find myself in a desert scene, watching patterns rippling in the sand. A crater opened in the sand, and a being I saw as the Dragon took me down to a world below. I saw hundreds of raised hands, working on something huge, and realized that these were builders maintaining and reconstructing my body."

"I focused my intention on learning about the lights. A Little Person told me, 'Each of us has twelve life stories. We have life and strength as long as the potential of these stories is strong. When the stories die — because we give up on them or because we are truly done with them — we move closer and closer toward death. Our strength depends on how much story potential we are carrying.'"

"I asked a guide, 'How are my lights?' I was immediately taken to a dark, murky place where the light was dirty brown. There was a very young boy there eating something. I realized he was eating my light energy in this place inside me. I was shocked when I recognized him as an infant version of my son, a part of my son that refused to be born and has been inside me since the difficult C-section that got him out." (We discussed and agreed on a ritual for soul return to get that part of her son back where it belongs.)

"I was surprised and saddened to find that my heart light was dim because it was shut up inside something like a lantern with sides of smoky glass. I felt my heart light needs more room and more air and that the container needs to be cleansed because it has been allowed to become dirty and has suffered from events that burned me emotionally."

"I kept counting the lights I found, trying to get to the magic number twelve. I was excited, after much searching, to find a light that was carefully hidden. It is associated with the thymus. I also thought of it as Daat on the Kabbalistic Tree of Life. It was a deep blue, contained in something like a glass globe. I want to learn how to work with it."

I have continued the experiments in other circles. Everywhere the idea of the twelve lights seems to spread hope. One of our shamanic dreamers, guided by a cat, discovered three of the lights were meant to be centered on the heart. The other lights were available to be whirled out in a certain way to go to places in need of healing, and they were not to be overused. The movement of the lights was to be alternated with periods of restoration and energy building, which was an interesting discovery.

Another of our active dreamers quoted Bonnie's story at a large meeting of cancer survivors. A despondent elderly man, blind for several years, was immediately wreathed with smiles. He said, "When you spoke of the lights, I felt you had given me my sight back!" He declared he was going to work with the twelve lights in meditation every day.

Experiment: Tracking the Twelve Lights

Would you like to try this as a personal meditation? You will begin, as always, by getting your body in a comfortable position and relaxing into the flow of your breath. As you exhale, release anything that may be holding you back. As you inhale, breathe in a sense of expanding possibility and potential healing.

If you have made friends with the animal spirits, invite them in.

Where are you going? Inside your body, so you can't get lost. I would go straight to the heart to begin the journey, as the cat advised.

How many lights can you find? Where are they? How are they? Do they move around, do they swirl? Can you now identify places within you that are in need of light and healing?

When you come back, write a brief report. Maybe you want to draw an energy map of your body showing the placement and condition of the twelve lights.

Here's one more report to encourage you to pursue this experiment, from a natural healer and counselor who found herself guided by the benign feminine presence she calls Ancient Mother: "The lights, the galaxies move throughout the body. Several of them pool in a place that needs healing. My guide told me to join my consciousness with the lights as they pooled in that area that needed healing. That area felt like it was buzzing, vibrating, humming. I was thrilled that I could join consciously in the healing. I wasn't exactly directing it, but my desire for healing seemed to be acting in concert with the lights."

It was fascinating how waves of resonance spread from this experiment. Soon groups all over the map were trying it out, and people who had heard only the briefest account — like the blind man at the elder hostel — were giving it a try in private meditation. It's an example of the secret of life and imagination we will explore in chapter 7: *you are magnetic.*

6

Your Big Story Is Hunting You

We live by stories. Our first and best teachers, in our lives and in the evolution of our kind, instruct and inspire by telling stories. Story is our shortest route to the meaning of things and our easiest way to remember and carry the meaning we discover. A good story lives inside and outside time and gives us keys to a world of truth beyond the world of fact.

Consciously or unconsciously, our lives are directed by stories. If we are not aware that we are living a story, it's likely we are stuck inside a narrow and constricted one, a story bound tightly around us by other people's definitions and expectations. When we consciously reach for a bigger life story, we put ourselves in touch with tremendous sources of healing, creativity, and courage.

You know this moment: your life is trembling on the edge of a greater drama. You feel things stirring behind the curtain of everyday perception, moving pieces around you, bringing elements together in astounding moments of synchronicity. You feel yourself driven, defended, or thwarted by greater powers. Your life rhymes in inexplicable ways. You become aware that what is with you and around you — in what Jung called your "circumambient atmosphere" — has been charged with the energy of an archetype, call it a goddess or daimon, an angel or elemental.

You have been prepared for these awakenings by dreams and by stories you heard in childhood. As the mythologist Joseph Campbell said so clearly: "A dream is a personal experience of that deep dark ground that is the support of our conscious lives, and a myth is society's dream. The myth is the public dream and the dream is the private myth."

Australian Aborigines say that the big stories are hunting the right people to tell them, like predators stalking in the bush. The trick is to put ourselves in a place where the big stories can find us.

When we are seized by the big story, we step beyond limiting definitions and beliefs. Great healing becomes available because we can now draw on the immense energy that is generated by the sense of serving a larger purpose and living a mythic life. The muse, or creative genius, and the intelligences of the world behind the world come to support our life projects, because we are following a deeper call.

Powers of the deeper world move among us. Most of the time we are unaware of their presence. When they are in the field — noticed or invisible, invoked or uninvoked — their presence has a shimmer effect on the ordinary world. The fabric of physical reality in their vicinity becomes fluid and unstable. We experience the shift as a synchronicity or anomaly. If we become alert to the shimmer effect and make the right moves in that moment, we can manifest extraordinary things.

Know the Myth You Are Living

As some people use the word, *myth* is synonymous with fake news, or superstition, or outmoded hand-me-down beliefs. A myth may be a prevailing worldview: that the earth is flat or the still center of the turning universe, that humanity begins with Adam and Eve, that the world is enthralled by a dark Demiurge. A myth may be a sacred teaching story that explains how the world came into being, and what is beyond it, and why bad things as well as good things happen, and what it means to be human. A myth may justify the ways of gods to humans or those of humans before their Creator. A myth may introduce you to essential members of your archetypal family, like the major arcana of the tarot: personified forces at play in your life and your universe.

A myth may invite you to consider who among the gods defends you and who has it in for you. A myth may be a living reality beyond the realm of facts, a source of truth that cannot be confirmed in a laboratory experiment but may be evidenced by the data of raw experience.

In Greek theater, *mythos* is the underlying story, the pattern or spirit of the play, familiar to the audience yet as unpredictable as the gods in how it will unfold in each fresh production. You may think you know the plot, but you don't know exactly how it will develop this time. This is a marvelous analogue for living myths on the stage of our lives.

Your dreams can be a nightly screening of gods and archetypes. A dream may be your place of encounter with a big story that is looking for you. It may call you to a tradition about which you previously knew nothing. "In the absence of an effective general mythology, each of us has his primary, unrecognized, rudimentary, yet secretly potent pantheon of dream," Joseph Campbell wrote in *The Hero with a Thousand Faces*. Psychologist Betty Meador was called to study the great Sumerian goddess Inanna and her high priestess after a dream that involved the prayer flags of the Queen of Heaven and Earth that were previously unknown to her.

I was seized by the Hindu goddess Kali in a terrifying night vision — beginning with what is often called sleep paralysis, when you wake but can't move your body — when I was fourteen. I wrote a cycle of poems in her honor. Later her brother-consort Kala, better known as Yama, became one of my principal mentors, reminding me to consider every life choice in the presence of Death. A little-known

Celtic deity came into my ken in a series of dreams in which I was defending my property with a long-handled hammer, like a weaponized croquet mallet. Some shelf elf produced a Gallo-Roman statue of a god with a similar hammer, named in the inscription as Sucellos, which means the "good striker." He seems to share some qualities with Thor. He is also the consort of a great goddess of abundance, called Rosmerta by the Gauls and Abundantia by the Romans.

Myths are a cauldron of stories and symbols that hold superabundant energy for life. You want to become conscious of the myth you are living. If you are unconscious about this, then the myth is living you, and you may be driven into confusion and disaster, like Odysseus when his men lost control of the winds. In different phases of life, we may inhabit and be inhabited by different myths. We may find ourselves in the play of rival stories. We may be able to match and mix.

The great scholar of religions Wendy Doniger writes about the "seed text," *bija mantra*. She describes how she found this in the story of an Indian goddess, Saranyu, who cloned herself in order to get away from a husband she detested, leaving a compliant Hindu version of a Stepford Wife at home while she ranged free as a wild mare. This story kept after Doniger for decades, prompting her to reach deeper and deeper into its well. Whenever she heard it, she would say, "That's the story of my life."

"Myth, by design, makes it clear that we are meant to be something more than our personal history," declared P. L. Travers, the author of *Mary Poppins*.

The myths we are living now swing on hinges into other lives, whose myths swing back at us. Because our present life dramas are connected with those of other personalities, in other places and times, within our multidimensional family, it is not surprising that "old" gods and "dead" religions feature in our spontaneous mythology, as mediated by dreams and visions and by moments on the roads of this world when we experience a hidden hand, pushing us forward or holding us back or rearranging the stage set.

Reclaiming the Book of the Grail

The big stories must be lived. This is a lesson we may derive from an old story about the *story* of the Grail. It is in the introduction to the *Lancelot Grail*, also known as the *Cycle de Walter Map*, which was composed around 1200. The text explains that the author was alone in a hut "in one of the wildest regions of Britain," troubled by questions of faith, when Christ appeared to him and gave him a small book. Christ said it would resolve his doubts, but he would not be able to read it until he had cleansed himself.

In the morning, the writer opened the book and read the titles of its four parts:

1. This is the book of thy descent.
2. Here begins the book of the Holy Grail.
3. Here begin the terrors.
4. Here begin the marvels.

His reading was interrupted by a tremendous thunderstorm. Then "an angel caught him up in the spirit, into the third heaven," and his religious doubts disappeared. But when he wanted to return to the book, he found it had vanished. A voice told him that to reclaim it, he must suffer and follow a strange animal to the far north.

He embarked on his quest. He followed the beast to a pine tree of adventure, and a knight's castle, and a queen's lake, and to the home of a hermit sorcerer possessed by a devil. After the writer exorcized the devil, he found the book. Christ appeared to him again and commanded him to make a transcript. "Thereafter follows the legend of the Holy Grail."

We learn that the essential things cannot be learned or written in a book until they have been lived. This requires a dangerous journey beyond the tame and settled places of the mind, and direct visionary experience, and the power to cast out demons that are in the way.

Call of the Goddess

I have decided to devote most of this chapter to stories of the call of the goddess in contemporary lives, because we so desperately need the Divine Feminine to balance the greed and brutality of hollow men who do not hear the voice of soul, of conscience, and of nature.

Inanna at the Breakfast Table

Inanna took possession of the breakfast table at the retreat center where I was leading a weekend adventure in Active Dreaming.

"How is your dream recall?" I asked the first person to join me at the table.

She proceeded to recount a dream in which she was traveling through a dusty landscape to the home of a tarot reader. Instead of spreading the cards, the tarot reader showed her two fish tanks, each containing elaborate dioramas. At the center of each was a statuette of a goddess. The dreamer recognized the goddess forms: Isis and Inanna. The tarot reader told her she must choose one. She chose Inanna. Immediately a great tornado whipped up, swirling everything around her. She awoke excited and curious to know more about the power and the attributes of the goddess she chose.

We started talking about Inanna and the great cycle of poems composed in her name in ancient Sumer. I spoke of the terrifying praise poems in which Inanna goes forth into battle with the force of a tornado, with a flashing carnelian at her throat and the mace of a warrior raised in her hand. I mentioned that in my carry-on bag for this trip there just happened to be a copy of the beautiful versions of the Inanna poems composed by Diane Wolkstein and Samuel Noah Kramer.

We were joined by a psychologist who had made a close study of the myths of Inanna and spoke about the story of the descent of the goddess as the model for a woman's journey to the depths to meet and integrate her shadow side. She reminded us that one of the mysteries in this mythic cycle is that we are not given a clear reason why Inanna chose to make her descent to the darkest level of the underworld, the realm of her dark sister, Ereshkigal, to be hung on a meat hook. We do know that she did this of her own volition. It was a choice she made freely.

Now our company had grown with the arrival of many other dreamers, all eager to contribute to the weave of mythic associations that was taking place over the waffles and coffee. One woman shared that she was in the midst of a ritual journey through the descent of Inanna organized by a women's group and unfolding over many days. Through visualization and ritual, she had journeyed down through the seven gates of Inanna's descent, at each of which she was required to give up an aspect of her power and protection. As she made this mythic journey, she realized that it evoked many of her personal life dramas and passages — for example, losing a job and leaving a home — and they now assumed even deeper resonance.

I confessed that Inanna, in full warrior mode, makes me, as a mere man, a little nervous, since she so supremely embodies the take-no-prisoners wrath of a woman giving vent to her righteous rage. At that moment, a woman named Moon took the place at the table that someone had just left free. I smiled. Inanna is the daughter of Nanna, the Moon god, and I am a very lunar man. We were at a mythic edge — with all the juice that brings — that was also a family situation.

Inanna
daughter of the Moon
silken bud unfolding

riding out on your wild blue bull
through the Gate of Wonder.

I am riffing on a version of "Inanna and Ebih," written by the high
priestess of the moon god at Ur around 2300 BCE. The literal translation is in Betty De Shong Meador's brilliant *Inanna, Lady of Largest
Heart*.

As mentioned earlier, I was excited to learn that Meador was called
to the great Sumerian goddess Inanna by a dream. She dreamed she
saw two fellow Jungian analysts — conservative, by-the-book types —
being buried. Strange sticks with loops at the top were planted in the
earth around their graves.

At the time, Inanna was unknown to her, and she made no as-
sociation between the dream and the goddess. Long after, in one of
Erich Neumann's books, she found a picture of the looped poles like
the ones in her dream. She read that they were symbols of Inanna
and the earliest way of writing her name in pictographs. They were
reed posts. They may have represented doorposts or the props for a
curtain. In pictographs, reed pieces hanging down from rings sometimes look like women's hair or ribbons.

Why would doorposts made from reeds be a symbol for the
Queen of Heaven and Earth? Doorposts of this kind could denote
the passage to the storehouse, the place of the fertility and abundance that are the gifts of the goddess in her beneficent mode. Doorposts could also symbolize the passage between the worlds. Inanna
herself passed through a series of doorways in her famous descent to
the underworld. So the reed doorposts, in a country with little tim-
ber or stone, could be the Mesopotamian version of the pylon gate in
Egypt or the dolmen arch in Celtic lands.

The reeds have further significance. In ancient Mesopotamia,
dream incubation took place in reed huts. You would step between
reed doorposts to dream with intention, maybe to dream yourself
into a close encounter with the goddess herself. The marshes of

southern Mesopotamia, full of reeds, offered a liminal dreamy landscape. Legend has it that Sargon of Akkad, the father of the priestess who wrote poems and hymns to Inanna, was abandoned on a river in a reed basket, sealed with pitch, to be found by the gardener who then raised him. A baby from the reeds, long before Moses.

Meador waxes poetic about the reed posts of Inanna. In her words, "Inanna's symbol standing tall on the graves was an image of strength and courage from a culture outside of and alien to patriarchal thinking....Inanna's tall reed standards stand like insurgent flags amid the bastion of traditional beliefs that restrict women." The meetup between the old dream and new research into the mythic cycle of Inanna led the Jungian analyst to make a huge leap in her work and understanding, into goddess realms. "This new perspective propelled me onto my future path."

As Meador studied the texts, she found Inanna's wild call for her chosen lover to plow her field. The goddess calls for Dumuzi, who is both the "wild bull" and the plowman:

My field needs hoeing
Dumuzi, I call you
It is you I want for prince.

Inanna is many, a great goddess who refuses all boundaries and limitations. For Meador, she is the Sumerian "personification of the whole of reality."

You wear the robes
of the old, old gods.

Meador discovered a soul friend in ancient Mesopotamia. She happens to be the first named author in all of human history. Her name is Enheduanna. The "en" in her name means "ruler." She was the daughter of King Sargon of Akkad and high priestess of the moon god Nanna. She was also a poet of the first rank, and the most passionate of her poems were devoted to presenting Inanna in all her faces. She composed forty-six temple hymns that have survived and the "Exaltation of Inanna" ("Nin-Me-Sar-Ra"), which is infused with her passion for the goddess.

Enheduanna signed her name to her cycle of temple hymns. She is a great poet. She is advancing a whole theology and philosophy that promotes the great goddess as the one beyond the many. She writes with searing passion and eloquence about the many aspects of the self. The goddess she praises — in all her dark and light — is within her and within the whole of nature and the whole cosmic order. Both contain multitudes.

Meador writes that "in Enheduanna's writing, we witness that moment when an individual is selected out of the mass of humanity into a new consciousness of self-definition and self-worth.... Enheduanna begins to understand emotion as the graze of the goddess' hand across a person's soul. Image and emotion become the language of the goddess to the particular individual."

Called to the goddess and the ancient poet through the doorway of a dream. Goddesses and dead poets can make that happen. I know something about this.

Hoofprints of the Goddess

Horses run through our dreams. We wake, hearts pounding, still feeling the thunder of the hoofbeats. With all that horsepower, big stories often rush in on us.

Not everyone's dream horses are the same, of course. Some people are oppressed by dreams of a black horse that seems like a figure of death, or a red horse foreboding war and bloodshed, or a ghostly pale horse that brings a sense of sorrow and bereavement. Such dreams — and Henry Fuseli's famous painting *The Nightmare* — have encouraged the belief that the nightmare has to do with a mare, whereas in fact (the etymologists tell me) the "mare" part here is most likely derived from the Old Germanic *mer*, meaning something that crushes and oppresses.

In dreams, the state of a horse is often a rather exact analogue for the state of our bodies and our vital energy. When you dream of a starving horse, you want to ask: *What part of me needs to be nourished and fed?* You dream of horses flayed and hung up under the roof beams (as did a dreamer in one of my workshops), and you need to ask: *Which parts of me have been flayed and violated in the course of my life? And how do I heal and bring those parts back to life?*

Such a dream also evokes the ancient rituals of horse sacrifice, common to many cultures, and might require a search back across time into primal material from the realm of the ancestors, lost to ordinary consciousness, but alive in the deeps of the collective memory. In the opening of the Brihadaranyaka Upanishad, the whole universe is likened to a sacrificial horse.

In Greek mythology, horses are the gift of Poseidon, and they come surging from the sea, their streaming manes visible in the whitecaps. Or they irrupt from the dark underworld, from whence Hades charges on his black stallions to abduct the Maiden and brings her into a realm of initiation and sacred union that makes her Persephone in a story we are going to explore in depth. Yet in Arcadia, Persephone's mother, Demeter, the great goddess of the seeded earth and grain and beer, was depicted with a horse's head.

Go to the British Isles, and you find the white mare revered as the mount and form of the goddess. Her prints still mark the land whichever way you ride, even if only by train or car or shanks' pony. In ancient Ireland, a true king was required to mate with the white mare, as the living symbol of the sacred earth. (It would take a manful king indeed to couple with a mare; I suspect a priestess was substituted for the horse.) In Wales, she is Rhiannon, and she comes mounted on a white horse out of Annwn, the underworld, to marry a prince.

In Gaul and throughout the Roman Empire, she is Epona, a name related to the Gaulish *epos*, "horse." She is usually depicted riding sidesaddle on a mare or between twin horses. She was hugely popular in Gaul and the Rhineland but was also known in Britain. She was regarded as a patron by cavalrymen. The Aedui, used as auxiliaries by Julius Caesar, prayed to her to protect their horses (and themselves) in battle. To the wider community, she was a mother goddess, and her imagery often suggests fertility. On a stone relief of Epona in Burgundy, a foal is beneath the mare she is riding, possibly suckling. She often appears carrying baskets of fruit or loaves of bread. She was awarded her own official festival in the Roman calendar, on December 18.

Miranda Green comments, in her excellent book *Animals in Celtic Life and Myth*, "The horse is absolutely crucial to Epona's definition: the equine symbolism gave rise to many different levels of meaning, with the result that Epona was worshipped not only as patroness of horses but also as a giver of life, health, fertility and plenty, and as a protectress of humans even beyond the grave."

Epona was associated with death and rebirth. She is often depicted in Gaulish cemeteries. At a burial ground of the Medioatrici near Metz, images of Epona were offered by relatives of the deceased; one shows the goddess on her mare, leading a mortal to the Otherworld.

We know the horse in living myths as healer and teacher, as vehicle for travel to higher realms, and as the source of creative inspiration. It is the hooves of Pegasus, rending the rock, that open the Hippocrene spring beside the grove of the Muses, from which poets have drunk ever since. It is Chiron the centaur, the man-horse, who is the mentor of Asklepios, the man-god synonymous with healing, especially through dreams. In fairy tales (the Grimms' and others) it is often the horse that can find the way when humans are lost.

I dreamed of rounding up a great herd of wild horses, and

understood, waking in excitement and delight, that this was about bringing vital energy back where it belongs and helping to shape a model of understanding and practice of soul recovery for communities as well as individuals. The wild horse racing through our dreams may be the wind horse of spirit, or vital essence, that needs both to run free and to be harnessed to a life path and a human purpose.

Of all the shamanic terms I have heard, *wind horse* is my favorite. It is native to at least three traditions of Central Asia, where the word *shaman* and the shaman's frame drum (often made with horse hide and commonly called the shaman's "horse") originate. In Buryat (Mongolian) the word for "wind horse" is *khiitori*; in Old Turkic it is *Rüzgar Tayi*; in Tibetan it is *rlung ta* (pronounced *lung ta*).

When you think about it, the horse is unlike any other animal. Stronger than man, it yet allows itself to be gentled and bridled; it provided humans the main form of locomotion for all those centuries before the invention of the internal combustion engine. As in Plato's image of the charioteer of the soul, challenged to manage the rival energies of a horse that wants to go *down* on a rampage, wild and sexy and possibly violent, and the steady horse whose instinct is always to go *up*, to rise higher, we are challenged by our dream horses to recognize, release, and temper the horsepower within us.

In some of my workshops, I lead people on a journey to find their spirit horses and ride them to a very special place where they can reclaim vital soul energy and identity, from a child self who went missing when the world seemed too cruel or a younger self who separated because of a wrenching life choice. Sometimes these journeys of soul healing result in the beautiful transformation I call spiritual enthronement, when we are able to receive and embody a part of the Greater Self — sometimes the goddess self — because we are now ready to live a greater life.

Follow the hoofprints of your own dream horse, and you may find you are on the trail of the goddess.

Lady on the Shore

There are moments when a big story steps out of a dream and confronts you in ordinary life. I was leading a workshop in Brazil, on the wild Atlantic coast of Santa Catarina Island. On my first night on the island, I dreamed I was introducing people to the Great Mother Goddess, counseling them to treat her with respect.

On my last day there, I agreed with my host that we would take a drive around the bay side, to an area of Azorean fishing villages and oyster beds. The drive was wonderful. On the forested hills, indigenous garapuvu trees put up vivid yellow canopies, like floral umbrellas.

Just short of the village of Ribeirão da Ilha, I saw a wonderful female figure in a flowing blue gown, arms raised, a star in her hair.

"Stop the car," I said to my friend. "That's Yemanjá." In Spanish-speaking countries she is Yemaya, but here I gave the great goddess of the sea and of motherhood her Brazilian name. In both versions, her name is a contraction of the Yoruba phrase *yeye omo eja*, meaning "mother whose children are like fish." The phrase evokes her endless fecundity; she embodies the sea of life, immense and universal and giving and forgiving.

In other parts of Brazil, Yemanjá's presence by the water would be no surprise. Hundreds of thousands of people gather by the sea in Rio de Janeiro and São Salvador da Bahia for her festivals. But here in the south, I was in a very white part of Brazil, settled by Germans, Austrians, and Italians after the Portuguese sent early colonists from the Azores; signs of the Afro-Brazilian tradition had been absent until now.

We noticed a sign across the street from Yemanjá for the *ilé de Shangó*, the temple of Shangó, the thunderer among the *orixás*, the African gods who crossed the Atlantic with those brought to the New World in captivity. We crossed the road and were greeted by a friendly, maternal black woman who proved to be a *filha de Shangó* (a daughter of Shangó). She gave us an informal tour of the temple and explained that it had required a long campaign to get permission from the conservative white town fathers to place a statue of a black goddess at the edge of the bay. Pleased by my enthusiasm and my familiarity with some elements of her tradition, she invited me to take off my shoes and enter the sanctuary, where I was received with kisses and embraces as one of the family.

I studied photographs of the *pai de ilé* (the father of the temple) with drummers in Nigeria and recalled how, thirty years earlier, I nearly gave up my familiar life to go to West Africa to be trained and initiated in this tradition.

The priestess expanded her tour to the kitchen, where her daughter-in-law was nursing a baby, and showed us the pots used for cooking the feasts that accompany their nights of ritual. I thanked her, and the Great Mother by the bay, with respect for what felt like a happy homecoming.

I had been uneasy until now about my return flights to the United States, receiving broken reports of the progress of Hurricane Sandy. I now relaxed, feeling all would be well. All three of my flights went almost impossibly smoothly; I arrived a few minutes early at my home airport. On my first night home, I dreamed again of a Great Mother, this time in the guise of a Native American spirit woman who opened and held a marvelous space for healing within the gathering I was going to lead on a mountain in the New York Adirondacks the following weekend.

As I look over my wanderings in this world and the traffic from the mythic world that is forever part of this story, I see I am always coming home to the goddess.

Goddess Rising

I would encounter darkness as a bride and eat the pomegranate.
— P. L. TRAVERS

With the coming of spring, as the earth bursts into fruit and flower, many societies have honored the dying and returning god or goddess who embodies the cycle of life, death, and rebirth. For ancient Greeks, this was the time of Persephone, whose story resonates with many of us. Persephone is picking flowers in a spring meadow when the earth bursts open and a dark lord, strong and lusty as his stallions, drags her down to the underworld. At this point she is known only as Kore, the Maiden. In this part of her story, many of us will recall a time when we were victimized, abused, ripped out of a familiar life.

Her mother, Demeter, searches for her everywhere and finally locates her in the Great Below with the help of the crone goddess Hecate and the sun god Helios. She is enraged to discover that the father of the Maiden, Zeus, gave his brother Hades permission to abduct Kore; no doubt many would see this as the arranged marriage, enforced by the patriarchy, of a nubile girl to an older male. In her grief, Demeter wanders off to a small town, Eleusis, where she works as a nanny until she remembers she is a goddess, and not just any goddess, but the One Who Brings Things to Fullness, the goddess of the fruitful earth, of the crops, the nourisher and provider.

Now her grief and rage blight all growing things. Humans are going to starve, and the gods on Olympus will no longer receive their offerings. Thunderous Zeus, the top god, is made to yield; he will send Hermes, the divine messenger — and the only Olympian who can pass easily between the underworld and the worlds above — to bring the Maiden back to the Great Mother.

At this point the story shifts in ways that invite us to claim its power in our own lives, from whatever angle and whichever player's perspective call to us most directly. The pivotal incident is well-known, but its deeper meaning is often lost. It involves the pomegranate seeds. Everyone knew back then that if you eat the food of the underworld, you can never escape it. We are then told, in the classic version of the tale in the Homeric Hymn to Demeter, that Hades tricks Kore into eating six pomegranate seeds (the number matters) so she will be bound to return to him for six months of the year. But what follows suggests a deeper game and even that the artifice was not Hades's, but the Maiden's.

When the Maiden comes up from the underworld, she has a new name: Persephone. Its meaning is disputed, but we know this is a great name, a goddess name, that comes from Crete. We see this full-fledged goddess power when Persephone takes her first steps back on sunlit earth. Shoots spring up and flowers blossom wherever she walks. She has changed in another way. She is proudly, radiantly pregnant with the child who will be Dionysus, god of joy and ecstasy, of wine and abandon. This is no haggard survivor. This, surely, is someone who brought treasures from darkness. We soon learn that her marriage to Hades is not that of a captive or an archaic version of a Stepford Wife. It is a true union — indeed, in the dysfunctional family of the Greek gods, this is one couple that stays together. She will leave Hades's kingdom every spring, rising like the barley and the maize. She will return to the underworld every fall, when the seeds are planted after the harvest, to sprout in the darkness and rise again. And when she goes back to Hades, it will not be as the little woman who has spent half the year with mommy. She will go down as queen of the underworld, enthroned beside Hades as his equal. We see her like this, in splendor, on votive plaques from the Greek colony at Locri in Calabria. Here the temple of Persephone was one of the wonders of Italy; brides-to-be went down the steps into a sacred cave to seek her blessing as patron of marriage, fertility, and childbirth.

When she is in Hades (which is a place as well as a person) it is her function, together with her husband, to receive and supervise the newly dead and prepare them for their next transits. Let's notice that Hades is not simply a death lord; he is charged with the care of the dead in the realm of the dead, where he rules with his queen.

After her own underworld initiation, Persephone becomes an initiator in the realm of those who live after death and those who are reborn after ritual death. With Demeter, she presides over the most famous and most secretive mysteries of the ancient world. They are named for Eleusis, the town where Demeter concealed her divinity until she remembered she was a goddess. The lesser mysteries, dedicated to Persephone, are held in early spring. The greater mysteries are held in the fall, and it is a capital offense to reveal the content of the "things done," "things seen," and "things said" in the nine days of transformative ritual and sacred dreaming. No one in ancient times broke the taboo, unless we read what Apuleius, shifting from bawdy farce to sacred witness, wrote of a manifestation of the great goddess and a moment when the sun shone at midnight, in a later chapter of *The Golden Ass*.

"The Mysteries do not only give us pleasure in this life but give us still better hope when we die," wrote the great Roman statesman and philosopher Cicero, himself an initiate. Cicero said that initiation into the Eleusinian mysteries gave him reason to live in joy and die with hope.

Candidates for the greater mysteries walked the fourteen miles from a cemetery in Athens to the great temple that Demeter ordered to be founded at Eleusis. Along the way, they sacrificed piglets and jumped into the sea, both elements in ritual cleansing. On their way to and inside the temple, they were expected to incubate sacred dreams and be ready to share them in the morning. Again we see the interweave of private myth and collective dream.

Modern investigators, especially enthusiasts for entheogens, suggest that something added to the *kykeon*, the barley brew aspirants drank on the way to full revelation at Eleusis, was doctored with some psychoactive substance, maybe ergot, to guarantee results. This is a false trail for those of us who want to seize or be seized by the heart of the story, and anyway dreamers know we can manufacture our own chemicals inside the body by using the imagination.

At the close of the mysteries a priestess held up a mown sheaf of wheat or barley in front of the new initiates, who sometimes numbered in the thousands and were of every social degree, men and women together, outside rank and status forgotten. This confirms that the rites were connected to the cycles of the seasons — in the myth Demeter and Persephone are actually responsible for the seasons — and to regeneration, the renewal of the fertility of the earth.

The mysteries of the goddesses — Mother and Maiden and Crone (if we include Hecate) — always involve connecting and reconnecting humans with the seeded earth. The mysteries are also about regeneration in a deeper sense, the sense expressed by the mystic Abraham of Santa Clara, who said that "he who dies before he dies does not die when he dies." In ways we can only dream on — but dream we can — the mysteries took participants through a personal experience of death and rebirth. Here again we see the initiate, Kore, become the initiator, Persephone.

Let's return to the pomegranate seeds. Many of us know the pomegranate as a juicy, flashy globe of sweetness, almost shockingly sexual when opened to reveal the seeds floating like eggs in the ovaries. In many traditions, the pomegranate is a symbol of fecundity. Sometimes it even offers a promise of immortality. In Persian mythology Isfandiyar eats a pomegranate and becomes invincible. Herodotus states that golden pomegranates adorned the spears of warriors in the Persian phalanx. The Song of Solomon compares the cheeks of a bride behind her veil to the two halves of a pomegranate. The pillars of King Solomon's temple are decorated with pomegranates, as are the robes and regalia of Jewish kings and priests.

Persephone is shown in the iconography with a pomegranate that looks like an orb of sovereignty, not a food choice made fast down below. Let's suppose that she chose to eat the food of the underworld and that her selection of the pomegranate, and the number of seeds she swallowed, was calculated, not casual. What would that tell us about Persephone as a character who is turning into an archetype?

The sweetness and sexual appearance of the pomegranate suggests that the Maiden is now a full, ripe, sexually mature woman who is sealing her marriage to Hades. However their relationship began, it is now a true union, a *theogamy,* or sacred marriage, between equals. Hades no longer seems like a sexual predator — it is mostly agreed in the sources that he is handsome and sexy as well as lustful — and more like Ploutos, the Wealthy or Abundant. Their marriage table is richly spread. In the way she approaches the pomegranate, the Maiden not only affirms her choice of husband and her power to grow her man and her marriage. She also asserts her autonomy from her mother. Demeter has forced the gods to bring her back, but she is not going back to be mommy's girl or live the old life. She reserves six months of the year for the underworld, not because she has been duped, but because she *chooses* to live in two worlds.

I know many women who have found themselves in some version of the story of Persephone and men who have discovered that it is hounding and sometimes awakening them. We are in the presence of a powerful archetype, as psychologists, following Jung, like to call the mythic figures who walk close to us and sometimes irrupt into our lives. Like dreams, archetypes are both personal and transpersonal. They are aspects of our own psyche and potential, yet they are also *out there*. Tell yourself that the gods and goddesses are dead, and they will surprise you.

Like Persephone, who chooses her relationship with her husband and her mother and will awaken to a deeper life on both sides of death, we can choose what we make of a story like this and what we take from it. Many of us will find a profound, emboldening example of the gift in the wound. In this story of a goddess rising, we may discover an analogue for dark passages in our own lives from which we were able to achieve resurrection.

You may see mother and daughter as inseparable, two faces of the great goddess, as Jane Ellen Harrison, the pioneer feminist scholar of ancient Greek religion, did in citing the iconography: "Mythology might work its will, but primitive art never clearly distinguished between the Mother and the Maid, never lost hold of the truth that they were one goddess."

The novelist Sue Monk Kidd cowrote *Traveling with Pomegranates: A Mother and Daughter Journey to the Sacred Places of Greece, Turkey, and France* with her own newly engaged daughter.

As they traveled to sites of goddesses and Black Madonnas, they planned the daughter's wedding and focused on the idea that the death of their old mother-daughter relationship was required. They acted out severing previous codependency with a clean cut of a silver umbilical cord.

The Persephone-Demeter story may draw you into a prolonged engagement, to years of study and self-examination, as happened to Carol S. Pearson, who describes the inspiration for her excellent book *Persephone Rising* like this: "It was Persephone who demanded that I write this book."

Or you may be drawn to a figure in the story other than Persephone. The literal or instinctive mother in you may be pulled to Demeter. You may glean the lesson that, when you remember you are a goddess and drink from the full strength of that power, you can gentle the force and end the abuses of men of power in your field. As a man, you may recognize something of yourself in the figures of Zeus or Hades, and that may help you to appreciate the deep healing that men can find in the realm of the Divine Feminine. As a man or a woman, you may be called to Hermes, who can travel like a shaman between the lower world, the middle world, and the upper world, to guide souls and carry the messages of the gods.

Dreams are personal myths; myths are collective dreams. I have listened carefully to how the Persephone story plays in the dreams and lives of some of the people who have joined me in my workshops over the years. Here is a sampling:

Laurie: "For me Persephone represents the courage to move through uncertainty while releasing without regret that which is familiar, trusting that whatever darkness she faces provides the transition into wisdom and self-actualization."

Meredith: "Persephone does not allow herself to become a victim of abduction, but through resilience and inner strength she descends into the wilderness of loss, knowing what she does will matter.

Unlike the tame flower-filled fields of her mother's creations, the underworld with Hades is full of uncertainty, a terrain she must navigate without giving up on life. Her initiation in the uncharted regions are invitations to gifts beyond her wild imaginings and provide doorways to mysteries she opens to others. She is fond of her husband, perhaps even loves him. Yet she will not allow herself to become captive to him. Finally, she will not allow Demeter's needs to take priority in her life. When Hermes comes to retrieve her, she consciously chooses not only to eat the pomegranate seeds but *how many* to eat. She doesn't need to be rescued, taken care of, or fulfilled by another. She uses discernment to know what is right for her."

Exercise: Who Is Persephone to You?

I must confess, blushing a little, that as a mere man, I am most drawn to — and most disturbed by — the male characters in the story, to Zeus and Hades, Hermes and Dionysus. I like the versions of the myth in which the top gods are gentled without losing their potency. I asked myself the question *Who is Persephone to me?* I jotted down the following responses:

> The one who gentles the predatory male
> The one who turns adversity into initiation
> The one who finds treasure in darkness
> The initiate who becomes initiator
> The one who lives two lives in two worlds and holds them
> in balance

You might want to do this quick little writing exercise. Think about what elements of the myth you recognize in your own life and perhaps your own dreams. Then write, as fast as you can, your immediate responses to the question *Who is Persephone to me?* If names from your own family or your personal history come up, so be it.

Oh, yes. You may want to eat some pomegranate seeds.

Shaping the Storm

Dion Fortune, a true priestess of the Western mysteries, maintained that "the true nature of the gods is that of magical images shaped out of the astral plane by mankind's thought, and influenced by the mind." Our ancestors used the power of story to make sense of the world around them, and to give it shape. There is a marvelous story about this use of story from one of the first peoples of North America, who call themselves the Omushkego. In English they are called the Swampy Cree.

This is how it was, says one of their elders. There were forces much more powerful than humans that humans did not understand and could not control. Like thunder and lightning. People were terrified of the sound of the thunder and the flash of fire from above. What could they do to make this less wild, less overwhelming?

The dream shamans went to work. They dreamed that thunder and lightning could take a form humans could recognize and deal with. The form was still scary, but it had a shape and a personality that could be seen and with which conversation was possible.

The shamans dreamed that thunder took the form of a giant eagle. It had to have wings because it came from the sky. The eagle was the right bird because it is a fierce, high-flying predator that can seize other birds in midair. All the winged ones respect it.

When the shamans dreamed the thunderbird into being, things changed. Now people could talk to the elemental powers of thunder and lightning as relations that had a name and a shape:

> Through their dream they were able to control this thunderbird and use it when they wanted to. The highest level a shaman could reach was when he could control the thunder, when he could form it into a thunderbird so he could use this power from thunder and lightning. He wanted to form this energy into a being, a bird — something he could handle here on Earth. They didn't use any substance to harness this power. Instead, they formed it in their minds.

This is how Louis Bird, an extraordinary storyteller of the Swampy Cree, recalls the traditions of the *midewiwin*, the shamans of his people.

His account is marvelously provocative, goading us to think about all the ways humans and beings other than human may have agreed to converse with one another in an animate universe where everything is alive and conscious.

I was once swimming in a lake when thunderheads came rolling over the scene. Everyone left the water except me. I wanted to go on swimming as long as possible, because my body loves it. Then a great humanoid figure took shape among the clouds, blacker than the rest, except for the two patches of light that seemed to be eyes glaring down at me out of an angry, commanding face. I got out of the water pronto. Now *that* felt like a personal encounter with an elemental power.

Louis Bird describes how the training of a dream shaman of his people, from the earliest age possible, emphasized learning to give shape to elemental forces in order to manage relations with them and how this art was mastered through "dream quests":

The elements — the atmosphere, the air, and the water — can be dangerous. One must understand how to deal with them. In his dream quest, one had to develop the ability to solidify elements that are not yet solid. For example, there are times when the wind is very destructive — it can kill you. And so some people dreamed of the north wind and the north direction as a very powerful being. A dreamer on his dream quest had to visualize the north as a being, a human form, so he can speak to it and come into its favor, so he could use it during his lifetime if possible. It could help him and be kind to him during his lifetime.

I know how this works too. When I was living on a farm in upstate New York, a fire caused by a neighbor's effort to burn trash in big kerosene drums came raging over the hill on the north side of my property and soon claimed twenty acres of tall, dead grass. Pushed by a strong north wind, the fire raced to the edge of the drive in front of my house. I called the fire department, but there was no help in sight, and I had only a garden hose and a bucket and was facing what was now a major wildfire. I was ready to jump in my car with my dogs and the unfinished typescript of my new book when I remembered that it never hurts to ask for help.

I walked to the western edge of the fire and did just that. I asked the elements for help.

The wind shifted in an instant. Now it was blowing hard from the west instead of the north. It drove the fire toward the main road, and dry spruce and pine made the noise of popping firecrackers as the flames took them.

The local fire chief turned up ten minutes later. He told me, "We didn't save your house."

"I noticed that," I told him.

"Your house ought to be on fire. You must have some powerful protection."

What do you say about an episode like that? I said to the animate universe, "Thank you."

Exercise: Hunting the Story That Is Hunting You

If your big story is hunting you, all you need to do is place yourself where you can easily be found. That place is at the edge of your comfort zone and your familiar rounds. Everything interesting happens on the boundaries, and the great beasts don't bother with gated communities unless they are very hungry indeed. We have seen how your big story may be hunting you in dreams, on hooves or in winged flight. We are going to look more closely in the next chapter at how the big story may irrupt in the midst of everyday life, through the play of synchronicity.

Perhaps you want to be more than available; you are ready to make an expedition.

A dream that has some real juice for you may give you the very best starting point if you are ready to seek a close-up encounter with a big story. You know the essential things about this kind of shamanic dreaming now. You call up a dream that has power for you. You set simple intentions for what you want to know and what you aim to do once you project yourself back inside the dream scene. You lie down or lie back in a quiet space, shut out external light and noise, and maybe put on a drumming tape or a recording of nature sounds to fuel and focus your expedition.

You can also journey to a place where many stories may be waiting. The magic library is a real place in the imaginal realm (we'll learn more about this in chapter 8) that is available to you. If you are new to this kind of locale, you can go there through a portal you build from your own life memories. Like this.

Imaginal Exercise: Journey to the Magic Library

You are thinking about a place you remember from your life — a library, a bookshop, a museum or gallery — where your imagination has been fired up by new images and ideas and discoveries. You may be back in elementary school, or in the Louvre, or in a gallery of glass art in Tacoma, Washington, or in a composite of several places.

You let the scene become vivid on your inner screen. You look closely at the entrance to this place.

You see yourself going through the door. You are received by a librarian or custodian who may ask you to put something down that you have been carrying. You may be surprised to discover that you have been going around with some old stuff. Don't skip this bit. In the inner work of transformation, we get to the good stuff only if we are willing to put down old baggage, which may contain the tired old stories it is time for us to leave behind.

The librarian is waiting for you to state an intention. Say something like, "I am here for the story I need for my life right now."

Let yourself be guided, effortlessly, to a place of discovery and encounter. Expect the unexpected. The building you are in may soon look nothing like the place you remember. It may have previously unsuspected wings and levels. A wall of books may roll back, revealing a courtyard and a wild wood beyond it.

Remember why you are here: you are hunting the big story that is hunting you.

Be ready to encounter it in whatever form it chooses.

7

You Are Magnetic

Whatever you think and feel, the universe says, "Yes." The more strongly you think and feel, the stronger and faster the response is likely to be. It may come in ways you do not expect, since quite often you are unaware of the thoughts and desires you are carrying below your surface mind. The response may knock you back, because you live in a world of contending energies and the force lines of your hopes and fears and ambitions may excite opposition.

You may be frustrated because you have been drilling yourself to think yourself rich or successful or forty pounds lighter and the universe is not giving you any encouragement. That may be because your Greater Self is uninterested in your ego agendas or is flat out against them. It may be because the grocery lists of wants and needs you put together in your little everyday calculating mind have nothing much to do with what stirs your soul.

"All things which are similar and therefore connected, are drawn to each other's power," according to the medieval magus Heinrich Cornelius Agrippa of Nettesheim. It is a rule of reality that we attract or repel different things according to the emotions, attitudes, and agendas that we carry.

Before you walk into a room or turn a corner, your attitude is there ahead of you. It is engaged in creating the situation you are about to encounter. Whether you are remotely conscious of this or not, you are constantly setting yourself up for what the world is going to give you. If you go about your day filled with doom and gloom, the world will give you plenty of reasons to support that attitude. You'll start looking like that cartoon character who goes about with a personal black cloud over his head that rains only on his parade. Conversely, if your attitude is bright and open to happy surprises, you may be rewarded by a bright day, even when the sky is leaden overhead, and by surprisingly happy encounters.

Through energetic magnetism, we attract or repel people, events, and even physical circumstances according to the attitudes we embody. "We are magnets in an iron globe," declared Ralph Waldo Emerson. If we are upbeat and positive, "we have keys to all doors.... The world is all gates, all opportunities, strings of tension waiting to be struck." Conversely, "a low, hopeless spirit puts out the eyes; skepticism is slow suicide. A philosophy which sees only the worst... dispirits us; the sky shuts down before us." This requires us to do a regular attitude check, asking ourselves, *What attitude am I carrying? What am I projecting?*

It is not sufficient to do this on a head level. We want to check what we are carrying in our body and our energy field. Attitude adjustment requires more than reciting the kind of New Age affirmations you see in cute memes with flowers and sunsets on Facebook. It requires deeper self-examination and self-mobilization.

The poet and philosopher John O'Donohue reminded us, in beautiful language, that

> each of us is responsible for "how" we see, and how we see
> determines "what" we see. Seeing is not merely a physical
> act: the heart of vision is shaped by the state of soul. When
> the soul is alive to beauty, we begin to see life in a fresh and
> vital way. The old habits of seeing are broken. The coating
> of dead dust falls from the windows. Freed from their dead
> forms the elements of one's life reveal new urgency and pos-
> sibility.

To let dead dust fall may require us to recruit the help of the natural world around us. On a morning walk in the woods around a lake, I watched a thousand tender green ferns rise together from prostration to catch some dappled sunlight and thought: *We can do that too.*

Up from under the Rubble

Farrah was going through a period when she was worried about paying her bills and found that her worry spilled over into other aspects of her life, leaving her doubtful and insecure. Dark dreams seemed to mirror her anxieties. A nightmare scene recurred in which her body was crushed under heavy stones and there were stones in her mouth, leaving her unable to call for help or even to breathe. The scene shifted when a giant white owl swooped down and pulled her out from under the rubble with its claws.

Leaving the dream, she felt a surge of hope she carried with her on a trip into the English countryside. In a café, an owl-like elderly woman, who was sitting alone, struck up conversation. She was so friendly and familiar that Farrah found herself talking openly about her worries. The owl woman told her she needed to let go of her worries in order to receive the gifts that were waiting along her path. "You have to give yourself permission to be, and only from being can come knowing, and from there you will have."

Farrah recalls, "Her words were so wise. They affected me like the barn owl that rescued me from the rubble. I carried those words with me and tried to make it my practice to relax into a state of being. As I relaxed, the troubles in my mind began to dissolve. Within a few weeks, I stopped thinking about my financial worries. As soon as I made that shift, I started receiving job offers, seemingly out of nowhere. I had not applied for these jobs; the offers came from meeting friends of friends or being headhunted by people I did not previously know about. No more money problems."

We see in Farrah's story the practical truth of Henry David

Thoreau's observation that someone who stands in their own way will find that the world stands in their way. When she changed her attitude, her situation changed. And she had helpers — in the dream of the owl rescue and the way that dream seemed to come fluttering into the waking world in a café in the home counties — to make sure she got the message.

Story Magnets

One of my secrets of survival in my very frequent travels around the world prior to the pandemic was that I was (and am) always on the lookout for a new story. I have noticed that the best stories sometimes present themselves when my plans are scrambled. As they say of fiction, film, and nonfiction narrative, unless you have trouble, you don't have much of a tale. So whenever I missed an airport connection and found myself in the wrong seat on the wrong plane, seated next to someone I would not have met except for the screw-up, I would look for an opportunity to harvest a story. If the person next to me was sentient, I often asked, "What is your story?"

This triggered a fascinating range of responses, including life stories that the stranger on the plane may never have confided to anyone before. Occasionally I struck out. Stuck in a middle seat on the wrong plane, I asked the woman on my right, "What is your story?" When she goggled at me, I added, "You must have a story for me, because I'm in the wrong seat on the wrong plane."

She considered this, then said, "I don't have a story. I'm an auditor. I do everything by the book." Her jaw snapped shut like a steel trap.

I turned to the lugubrious, skinny young man on my left, whose body language suggested he was trying to roll himself up like an umbrella.

"Oh, I have a story," he was quick to say. "But you don't want to hear it. It is terribly depressing."

There was a story, of course, in these responses. However, the story I want to share here is about how, when you have established a certain kind of magnetic field, it continues to produce effects even when you have not asked for them and may not want them.

After an especially grueling set of travel misadventures that left me exhausted, I arrived at Oakland International Airport and said to the sky and the field, "I don't need a new story today." I just wanted a smooth ride home and maybe a nap.

I had time before takeoff, so I headed to an airport bar and ordered a beer. A cheery, ruddy-faced man on the stool beside me gave me an affable but appraising look. He then said, "You look like a guy who likes a good story."

"I am."

"Well, I have one for you." He began by introducing himself. He was a retired police detective from the East Bay area, now living on what he called a "gentleman farm" in Oregon. This was already fascinating.

"So I was taking a walk in a graveyard in a part of Oregon I had never visited before. I had no reason for going into that cemetery except that it looked like a nice place to take a walk. I was thinking about a girl I loved thirty years ago and could never have. I looked down at the headstone, and there was her name, all three parts of it. The date of death was last summer. I couldn't believe it was her. As far as I know, she never went to Oregon. But when I called mutual friends I discovered it really was her. I've been waiting a week to find someone I could tell about this. What do you think?"

"I think it's a great story."

We could look at this retired policeman's tale as an example of the role that a hidden hand may play in synchronistic events, in this case that of a departed sweetheart calling a survivor to her grave site. All I want to do here is to give a personal example of how human magnetism works. I love stories, and the world gave me a new one even on a day when I asked not to receive one.

When the Universe Gets Personal

Synchronicity is when the universe gets personal. Though the word *synchronicity* is a modern invention — Jung made it up because he noticed that people have a hard time talking about coincidence — the phenomenon has been recognized, and highly valued, from the most ancient times. The Greek philosopher Heraclitus maintained that the deepest order in our experienced universe is the effect of "a child playing with game pieces" in another reality. As the game pieces fall, we notice the reverberations in the play of coincidence.

When we pay attention, we find that the world around us gives us signs every day. Like a street sign, a synchronistic event may seem to say, "Stop" or "Go," "Dead End" or "Fast Lane." Beyond these signs, we find ourselves moving in a field of symbolic resonance that not only reflects back our inner themes and preoccupations but provides confirmation or course correction. A symbol is more than a sign: it brings together what we know with what we do not yet know.

Through the weaving of synchronicity, we are brought awake and alive to a hidden order of events, to the understory of our world and our lives. You do not need to travel far to encounter powers of the deeper world or hear oracles speak. You are at the center of the multidimensional universe right now. The extraordinary lies in plain sight, in the midst of the ordinary, if only you pay attention. The doors to the Otherworld open from wherever you are, and the traffic moves both ways.

Look for the Hidden Hand

In his essay "The Alchemical Interpretation of the Fish," Jung suggests that "the self is an archetype that invariably expresses a situation within which the ego is contained. Therefore, like every archetype, the self cannot be localized in an individual ego-consciousness, but acts like a circumambient atmosphere to which no definite limits can be set, either in space or in time. (Hence the synchronistic phenomena so often associated with activated archetypes.)"

"True realism consists in revealing the surprising things which habit keeps covered and prevents us from seeing," observed the French playwright and filmmaker Jean Cocteau. To be realists in this sense, we must be alert for the hidden hand behind meaningful coincidence. All our ancestors understood this, and some of those traditions have continued without interruption.

Who Defends You in Front of the Greater Powers?

I am sitting on a rush mat in a small room that smells of chicken blood. In front of me is an African divination priest, a *babalawo* of Ifá, the sacred and poetic oracle of the Yoruba people. His job description means "father of the mysteries." He casts a set of bronze medallions hung on a chain and records the patterns that emerge in a binary code, one vertical stroke or two. In his tradition, the *odu* — the patterns he will proceed to read — are not random, are not just the effect of the flick of his wrist. They are an agreed vehicle through which the orishas, gods of West Africa, and the ancestors will communicate with us.

The divination priest poses a big question to his gods: "Who defends Robert in front of the orishas?"

He receives an immediate answer. He needs to confirm something before he speaks. Usually the oracle gives the name of one deity, but this time it has given two. I am defended by two orishas before the council of the powers. Their personalities are quite different. One is lusty, boisterous, eloquent, with a temper that can incinerate a village. The other is cool, reflective, cerebral, always wanting a clear head.

Fine, I can live with this sacred psychology. I can recognize both personalities in myself, vying for dominance most days. I hope I won't have to pay to croak a chicken or a goat to maintain friendly relations, now that I have sought to inquire into these matters by solemn ritual.

"Sacrifice given. Sacrifice accepted. Sacrifice returned." A loose translation of words for the transactions that usually result from this oracle. What sacrifice is demanded of me?

The babalawo is surprised by what the oracle tells him. He questions his reading, and the response from the unseen powers is firm. "All the orishas require of you," he tells me, "is your love."

That first big question, "Who defends Robert in front of the orishas?," has lived with me ever since that consultation with a diviner of the old ways who truly knew what he was doing. To put it in more colloquial language and apply it to anyone, the question becomes: "Who defends you in front of the gods?" Or, if you are uncomfortable about the word *gods*, you might simply say: "Who defends you in front of the greater powers?"

Paging Odysseus

I dreamed I discovered an epic poem, in a neat typescript of maybe two hundred pages, that I had started composing many years before. This seemed just-so. I emerged from that dream feeling that the epic was complete; it was only a matter of reclaiming those pages and getting them to the right people. My epic began, like Homer's *Odyssey*, with a poem invoking the Muses. To honor my dream, I wrote my own invocation, beginning, "Sing in me, creative spirit."

I packed translations of *The Odyssey* and *The Argonautica* in my carry-on bag for my next trip, which was going to take me to Colorado for a reading from my new poetry collection, *Here, Everything Is Dreaming*, at the Boulder Book Store.

My row mate on my flight to Denver was a feisty older woman with energy to burn. When we struck up conversation, I was surprised to find that her accent was the same as mine, a kind of Anglo-Australian with a few American touches that most Americans don't notice.

"You sound just like me," I told her.

"Of course," she replied. "I am Helen of Troy. Have you heard of Troy, New York?"

This astounding introduction had a double meaning. Helen explained that — after a life odyssey similar to my own, in Australia, Britain, and various parts of North America — she had just moved to the city of Troy, New York. It was my turn to reveal to her that I had lived in the same Troy for ten years, in a Greek revival house, inspired by a series of dreams. But it was the older Troy, the scene of a legendary war that inspired Homer's epic *The Iliad*, that claimed prime attention on my trip.

We had to pause in our conversation because a younger man was standing over us. "You are in my seat," he told my neighbor, brandishing his boarding pass. "But the flight attendant brought me here," my row mate protested. When we checked her boarding pass, we saw she was supposed to be sitting two rows back. She offered to swap seats with the man, and he agreed. "Things could get really good now," I remarked. "When seats get mixed up and plans get screwed up, the trickster comes into play."

She recounted some of the passages of her life with remarkable verve and humor. She had lived in Montpellier in southern France, where I had taught for several years and where I would be traveling again later that month.

"My middle name is Hypatia. Do you know about her?" Indeed I did know about the great philosopher and scientist of Alexandria in the fourth century. She was the mentor of Synesius of Cyrene, the philosopher and early bishop of the church whose treatise on dreams is my favorite book on the subject before the modern era. The list of parallels between our lives grew and grew. The matchups were amazing.

Where was she going today? To Colorado Springs, to take part in an Olympic-level springboard diving meet. At seventy-six and using a cane? Absolutely. The vital energy of Helen Hypatia was astounding. She seemed to have more of that than all the people on the plane put together, and I told her so.

The gods and heroes of the Greeks were on my mind when I arrived at the Boulder Book Store. I was greeted at the desk by a young woman named Athena.

In a heartbeat, I said, "Athena, where is Odysseus?"

"Odysseus works for the store," she said, not batting an eyelid. "I'll have him paged."

A minute later, the store's intercom boomed, "Paging Odysseus."

Very soon a well-made young man with flowing hair and beard — very plausible as one of Homer's "strong-greaved Achaeans" — appeared at the desk.

I asked if he had chosen his own name. Oh, no, his parents were traveling in Greece when he was born and reading *The Odyssey* to each other at night.

Helen of Troy, Athena, Odysseus. I felt the laughter of some hidden directors behind the stage curtain of the world.

That evening I read some of my poems inspired by Greek myth — "Proteus," "Birth of Apollo," "Becoming Caduceus" — to a warm and welcoming crowd at the bookstore.

The next morning, I went over to Gaia media network to record a television interview. I was given a cup of espresso by a young woman named Gaia, with a magnificent tattoo of the serpent of the earth goddess undulating down her left arm.

In the studio, they asked me to describe what it is like to live consciously at the center of the multidimensional universe. I started to tell the "Paging Odysseus" sequence.

"Hold on!" someone cut me off. "We've got to get Icarus in here."

Yes, they actually had a studio producer named Icarus. "Don't fly too close to the sun, Sonny," I kidded him.

"Oh." He adopted the posture of an archaic statue, firm and masterful. "There is no evidence that I fell to earth. I flew on, shining in my own power, once I dropped those trainer wings."

Now a character had stepped out of the old stories and was telling a fresh version.

That's what happens with living myths.

Live in the Speaking Land

Australia's First Peoples say that we live in the Speaking Land. Everything is alive; everything is conscious; the codes of the larger universe are in the country around us. Everything is speaking, and we will hear if we pay attention. The river is speaking; the bird is speaking; even a modern automobile has something to say beyond engine noise and what is playing on the radio. "There is a Toyota dreaming," says Aunty Munya Andrews, a wisdom carrier for the Bardi people of the Kimberley.

"Nothing is nothing," they say in the Cape York Peninsula. Everything speaks of something else and to something else. The spirit world and the physical world are interfused. The distance between them is the width of an eyelid — and no distance at all if the *strong* eye is open.

Knowledge is in the land. In the language of some Aboriginal peoples, there is no equivalent for the English word *knowledge*. Tex Skuthorpe, an artist of the Nhunggabarra people of New South Wales, explained that "our land is our knowledge, we walk on the knowledge, we dwell in the knowledge, we live in our thesaurus, we walk in our Bible every day of our lives. Everything is knowledge. We don't need a word for knowledge, I guess."

You know when it is the right time to do something by

listening to the land, by recognizing those things that like to happen together.

You learn that the birds are a whole telephone system.

You listen to water as well as earth, to the voices in a billabong, to the song of a river.

Releasing the Black Swan

Kurnai Aboriginal artist Ellen Harrison recalls an incident from childhood when she was out on a Gippsland lake with family. Someone caught a black swan and put it in a bag. Her uncle thought this was bad luck, but no one listened. A violent storm whipped up on the lake, threatening to sink their rowboat. The uncle struggled to the front of the dinghy, reached under Ellen's seat in the corner where the swan was in the bag, and released the bird. The wind dropped, the water calmed. They were safe.

"Maybe the swan became my special symbol. Just for me alone," she recounted to authors Carolyn Landon and Eileen Harrison in the book *Black Swan*.

> I was the youngest. I was the one who was sitting in the corner of the boat and it was under my seat. I got to thinking that I wasn't the one on the boat who could harm the swan. I was feeling something for the bird because, like, I felt it should have been me who would go to the bag and set it free. So maybe it was for me. I did often have thoughts on why that bird was there. Could it have meant for me to know something? Could it have been just for me?

Australian anthropologist Philip Clarke observes that "to Aboriginal people anything unusual in the environment could be an important sign, but only if you have the cultural knowledge to interpret it. Particular 'clever' or spiritually powerful people are believed to have received training from knowledgeable elders to develop skills in reading these signs."

We are challenged to become our own "clever people" in reading the sign language of the world around us, as we are in coming to know what is going on in our own dreams. As always, the key is practice, practice, practice.

Call of the Hawk

Many years ago, I spent a weekend driving around the Upper Hudson Valley of New York. I was profoundly dissatisfied with my life. From the outside, that life may have looked like a dream fulfilled. I was a bestselling thriller writer; publishers competed to offer me high six-figure advances, laid on stretch limos, and made sure the Dom Pérignon waiting for me in the hotel suites they paid for was perfectly chilled. And my life felt hollow. I knew I had to make a break with big cities and the fast track I had been on and get back in touch with the spirits of the land and my own deeper creative spirit.

On that upstate weekend, a few miles from the village of Chatham, a realtor showed me some land with a run-down farmhouse that might be available. The house would need a ton of work, but as I walked the land, half of it still primal woodlands where the deer moved in great droves, I knew in my gut this was a place I needed to be. I sat under an old white oak behind the house, feeling the rightness of the place but also that I needed a further sign.

A red-tailed hawk circled overhead, dipping lower and lower, screaming urgently at me in a language I felt I ought to be able to understand. I did not speak hawk, but I could not fail to get a message when she proceeded to drop a feather between my legs. That visitation by the hawk was the clincher. I purchased the farm, moved to the country, and soon found myself changing worlds, which is what can happen when we radically alter the way we inhabit the world.

When we had restored the farmhouse and moved in, I was drifting one night in that in-between state of consciousness the French used to call dorveille, sleep-wake. I found myself gently rising from my dormant body on the bed, in a second body, a dream body — not an exotic experience for me, as far back as I can remember. I floated out over the night landscape and discovered that in my dream body, I had wings — the wings of a red-tailed hawk, scaled to my size. I had a marvelous time enjoying a highly sensory experience of flying, riding thermals, swooping and soaring, seeing the world at different angles.

I found myself flying north, over Lake George and then Lake Champlain. I noticed the Adirondack Northway, and modern towns were missing from the landscape below me. I felt the tug of someone else's intention and followed it, out of curiosity, to a cabin in the woods somewhere near Montreal, where I was received by a beautiful, ancient indigenous woman. She spoke to me for a long time in her own language, her words coming wave upon wave, while she stroked a beaded belt that hung from her shoulder, with the design of a she wolf and human figures. I was fascinated but did not understand a single word, any more than I had understood the language of the hawk. I knew I was in the presence of a woman of power, and I hoped that, since this felt urgent and important, more would be revealed.

This was the start of my relationship with the ancient arendiwanen, or woman of power, I introduced in the first chapter. She called me to the path of a dream teacher. But before I heard her call, I heard the call of the hawk.

The design of her belt, in my night vision, proved to be the equivalent of the hawk's feather: a way I could receive and confirm a message even though I lacked a necessary language. My first Iroquois friend — whom I met later through an interesting series of coincidences — was able to show me a wampum belt identical to the one in my vision. It was in the archives of the New York State Museum at that time; since then it has been returned to Onondaga, the traditional capital of the Confederacy of the Six Nations of the Iroquois, or Longhouse People, among whom the Mohawk are Keepers of the

Eastern Door. He told me it was believed that the belt was the credential of an ancient mother of the Wolf Clan of the Mohawk people.

I entered deeply into the study of the traditions of the ancient dream shaman who had called me when I was flying on hawk's wings. This opened to me ways of dreaming and healing that were possibly shared by all our ancestors but that have become atrophied, when not actively suppressed, in modern society. I came to call the ancient shaman Island Woman; this reflects the fact, which I was able to confirm through historical research, that she was captured as a young girl from the Huron/Wendat, called by the Mohawk the Island People, to be raised as Mohawk. In order to receive her teachings fully, I had to study the Mohawk and Huron languages and reclaim terms from early sacred vocabulary.

New dreams eventually called me to leave the land to which the hawk had called me and teach what I had learned about dreaming the soul back home and dreaming for our communities. We sold the farm to a woman who promised to conserve the land.

As we were leaving the house, after our final checks, I was inspired to go back inside for no reason I could express. I heard a scuffling in the family room we had built overlooking the old white oak. The noise was coming from the hearth. When I removed the fire screen, I found a young red-tailed hawk, a fledgling, that had somehow managed to fall down the chimney between my last two visits. My final action, on the land I acquired because of the hawk, was to carry the young hawk outside, next to my heart, and release her. She flew straight into the branches of the white oak where the first hawk had delivered her message.

The red-tailed hawk has become my most important bringer of omens. A hawk in good shape, flying my way or grabbing a good meal, will give me a surge of confidence for the day that has yet to be disappointed. A dead hawk in power lines will make me batten down the hatches and watch out for challenges.

I was once very late for a phone interview with a California journalist who was irritated and pressed for time. I wasn't sure the interview was going to go well. She asked me to give an example of how I navigate by synchronicity.

I was standing on the balcony of a villa overlooking Long Island Sound. Right below me, three bunnies had been scampering about in the grass. As I considered my response to the journalist's question, a red-tailed hawk made a vertical descent, talons outstretched. It grabbed a bunny and shot straight up with its dinner in its clutches.

Given my affinity with the hawk, I took this as a good sign, indicating that despite our bumpy start the interview would turn out fine. I was about to recount what had just happened when some inner caution made me pause. I was talking to a journalist for a Californian holistic magazine; for all I knew, she was a vegan who might be horrified by the scene of the hawk taking the bunny rabbit, especially if I reported it with the relish I was feeling. So I told her a black dog story, and she loved it, and the interview came out just fine. The hawk sign was, once again, reliable.

Everyday Practice: Walk in the Speaking Land

Schedule twenty minutes of your day, wherever you are, to attend to what is going on around you. Use all your senses. Close your eyes for a little while. Listen, smell, feel the air on your skin. "To attend," as I mentioned before, means literally "to stretch yourself."

Symbol Magnets

The magnetic power of a symbol in our lives can bring together inner and outer events in ways that shift our perception of reality. We learn best about these things through direct experience and through stories — like Jung's fish tales — that we can trust.

When Jung was immersed in his study of the symbolism of the fish in Christianity, alchemy, and world mythology, the theme started leaping at him in everyday life. On April 1, 1949, he made some notes about an ancient inscription describing a man whose bottom half was a fish. At lunch that day, he was served fish. In the conversation, there was talk of the custom of making an "April fish" — a European term for "April fool" — of someone.

In the afternoon, a former patient of Jung's whom he had not seen for months arrived at his house and displayed for him some "impressive" pictures of fish. That evening, Jung was shown embroidery that featured fishy sea monsters. The next day, another former patient he had not seen in a decade recounted a dream in which a large fish swam toward her.

Several months later, mulling over this sequence as an example of the phenomenon he dubbed "synchronicity," Jung walked by the lake near his house, returning to the same spot several times. The last time he repeated this loop, he found a fish a foot long lying on top of the seawall. Jung had seen no one else on the lake shore that morning. While the fish might have been dropped by a bird, its appearance seemed to him quite magical, part of a "run of chance" in which more than chance seemed to be at play.

If we're keeping count (as Jung did), this sequence includes six discrete instances of meaningful coincidence, five of them bobbing up, like koi in a pond, within twenty-four hours, and all reflecting Jung's preoccupation with the symbolism of the fish. Such unlikely riffs of coincidence prompted Jung to ask whether it is possible that the physical world mirrors psychic processes "as continuously as the psyche perceives the physical world."

In her discussion of how inner and outer events can mirror one another, Jungian analyst Marie-Louise von Franz suggested that "if the psychic mirrorings of the material world — in short, the natural sciences — really constitute valid statements about matter, then the reverse mirror-relation would also have to be valid. This would mean that material events in the external world would have to be regarded as statements about conditions in the objective psyche."

Some of the greatest minds of the past century — Jung and the physicists Wolfgang Pauli and David Bohm — sought to model a universe in which mind and matter, subject and object, inner and outer, are everywhere interweaving. Events, both physical and psychic, unfold from a unified field, the *unus mundus* of the alchemists, that may be synonymous with Bohm's "implicate order." Their interaction escapes our ordinary perception of causation and of time and space. Jung said, "Precisely because the psychic and the physical are mutually dependent...they may be identical somewhere beyond our present experience."

Living symbols deeply ingrained in the imaginal history of humankind are charged with magnetic force, which can draw clusters of events together. For those familiar with tarot, it feels at such moments as if one of the greater trumps is at play in the world. Traditional diviners understand this, as do true priests and priestesses. Thus one of the odu, or patterns, of Ifá, the oracle of the Yoruba, is held to bring the fierce orisha Ogun into the space, while another is believed to carry spirits of the dead into the realm of the living. When that happens, you don't just study the pattern; you move to accommodate or propitiate the power that is manifesting.

To grasp the full power of a symbol, we need to go back to the root meaning of the word. *Symbol* is derived from the Greek *sýmbolon*, which combines *syn-*, meaning "together," and *bolē*, a "throw" or a "cast." A symbol is that which is "thrown together" or "cast together." This is very close to the root meaning of *coincidence*. In Latin, to coincide is to "fall together." So it's not surprising that when symbols are in play, coincidence multiplies.

The first literary mention of a symbol is in the Homeric Hymn to Hermes, in which the god Hermes exclaims, on finding a tortoise, "O what a happy symbol for me," before turning the tortoise shell into a lyre. In the ancient world, *sýmbolon* came to mean "a token, that which brings things together." Thus a symbol might be a pair of tokens that could be fitted together to make a single object. Such tokens might be broken halves of potsherd, a ring, or a seal. They would vouch for the truthfulness of a messenger or an enduring loyalty.

Jung noted in his foreword to his most important work on synchronicity that "my researches into the history of symbols, and of the fish symbol in particular, brought the problem [of explaining synchronicity] ever closer to me." His experiences of symbols irrupting into the physical world led him to sympathize with Johann Wolfgang von Goethe's magical view that "we all have certain electric and magnetic powers within us and ourselves exercise an attractive and repelling force, according as we come into touch with something like or unlike." Such powers are magnified when our minds and our environments are charged with the energy of a living symbol.

The Biography of a Personal Symbol

If you are keeping a journal, a great game to play from time to time is to track the evolution of a familiar symbol or theme, in dreams and in everyday life.

You've been dreaming of the bear or the fox for years; how has your relationship changed? You often dream of running into construction on the road; are you getting through, taking a detour, grinding to a halt, or remembering you can fly? Again and again, you find yourself exploring a dream house that has more rooms or levels than your regular house; can you make a floor plan, marking its changes?

A man in one of my dream circles tracked his dream encounters with the bear starting with a scary brush with a giant grizzly many years before; some of the tension lifted when he was reminded that "all mammals like to be close to warm bodies." In a later dream, he found himself snuggling with a big black bear in bed, which would have been more enjoyable had the bear not recently been in the trash, so that it stank. In the most recent of his dreams, he was playfully skipping along with his children in the tracks of a friendly bear walking in the snow.

Journal Practice: Make a Book of Symbols and Follow a Spiral Path

If you keep a dream journal, you will find it easy to track symbols and situations that recur. You'll find yourself developing your personal dictionary of symbols, the only one that truly matters for you, since the snake or the bathroom in your dream is not the snake or bathroom in my dream. You'll learn to distinguish a serial dream — a continuous narrative playing and developing over time — from a repeating or recurring dream theme that may be challenging you to make a leap in understanding or to take action on a situation your dream producers are dramatizing for your benefit.

Life in the ordinary world also presents recurring themes and situations. Life rhymes. You come to recognize personal symbols and private omens that come up again and again. You start to notice when the wheel of time spins and brings you to a place you have been before.

To walk the spiral path in life is to notice each time you come to a choice or a situation that resembles one you have encountered before and then apply what you can learn from the past experience to avoid repeating mistakes. The secret logic of our lives is revealed through resemblances.

In the school of life, lessons are repeated until we graduate from each class.

In dreams, we often see a person or situation from our past before we find ourselves in waking contact with a new person or situation that resembles the old one. As the wheel turns in regular life, we find ourselves again at a familiar crossroads or in the presence of a new person who reminds us of someone we knew before.

Recognizing the similarity in either state of consciousness helps us to ask the spiral question, which is essentially this: *Do I want to repeat myself and go round again on the wheel of repetition, or, learning from the past, am I ready to make wiser choices and go upward on the spiral of growth as I circle around?*

When a Superhero Is Showing through Your Slip

Notice what's showing through the slip. This is one of my rules for navigating by synchronicity. I pay attention to any slip of the tongue or slip of the fingers that comes up, even in the most trivial cases, like a typo or getting someone's name wrong or not being able to remember it. Something of your own unconscious feelings or mindset may be showing through the slip. Sometimes the slip carries a message or suggests something in the field that goes beyond personal psychology. At one of my workshops, I kept calling a man named Charles by the wrong name, John. Since I am rather good with names, I finally asked him, "Who is John?" He burst into tears. He told us that John was his partner. John had died a few months earlier, and that day Charles was wearing his sweater.

In my journal I rediscovered a wild example of where following a slip can lead while preparing this chapter. On this occasion, the slip was made by a publisher — not, I hasten to add, the publisher of this book.

The art director at my then publisher sent me an email about problems with the rights to the cover art for "my" book. The cover image showed a man opening his shirt like Superman. There had been problems clearing any version of the Superman image. Clearly this message was not intended for me. I was intrigued to find out what was going on and whether there was some unintended message for me in the slip.

When I checked with the art director, I learned that the email concerned the reissue of a memoir by Alvin Schwartz, one of the creators of the Superman character in the early comics.

My sensors as a synchronicity sleuth were twitching. I soon found that Alvin Schwartz was leading an internet chat room. Under the heading "Alternate Realities," he had posted these words to a struggling writer:

> I have found that as far as work is concerned that will feed your soul and your body you must not let yourself be transfixed by what logic and common sense tell you you cannot do. If you look back carefully, you may discover that unlikely probabilities in the course of a lifetime were always the things that carried the day for you. We take defined reality too seriously. We must be open to more — that is, to the unlikely and the improbable....I'm just suggesting you allow yourself to be open to what you can't now see anywhere — some solution that comes from an aspect of reality that has been educated out of us. Open the door to the impossible.

Sterling advice! As I continued to track Superman's cocreator, I made ever more exciting discoveries. After leaving the world of comics, Schwartz exercised his creative imagination in many different fields. He became a marketing consultant to some of America's largest corporations. He wrote and lectured on religious symbolism in popular culture. He wrote novels, one of which (as *Le cinglé*) became a bestseller in France. And from inventing a superhero, he encouraged his audience to develop a "super-self." In a column titled "Where is Your Other You?" he recalled being asked, "Can there be a superhero without a double identity?"

His response was quite profound:

> My first thought was, there can be no identity for anyone without an accompanying super-self. That's right, we all have super-selves capable of actions beyond our wildest imaginings. But unlike Superman and his kin, we tend to live in our lesser identity, our Clark Kent self, if you like,

almost all the time. Nevertheless, we couldn't survive if we somehow didn't sense the presence of our super-self. The knowledge of that inner super presence gives the everyday a kind of panache.

As personal examples of the presence of that Greater Self, he cited episodes in which he faced near death on the road and felt that a hidden hand interceded to take control of the wheel and steer him to safety. Many of us can recall such moments. I was delighted to find that the man who gave us Superman came up with such super reflections on the super-self.

Magic behind Mary Poppins

P. L. Travers, the author of *Mary Poppins*, was a friend of Yeats and Æ (George Russell), the Irish visionary writer and artist, and was steeped in the same esoteric and magical traditions. All of them were very interested in the workings of what Æ called "spiritual gravitation." Æ summarized the law of spiritual gravitation like this: "I found that every intense imagination, every new adventure of the intellect [is] endowed with magnetic power to attract to it its own kin. Will and desire were as the enchanter's wand of fable, and they drew to themselves their own affinities. One person after another emerged out of the mass, betraying their close affinity to my moods as they were engendered."

We see how this plays out through chance encounters, through the dreamlike symbolism of daily events, when we turn up the right message in a book opened at random or left open by someone else on a library table. If the passions of our souls are strong enough, they may draw "lifelong comrades."

In his book *The Candle of Vision*, Æ gave a personal example. When he first attempted to write verse, he immediately met a new friend, a dreaming boy "whose voice was soon to be the most beautiful voice in Irish literature." This was, of course, William Butler Yeats. "The concurrence of our personalities seemed mysterious and controlled by some law of spiritual gravitation."

In his later life, Æ found a soul companion in Travers. He assured her their own connection was evidence that through mutual affinity "your own will come to you." In a letter to Travers, Æ said: "I feel I belong to a spiritual clan whose members are scattered all over the world and these are my kinsmen."

Yeats wrote that we will be drawn to our own according to our humors, "the sanguine, the spirits of fire, and the lymphatic, those of watery nature, and those of a mixed nature, mixed spirits."

Travers's beautiful essay collection *What the Bee Knows: Reflections on Myth, Symbol and Story* deserves to be better known. Her essay "On Forgiving Oneself" is a marvelous spur to seek to connect with a higher self. I would retitle it "Meeting the Blue Lady." Travers comes upon her again and again in the woods — a mysterious, beautiful woman in a blue mantle who reminds her of Demeter and of hyacinths. She is often dancing, or gathering woodland flowers, or meeting with strangers. The day comes when the Blue Lady blocks her path. "Then she thrust a hand under her veil and drew it down from head to shoulder, her face emerging from the blue as the moon slips out from the edge of a cloud. It was my face....And I knew that I had always known, and at the same time refused to know, what lay beneath the veil."

Travers got the idea that Mary Poppins came from a star from a childhood vision of her deceased father transforming into a star. Spiritual magnetism works beyond the apparent barrier of death.

Everyday Practice in the Magnetic Field

1.   **Check your attitude.** We really do attract or repel people, events, and even physical circumstances according to the attitudes we embody. So as a daily practice, especially when

you are meeting new people or entering a new situation, check your attitude. Listen to what is playing on your inner soundtrack. Check what you are telling yourself inside your own head, and if you don't like it, see if you can edit that inner voice.

2. **Put your question to the world.** If you need guidance on something, get that theme or question clear in your mind, go out into the world, and receive the first thing that enters your field of perception as an immediate response from the oracle of the world.

3. **Grow your poetic health.** To live fully in your field of resonance and possibility, you need to grow the poetic consciousness that allows you to taste and touch what rhymes and resonates in the world you inhabit and how the world behind the world reveals itself by fluttering the veils of your consensual reality.

4. **Seek your spiral path.** The wheel spins, and you are at a place of decision where you have been before. This may involve your personal life, your work, your family. Remember how things worked out before, and be conscious you don't have to go the same way or that, if you do, you can do so with greater awareness, leading to a different outcome.

5. **Notice that truth comes with goosebumps.** It's a rule of skin: truth comes with goosebumps (or chicken skin, if you like). There is a science of shivers. You want to learn to recognize and respect what is going on when something exceptional is in the air and your body responds before your mind can make sense of it.

8

There Is a World of Imagination, and It Is Entirely Real

A sudden stillness settles over the classroom. One by one, those who are ready rise from their bodies and gather in the corner, where a hearth fire is now burning.

The fire is extraordinary. It is electric blue. The flames stream and dance like shimmering blue silk. It is lovely and beckoning. Yet it is fire, and what is beyond it is unknown. So there is hesitation and some fear.

One who has passed this way before enters the fire like a dancer, becomes a figure of bright flame, and is gone. The others join the dance and move through the blue fire. There is no pain. The pain was on the other side.

Loving arms receive them. The angels have familiar faces. They are going to a new school, a pleasant place on a green hill, among beds of flowers and flowering trees. The course selection is amazing. Whatever they have learned already will be put to use, and their classes and assignments will be built around their curiosity, passion, and imagination.

They will want to communicate with those they left behind, to try to ease their grief by letting them know that there truly is a better place, beyond the pain of the world, where learning and growth continue, and where fun and adventure are encouraged, and where the most important skill is the ability to make things up.

Every experience is different, here even more than in the previous world. They are cheered by watching a graduating class, gathered on the green hill in front of a warm, ivy-wrapped brick building. They are dressed in simple white smocks. Their voices are achingly beautiful. Their songs are not hymns from church or what used to play on headphones.

Sunrise, sunset, evening star
What cannot be seen in the dream
cannot be seen in its glory

I walk and talk with some of the faculty. A donnish, tweedy man with a mustache reminds me of my favorite teacher in high school, eons ago, a British professor of ancient history who decided to come out of retirement to share his passion with hormonal boys in a burned landscape in Australia. What is the name of this school? Alma Mater, of course: Mother Soul.

I discovered this School of Mother Soul when I started teaching public dream classes some thirty years ago. I asked, in the night, to see what I most needed to teach and found myself leading a class through that blue fire. Since then, I have visited this Alma Mater many times and have found that its offerings are ever growing. Some students study communications, learning and inventing techniques to facilitate helpful contact between people on this side and those left behind in the physical world. There is great compassion among the faculty for the grief of the survivors and great eagerness among the students to alleviate that pain by reaching back to offer love and direct knowledge of life beyond life.

We are in the afterlife, then. But that is not a satisfactory description, because what goes on here is available to souls on both sides of physical death.

Will you allow yourself a taste of what you might be able to find here?

Imaginal Exercise: Through the Blue Fire

Picture this: You are in a pleasant classroom with people you enjoy. This isn't like regular school. You are presented with amazing books. When you open one, you enter a different world. You are instructed to swim with mermaids or to sing with an ancient tree. You are guided down into a cave of the ancestors, where you place your hands on a wall and great painted beasts come alive and you take their forms.

You've been in this school since you were very small, though your adult self may have skipped or forgotten most of the classes.

Now you are waking up to what dreaming can be. You're eager to make up for all the dreams you lost and get to graduate school. The way forward leads through blue fire. You hesitate, watching the electric blue of the leaping flames. You are encouraged by a teacher with a twinkle in his eye and by the presence of those lovely classmates who feel like family. You go dancing through the blue fire.

Now you are in a different landscape, green as the first day. You are welcomed by music, achingly beautiful songs. A scholar city rises before you. Its learned name is Anamnesis, which means "soul re-membering." You can call it simply the School of Mother Soul. You come here to remember what soul is, and what soul knows, and how to bring more of vital soul into every aspect of life.

Distinctions made in the ordinary world don't count for anything here. Great teachers and creators and beloved ancestors who were said to be dead are very much alive. The only time is now.

Oh look! Beyond the main building with its strange clock, students of all ages are learning to fly. Some are choosing their rides — a dragon, a flying tiger, a winged horse. Some are turning into bird people or flying Superman-style. You know they'll be safe. Everything is closely watched by the head of security, who appears to be a lovely little girl about five years old. But you know she has been around for longer than the moon.

Mundus Imaginalis ·

The School of Mother Soul and the scholar city of Anamnesis are real places in the world of true imagination. Henry Corbin, the great French scholar of Islamic mysticism, encouraged us to call this world the Mundus Imaginalis, or imaginal realm. It is a fundamental ground of knowledge and experience. It is a region of mind between the world of time and the world of eternity. In this realm human imagination meets intelligences from higher realities, and they co-construct places of healing, instruction, and initiation. Here ideas and powers beyond the grasp of the ordinary human mind — call them archetypes or Platonic forms — take on guises humans can begin to perceive and understand. It is a place beyond place where human minds meet intellects and intentions from beyond the human range. There are structures here: temples and palaces, schools and cities, pleasure gardens and places of initiation and healing.

The term *imaginal realm* is an attempt at translation of two terms used by medieval Islamic mystics who were frequent visitors: Alam al-Mithal, or Realm of Archetypes, and Alam al-Khayal, or Realm of Images. Corbin encouraged us to use "imaginal" instead of "imaginary" in describing this reality. If we call something "imaginary," we usually mean it is "made up," something other than real. Yet poets and mystics have always known that the world of imagination *is* a real world — a third kingdom between the physical universe and the higher realms of spirit — and that it is possible to travel there and bring back extraordinary gifts. Corbin described the imaginal realm as "a world as ontologically real as the world of the senses and the world of the intellect, a world that requires faculty of perception belonging to it.... This faculty is the imaginative power, the one we must avoid confusing with the imagination that modern man identifies with 'fantasy' and that, according to him, produces only the 'imaginary.'"

Imaginal may not be a household word in the English language — unlike in French, where you can speak of *l'imaginaire* without needing to explain — but it is worth getting to know it, because it affirms the reality of experience in realms beyond the physical where adventure and initiation, higher education, and deep healing are all available.

The Persian mystics also call the imaginal realm the Place Outside of Where, Na-koja-Abad. It is "a climate outside of climates, a place outside of place, outside of where." In its eastern region is the realm of the spirits who have moved beyond physical existence and "the forms of all works accomplished, the forms of our thoughts and desires." It is an "isthmus" between the realm of pure light and the darkness of the physical world. It is a realm of "suspended form" — dark as well as light — that may be renewed or destroyed, like images in a mirror, through the faculty of imagination.

In this realm we are beyond the physical, but we do not go about as disembodied thought forms. The Persian commentator Mulla Sadra Shirazi described the Alam al-Mithal as "the world of the subtle bodies...a world in which we have subtle or imaginal bodies as we have a physical body in this world." According to Mulla Sadra, the subtle world "has even more reality than the physical world."

The great Persian mystical philosopher Shihab al-Din al-Suhrawardi (executed by the judges of Islamic Sharia in 1191) insisted both on the objective reality of the imaginal realm and on the fact that the way to grasp it is the way of experience: "pilgrims of the spirit succeed in contemplating this world and they find there every object of their desire." Speaking with the authority of direct experience, he declared in his masterwork, the *Hikmat al-Ishraq* (*The Philosophy of Illumination*), "I myself have had trustworthy experiences, indicating that there are four worlds." To know the world of true imagination, you must go there yourself.

The imaginal realm may be the source of new creation in the physical world. It is related to what Seth, speaking through Jane Roberts, was content to call a "dream universe":

> Your universe and all others spring from a dimension that is
> the creative source for all realities — a basic dream universe

so to speak, a Divine psychological bed where subjective being is sparked, illuminated, stimulated, pierced by its own infinite desire for creativity.... The source of its power is so great that its imaginings become worlds, but it is endowed with a creativity of such splendor that it seeks the finest fulfillment, for even the smallest of its thoughts and all of its potentials are directed with a good intent that is literally beyond all imagining.

You are no stranger to the imaginal realm, even if you do not remember the dreams in which you may have traveled to its suburbs, at least. That curious house you keep visiting in night dreams may be your pied-à-terre in some quarter of an imaginal city. In this chapter you will be invited to visit some very interesting locales in the imaginal realm from which previous travelers have returned with reports of encounters with master teachers, privileged access to a total library, portals for time travel, and experiments in reality creation.

To the Moon Studio

The nearer regions of the imaginal realm are visible in the night sky. The astral realm of the moon is thickly populated, though it has the mixed character of any great city. I was once asked to consult with a young singer-songwriter who wanted both inspiration for new songs and guidance on how to get her work produced and published. I suggested that we might make a visionary journey to a music school in the astral realm of the moon. Instead of drumming, we would use a song to power and focus the journey — in fact, just part of a song. She had borrowed a phrase her mother had dreamed, "Dreams are moon babies," and set it to music. We lay on a rug, holding hands and singing this phrase over and over as we wished ourselves able to travel to the astral realm of Luna on the path of moonlight on water, visible to ordinary eyes earlier on the lake beyond the house.

There were Gatekeepers, of course, and a cleansing procedure, but we were not distracted by the thrumming hive of activity we found on first entering a lunar city, busy as downtown Tokyo or Hong Kong at night. We soon found ourselves at a building of warm brick, rising above gardens. I gasped when I saw the greeter who came to receive us at the top of the steps. She was Aunty Dick, as we called her — my mother's aunt, who had been a famous opera singer, a coloratura soprano who often performed with her friend Dame Nellie Melba. I had not seen Aunty Dick since my mother took me to visit her in Perth when I was three years old.

She was welcoming but also brisk and practical. She gave both of us some voice exercises. I remembered her telling me all those years ago, "Breathe from the diaphragm, dear." She escorted the singer-songwriter to a salon where a musical soirée was in full swing. I watched her rub shoulders with great chanteuses, some long dead to the physical world, some still very much in it. Then my mother's aunt guided my protégée into a recording studio. When we came back from the journey, the songwriter told me, in delighted amazement, "I got three new songs, with lyrics to two of them. And I saw who is going to produce the album." She proceeded to write the songs, and the album was released the following year.

Your Dream House as Imaginal Property

When you record your dreams, pay special attention to the dream locations. The settings may be familiar or completely foreign, vivid and sensory or cloudy and indistinct. You may be in a place whose physics appears quite different from that of ordinary reality. You may be at home with people you don't know in regular life. You might be living in a medieval castle that seems to have been constructed yesterday.

Again and again, you dream you are in the old place — back in the home you shared with your ex, or the office where you worked at the old job, or at Grandma's house, or in the schoolyard. Maybe you'll want to ask yourself: "Did I leave part of myself behind when I left that old situation?"

Maybe your dream house is a hybrid, melding elements from places you recognize from the past with novel architecture. The house may seem familiar at the outset but then prove to have more rooms and more stories than you remember. These may be stories of your life and levels of your psyche or Self. It can be fascinating to re-visit a dream structure of this kind through conscious dream reentry and learn more about what is going on. Jung found in his dream of a many-layered house (a dream Freud insisted on misinterpreting) a model for understanding connections between the conscious mind, the personal subconscious, and the collective unconscious. In his dream, he started out on a floor that looked like a normal bourgeois home. As he descended through successive floors, he found himself in primal territory, in a dirt-floor basement containing skulls and bones of distant ancestors.

I find it especially intriguing to go up on the roof of a dream house. Sometimes I discover levels beyond what I expected. Some-times, on a roof terrace or garden, I meet a benign figure I recognize as a slightly higher self, a witness self who can give me perspective on my life situation, since he is up above the scrum. I have called this figure the Double on the Balcony.

I dreamed I was in a house that I used to own, in another reality. It was quite familiar in the dream but does not correspond closely to any house I have occupied in this world. My dream house was a palace, with sections open to tour groups. It had sweeping marble staircases leading up to what used to be private family apartments and my library. I tried to go up the steps, but they petered out, and I realized the library and the private rooms had been long since aban-doned and sealed off. I did not give up on my detective work. I took another staircase to a balcony with wonderful views over green for-ests and meadows. I told ladies I met there, matter-of-factly, "I used to own this house." I knew I would come here again. I needed to get up that staircase and to understand what life story I was inhabiting in this palace that had seen better days.

By focusing on a dream location, we have an excellent portal for conscious dreaming, shamanic journeying, and astral travel. If you have been to a place in a dream, you can go there again, just as you might return to a place you have visited in ordinary reality. Your dream house may be a place you will visit in the future. I have been drawn again and again, in series of dreams, to houses I did not recognize at the outset but proved to be future homes that I would later purchase and occupy. We take real estate tours in our dreams.

The dream house may be a structure that the imaginal architect in you has constructed for various purposes: as a place for rest and relaxation, as a sanctuary or a study, as a place of rendezvous, as a pleasure palace. Such creations may have their own stability. They may be homes that await you in the afterlife or interlife. Your dream house may be a place where you are leading a parallel life with people you may or may not know in your physical world. It may be a construction or renovation site, a place waiting for your imagination to raise the walls or put on the finishing touches.

If your memories of your dream house are blurry, you can take comfort from Seth, as channeled by Jane Roberts: "If you have little memory of your dream locations when you are awake, then remember that you have little memory of your waking locations when you are in the dream situation. Both are legitimate and both are realities. When the body lies in bed, it is separated by a vast distance from the dream location in which the dreaming self may dwell."

Time beyond Time

The imaginal realm is rich in architecture, offering structures within the limitless space of what science now calls nonlocal mind. One such structure, the House of Time, is a created locale in the imaginal realm. It has been developed through the active imagination of hundreds of dream explorers and archaeologists who have traveled here over many years. It stands on the foundation of ancient structures dating back thousands of years. The House of Time is a creation, as is every structure built by humans on the planet Earth, from the pyramids to the Mall of the Americas. It is no less real than the Empire State Building or the Louvre because it stands on imaginal, rather than physical, ground. Structures in the imaginal realm sometimes prove to be more, not less, durable than those in the physical world. Think of how long people have being going off after death to heavens and hells generated by collective belief systems.

Reality construction in the imaginal realm is different than in the world of metal and cement, where plumbers or electricians may keep you waiting for days. Here schools and temples and palaces and pleasure houses are generated by imagination. You don't have to labor over every detail, unless that is your pleasure. And you don't have to wait for weeks or even days to see a finished building.

An imaginal creation becomes more solid and more complex when it is the result of an ongoing group project. With each visit or any set of visitors, the House of Time grows and shifts and changes even faster than Hogwarts in the Harry Potter series. Everybody who goes there adds to it and changes it in some way as a collective environment. Your own imagination, your own presence changes things. It's stable, but it's not static.

If you are ready to accept the invitation to visit this special place, you will learn something about the nature of reality construction in the larger universe. The lessons from this can be applied to how you construct your physical reality.

The House of Time is an excellent base for journeys to past or future or parallel times. You might want to scout out the future. You might want to visit the past. You might want to make contact with personalities in other times and places who may be ancestral connections, or part of your reincarnational dramas, or members of your multidimensional family.

Start by assuring yourself that the time is now. You are at the center of all times. In this moment of now, you may be able to access past time, future time, and parallel time, and you may be able to do some good. You may be able to change something for the better, at least in a mental state, at least in an emotional state. You could play advocate and friend to that younger self who needs support in her time. You could check in on a possibly wise older self. You could learn about how dramas from other lives in other times and places are relevant to your relationships in your present life, and you can do this in a fully conscious state, not through hypnotic regression, where you lose a sense of what's going on for a while. You will approach this adventure as an active dreamer and imagineer, ready to travel the multiverse fully lucid.

Are you ready to take to the road?

Imaginal Exercise: Journey to the House of Time

Picture this: You are cruising along a road on a pleasant day. Ahead, you see the mouth of a tunnel. It looks like a tunnel in a side of a mountain. You have seen something like this before, driving or riding in a train. You are moving forward at a steady speed, and you enter the tunnel. It's going to get quite dark inside, but you know you are fine. You are traveling at increasing speed as you follow the bends and curves of the tunnel. Here you go, *whoa*, this is getting exciting. Now there is light ahead, the light at the end of the tunnel.

You are outside again, but in a different landscape, looking across a beautiful, fertile valley. There are flowering trees and orchards and gardens on either side of a path that glows soft yellow. You inhale the aromas of flowers and ripe fruit. The air smells so good. You see the glint of water through the trees. That is the River of Time. Go there and look into the mirror-bright water, and another face will rise to meet you, bringing knowledge of another life in another time or another dimension that is relevant to your present life. Let yourself fall gently toward that face in the water, and you could find yourself

195

entering the life of that other person in their own time and place. But for now, your way is forward. You return to the yellow path. You notice the mountains on either side of the valley and their purple shadows. You may see the sun and moon together in the sky.

Straight ahead of you is an amazing building. It seems to be composed of many different architectural styles — a bit of Tudor, a little Frank Lloyd Wright, Gothic spires, a dome that belongs in Istanbul, a Greek portico. This could be a crazy chaos, but somehow it all fits together. There is a sense of harmony. You have to suspect that ordinary rules of geometry and physics don't apply here.

Tall steps lead up to a great doorway. Above it is a most unusual clock that does not display time in any way you can understand. You have arrived at the House of Time.

Go up the steps and meet your Gatekeeper, who will take a form appropriate to your perception and understanding. Your Gatekeeper is probably going to ask you to lay down some things you're carrying with you: that anxiety, that skepticism, that baggage from your life — whatever may prevent you from being fully present to this moment of now.

Your Gatekeeper may have questions for you. The first is likely to be: "What is the correct time?" I think you know the answer. Do you remember? The time is always now.

Your Gatekeeper might be friendly or severe and may even seem to be hostile to begin with. If your Gatekeeper seems surly or demanding, it's because your Gatekeeper's function is to make sure that you're absolutely primed and ready for the experiences about to unfold. What you discover in the House of Time may show you the deeper logic of your present relationships and life trajectory. You may awaken to patterns of connection between the dramas and challenges of your present life and those of other times and other lives. In the course of this, you may rise to the understanding that in a sense it's all going on *now*, past life, future life, parallel life.

Shall we assume that the Gatekeeper gives you permission to enter the House of Time?

The great door is opening into worlds of discovery and adventure. You go through the door and a lobby area into a vast, light-filled space we will call the Gallery of Time. It is full of interesting objects from many cultures, some known to you, some completely foreign. There are paintings and sculptures, furniture and fetishes, maps and musical instruments, icons and eyeglasses. You are drawn to many things, but one thing here seizes your attention. As you look into the picture or handle the statue or put on that hat or sit on that chaise longue, you are transported to the time and place from which it comes and into the life of a person associated with it.

You may find yourself deep inside this scene, seemingly inside the body and perspective of a person who is at home here. Or you remain an observer, taking things in without entering fully into another life drama. It's rather like what happens in dreams, where you might be an observer or you might be the center of the action in a role and even seemingly in a body that is not your usual one. In that scene of another life, your experience may be a kind of hybrid. You have access to the mind of that other person and may be able to set up an inner dialogue, sharing in their situation without entering it completely.

What is going on in that life is related to your current issues. So you want to learn everything you can about it. Who is this person? When and where are you? Who are the other people involved here? What are the challenges and gifts of this life experience? If the corresponding information does not come to you immediately, play detective. How are you and they dressed? Look for clues to identity. Follow the action that may start to unfold. ·

Are you ready?

Give yourself time to go through the Gallery of Time into that scene of another life and bring back strong impressions. When you come back to where you parked your body, write down three things you experienced or observed during your outing. You could draw a picture of the object that took you into that scene or the main character in that scene of a house or landscape you discovered. Can you identify elements in that other story that you recognize in your own life? Do any people in that other story remind you of people in your present life?

I know that recollection of past lives to which we are connected can be very healing. This is sometimes done through hypnotic regression. That is not our way. We try to do these things through lucid dream travel, the shaman's way. But let me give you a personal example of how this sometimes works. I seem to have grown up as a boy with the memories of someone who lived in England before World War II and fought in World War II. I was eventually able to connect those memories of a life in a slightly earlier time with the strange phobia that I carried for many decades in this life. I was frightened of going down at a certain angle, like the steep pitch of an escalator going down into the dark. I was especially scared of an escalator in the metro DC area, at the Bethesda subway station. My phobia grew so acute that on one occasion I had to sit down on the moving escalator. I was grateful no one else was there to witness my embarrassment.

This told me it was time to seek the source of that fear. I found it in my dreams. Over much of my life I had dreamed myself in the situation and seemingly the body of an educated, rather dashing young Englishman who joined the Royal Air Force in World War II. When I looked again into his life, I recalled that when his fighter bomber was shot down over the Netherlands, it went down at the same angle as that fearsome escalator. He did not die in the crash, but later he was betrayed to the Gestapo. With the returning memory of that past life episode, my escalator phobia disappeared. To see something as it is, including the roots of the situation, can be to change it for the better. Your dreams will take you there, and so will the portals of the House of Time.

Let's go deeper into this imaginal architecture. Beyond the Gallery of Time is a large atrium, tiled in black and white. High overhead in the domed ceiling is a large skylight or oculus. In the middle of the atrium is a bank of elevators of unusual design. They can transport you across time in different ways, to past or future or to a parallel time where you are leading a life on a different event track.

For now, picture yourself moving across the atrium, paying close attention to your surroundings. You look up at the skylight and see a pattern of stars that may or may not be familiar to you. Across the atrium are many doors. One is opening for you. You are about to enter the library of the House of Time.

You are greeted by a librarian. He often appears to me in a tweed suit with half-moon reading glasses, looking like an Oxbridge don, except that his shadow is that of a long-beaked bird revered in Egypt and well-known today (without much reverence, alas) in my native Australia. Your version of the librarian will guide you to what you are seeking. You may express a specific intention, for example, that you would like information or inspiration in a certain area, or to meet a master teacher in a certain field, or to find the big story you need for your life right now. Or you may simply trust that you will be drawn by affinity to the resources and counsel that you need and desire.

A landscape gardener who made this journey met Inigo Jones, the celebrated seventeenth-century architect and designer, who gave him surprisingly helpful advice on a project in the Hamptons. A yachtsman whose sights were set on winning a major race in the Pacific was shown blueprints for a new double-hull design; he proceeded to build the yacht and won that race.

When I had just started work on the book that was published as *The Dreamer's Book of the Dead*, I wandered among the stacks of the library of the House of Time while drumming for a group. I heard my name called in my inner field of perception, turned in its direction, and saw a spiral staircase I had not noticed before. At the top of the staircase, in a countryman's coat that floated like a cape, was the dead Irish poet William Butler Yeats. "What better guide to the Other Side than a poet?" he asked in a lilting voice.

This was the start of a deep inner communication that carried me through the crafting of that book and is described quite openly in it. One of Yeats's great ambitions was to write a Western Book of the Dead, and he tried valiantly in the two editions of his astonishing book *A Vision*, but he recognized that both times the content was flawed and inaccessible to most readers. Mutual affinity would certainly account for our convergence in the library of the House of Time and all the night seminars and excursions that followed. An inquiring mind will ask, *Was that really Yeats? Or an aspect of myself that identifies with Yeats, whose poetry I have loved and recited since boyhood? Or a mask for some other intelligence, leaning in?* I am ready to leave those questions unanswered and simply celebrate and create from the remarkable relationship that was offered to me by the man at the top of the spiral staircase.

In the library of the House of Time, you might be invited to ascend to a level where you find several advisers waiting for you. They may be an ad hoc committee that has come together to assist you with a particular project or transition. When I was temporarily between publishers and worried about where to find support for my work in a new genre, I guided a group journey to the library of the House of Time during which one of my familiar guides called me up to a mezzanine where several people were comfortably seated on leather chesterfields. Among them was Maxwell Perkins, famous in the history of American publishing as an editor who was always *there* for his authors (among them Thomas Wolfe, William Faulkner, and Ernest Hemingway), nursing them through their periods of self-doubt, their alcoholic binges, their blocks. The encounter made me keenly aware that instead of looking for a new agent, I must focus on finding the right *editor*. When I did, I became a constant author, delivering eight books to the same publisher over thirteen years.

Your version of the library of the House of Time may open into all kinds of unexpected spaces, not just nooks but entire wings and towers of possibility. One hint for now: there is a very secure area in the library where you may be able to access your own Book of Life. This will remind you of the contract you made before you embarked on your present life experience. I have come to suspect that all of us enter into this world on assignment. The mission may be large or small as viewed by others. It may be karmic in the sense that it is related to what was done or not done in other life experiences for which we are responsible. If you have the opportunity and the courage to look in your Book of Life, you may be able to better understand your life challenges and claim the deeper meaning of your existence.

Architects of the Imaginal Realm

The poet Rumi sings of Shams, his spiritual mentor, as an imaginal architect, creating a place from No-place:

> My heart flew up in joy and placed a ladder at the intellect's edge.
> It rushed to the roof in its love, seeking a tangible sign of that
> good news.
> Suddenly from the housetop it saw a world beyond our world —
> an all-encompassing ocean in a jug, a heaven in the form of
> dust.
> Upon the roof sat a king wearing the clothes of a watchman.
> An infinite garden and paradise within that gardener's breast.
> His image traveled from breast to breast explaining the Sultan of the heart.
> O image of that king, flee not from my eyes! Renew my heart for
> a moment!
> Shams-i Tabrizi has seen No-place and built from it a place.

I dream of scholar cities and pleasure domes, of temples and libraries in a real world that is constantly and delightfully under construction. "You are a space architect," one of my students told me. "You create tents of vision and bring us inside for shared adventures." I like this notion. I invite others to accompany me to the Moon Café, and the House of Time, to the Silver Airport and the Cosmic Video Store. I give them route maps and floor plans. I tell them how to deal with Gatekeepers, what to offer and what to leave behind.

I help invited visitors to frame their intentions: to meet a guide or an ancestral soul, to find a new song or look (if they dare) in their Book of Life, to design a home on the Other Side, to embrace a lover in an apple orchard at the edge of Faerie. I don't lead them around like a tour guide. I open space, then turn them loose to make fresh discoveries on their own.

The travelers add to the locations they visit. Their very presence makes the ground more firm, the structures more durable and more intricate. They are composed of subtle stuff, but may endure longer than buildings of steel and concrete.

The taste and imagination of visitors add flourishes and sometimes whole floors. In these ideoplastic environments, every visitor is a builder and decorator. A bronze mirror replaces a daguerreotype; a cello is heard in a music room that wasn't there before; a wall of books in the magic library rolls back to reveal a druid wood; golden carp gleam in the pool of the Garden of Memory.

I created a huge tent, the kind used for family reunions and elegant outdoor weddings, and told my invited guests that they could come here to encounter and reclaim multiple aspects of self and soul. I showed group after group the way to this house of gifts, and to make sure they did not get lost, I assigned the sheepdog of shamanic drumming to sort out their brain waves. These visits produced marvels. Then I noticed that the tent had grown in wondrous ways. From one side, it looked like a fairy-tale castle; from another, like a Victorian mansion with many wings and countless rooms to open one by one.

The act of observation, we are informed by quantum physics, makes things, even worlds. Looking brings definite events into manifestation out of a soup of possibilities, Heisenberg's "world of tendencies." Frequent explorers of the imaginal realm are quite familiar with the observer effect. I am constantly astonished, though rarely surprised, by how the travelers who follow my maps change what they look at. A pink woman with an elephant's head now staffs the ticket counter of the Dream Cinema, and a three-headed oracle is open for business on the dark side of the moon.

The Strand of Imagination

I love playing architect of the imaginal realm. This means helping to design or cocreate real places in the realm of true imagination where people can go — in lucid dreaming, shamanic journeys, and imaginal exercises — to have adventures in discovery and healing. As a book lover, I especially like traveling and guiding people to various versions of a secret library or magic bookstore where they may have access to any kind of information or inspiration and meet master teachers. I invite them to call up the memory of a place, like a bookshop or museum, where they were excited by the discovery of new ideas and images and then to use that memory as the portal for a visit to a space that will soon expand and deepen into something far beyond memory. Here is my account of what happened when I suggested to a circle of forty literate dreamers at a weekend workshop in Manhattan that we might travel together, fueled and focused by my shamanic drumming, to New York's iconic Strand Book Store and let it become our doorway to the imaginal realm where poets, shamans, and mystics have always wanted to go.

We agreed to meet at the Strand, the venerable, vast, and lively bookstore at the corner of Broadway and East 12th Street in Manhattan. The area used to be called Book Row, but of all the bookshops that flourished here around the time the Strand opened its doors in 1927, this is the sole survivor. It has remained a family business, ownership descending through the progeny of Ben Bass, the founder.

In the time when the Strand boasted that it contained eight miles of books, a wag stated that the eight miles of New York worth preserving were inside its walls. The bookstore has grown since; it now holds no less than eighteen miles of books.

In the year I lived in Manhattan, my arms were often sore from toting big shopping bags of twice-sold tales from the Strand up to my modest apartment in Yorkville. On flying visits to the city since, I have frequently failed to ration my Strand book buying sufficiently to pass the weight inspection for suitcases at airports. Besides the expected and unexpected treasures in all the cases of old books, the Strand is the place to get a new book at half price. The velocity at which review copies pour into the store makes it hard to believe that many of those reviewers even opened their copies before generating a little extra income.

The Strand has long been, for me, one of those magic bookshops where the shelf elves produce exactly the right book to guide or redirect a creative intent. When I was writing a chapter of a novella in which Yeats is at home in his rooms in the Woburn Buildings, off London's Tavistock Square, circa 1900, my youngest daughter — who did not know about my project — visited the rare book room at the Strand and brought me back a scarce prize, a memoir of Yeats by John Masefield in which the English poet evokes beautifully the experience of visiting the Irish poet in that London apartment.

The Strand has a place in my imaginal geography as well as my physical rambles. When I was writing about Harriet Tubman, who used her dreams and visions to guide escaping slaves to freedom on the Underground Railroad before the American Civil War, I found myself roaming the Strand in the middle of the night in my astral body, in that wondrously fluid state of consciousness that sleep researchers call hypnagogia and I prefer to call the twilight zone. Down in the basement, I met Tubman, wearing a hat pulled down over her forehead and a shapeless coat. She showed me that her skills as a tracker and guide owed a great deal to the shamanic ways of the

Ashanti, her father's people, and especially to the leopard, the favorite animal spirit of West African shamans and shapeshifters. I used the insights I gained in the basement of the Strand that night in my chapter on Tubman in *The Secret History of Dreaming*.

I shared this dream with the participants in the shamanic dreaming workshop I led at the New York Open Center. Most people in the workshop knew the Strand. There was great excitement when I suggested that all of us could use the Strand as a portal for an adventure in the imaginal realm, with the aim of contacting master teachers or practitioners in whatever fields most interested us.

I explained that we could use our memories of the physical bookstore in order to enter a space beyond it. We might find that by opening any book, we could enter the world it contained. We might discover that a bookshop in Manhattan could become the gateway to a secret library, where all knowledge is accessible.

When I was sure that everyone had been seized by the intention to explore and the workshop participants had placed their bodies in comfortable positions for journeying, I used my gee-whiz technology — a single-headed frame drum — to provide fuel and focus for our group adventure. I always journey for myself while drumming for the group; I immediately found myself at the corner of Broadway and East 12th. After a cursory look at the sale items in the stalls on the sidewalk, I headed into the store. I noticed a memorial display for Maurice Sendak, and I paused to check the prices of recycled review copies of a few novels I had recently purchased: Carlos Ruiz Zafón's *The Prisoner of Heaven*, Alan Furst's *Mission to Paris*, Joseph Kanon's *Istanbul Passage*.

I took the stairs to the basement and found Graham Greene waiting for me there. I have talked before to that grand English novelist and entertainer (or the part of myself that relishes him and puts on his mask), and he has given me excellent advice on the practice of writing, advice I have not always followed. Greene was a consummate professional, able to sit down and crank out his 750 words a day however many drinks he had shared with a Soviet agent, a whiskey priest, or a bevy of filles de joie the night before. I wondered if he would nudge me toward trying my hand again at a tale of intrigue; in a former life, back in the 1980s, I had published a series of popular spy novels. Ah, something more interesting. Greene offered me some tips on writing a memoir. I set my intention to reread his own autobiographical works, especially *A Sort of Life* and *Ways of Escape*.

Behind Greene, among the stacks, I saw a dark-haired young fellow in a trench coat. Who was that? It gave me a shiver to realize I was looking at a much younger version of myself, the 1980s thriller writer, seen now very much as he appeared on the dust jacket of a couple of my early novels. I did not engage with him directly.

Instead I went to the right, down book-lined passages, and met other figures, including a magical child with a treasure chest full of stories for children that I might yet write. As I continued drumming, I found myself in a passage where books rose to the ceiling. The passage turned and turned in a spiral until — *poof!* — I came out in a space where the first thing I saw was a spray of black feathers and the black embroidered hem of a woman's long dress.

I found myself in the presence of a gloriously over-the-top lady of a certain age, still desirable and very sure of her place in a social and literary world she had made for herself. She was dressed in a black feather boa and a magnificent black dress with plunging décolletage. She gave me her pen name and allowed me a glimpse of her life. Her admirers included American tycoons and European counts; she allowed only a very select few to share her intimate favors. There were those in high places who relied on her as a psychic medium; it was her special pleasure to connect people with their past lives. Out of this life, she had written a wildly successful series of romps that blended the metaphysical with the bodice ripper and the *policier*.

I was astonished, though not altogether surprised, to realize that I knew this lady writer. At the end of the 1980s, when I had abandoned the commercial path, I found myself held up for a long time at a customs check. While I submitted to questions and inspections, I noticed a flamboyant woman in furs breezing past compliant officials at a parallel checkpoint; they whisked her Louis Vuitton bags through, unopened. The lady in furs turned to me and blew me a kiss. She called to me, "Maybe we'll meet again."

That had been, of course, a dream. When I thought about it at the time, I chuckled, realizing that I had caught a glimpse of my inner Happy Hooker, the part of me that had been willing to put out my work for a price. Here she was again, in a black feather boa. Why?

"Write in my voice," said my Happy Hooker. "Write in my name, if you like. You can still write about the things that matter to you, while you give people even more fun."

Hmm. I'll need to think about that.

When I sounded the recall with the drum, our intrepid dream travelers brought back a marvelous set of personal reports, featuring encounters with dead poets and master chefs, with a children's writer and a Neoplatonist philosopher. Wonderful what one can find in the Strand of the imagination.

On the Cards

"The doorways to the invisible must be visible," declared René Daumal in *Mount Analogue.* You may find that your ability to access the inner worlds of imagination will grow if you practice using visual images as portals. A simple exercise designed to expand your inner sight is Step into a Picture.

Imaginal Exercise: Step into a Picture

Choose a picture that intrigues you — a painting, a photograph, a postcard, an oracle card. I prefer representational images, but you can choose whatever appeals to you, on one condition: the picture has a border or a frame.

Study the picture, memorizing as many details as you can. Close your eyes and try to bring the image up on your inner screen. Now open your eyes and see what you missed or transposed. Repeat until you are confident you have internalized the essential parts of the picture.

Now look at the border. Imagine that it is the frame of a door. In deepening meditation, you are going to picture yourself stepping through that door, into a scene beyond it. Are you ready? Close your eyes and go through the door.

You may find yourself far past what is shown in the original picture, sailing on an ocean beyond that headland or into a strange quarter of that city of cobbled streets. You could meet someone who is in the picture and now comes alive — Grandma, a girl on a swing, the Queen of Swords, or Aslan — or is now presenting themselves for the first time.

Enjoy your excursion. When you are ready to come back, turn around slowly. Look for the open door you came through, as the children in *The Lion, the Witch, and the Wardrobe* seek the door of the closet that opened into Narnia. Maybe, if only for an instant, you will see your body dormant in the place where you parked it.

Come back, open your eyes, stretch out, wiggle around.

This is everyday practice. In the old Western mystery tradition, there is an advanced practice for using pictures to access inner worlds that is known as pathworking. This is sometimes accomplished by deriving a map for a journey through the projection of the major arcana of the tarot on the Qabalistic Tree of Life.

Tarot Gate to Atlantis

Working the tarot can bring us in contact with past masters of this system. On a fall evening, I had been discussing tarot and did a personal reading in which the last two cards were the Hanged Man and the High Priestess.

When I lay down, relaxing into the twilight state between wakefulness and sleep, I had a strong sense of contact with a female personality. I had no doubt she was a priestess. I associated her with Dion Fortune, who had led a great esoteric order in Britain, and used the Qabalistic tarot in her teachings and rituals. She gave eminently practical advice on approaching tarot:

> To use the Tarot properly…requires a very great deal of preparation, and the preparation does not consist merely in a knowledge of the significance of the cards, but in getting in touch with the forces behind the cards.…Obtain a new pack of Tarot cards, for a used one will be too full of other people's magnetism to be reliable, and carry them on the person, and sleep with them under the pillow, and handle them and ponder upon the meaning of the pictures in the light of what the book of instructions has to say about them until the significance of each picture is realized. It does not matter greatly which pack is used.

She had died six months before I was born, but I had often dreamed of her and her circle.

My visitor in the twilight state invited me to go on an astral journey and instructed me to put on special vestments, black, white, and silver. She led me to an inner temple and showed me the gateway to the path of the High Priestess on the Qabalistic Tree of Life. This is the longest and most challenging of the tarot pathworkings, requiring the traveler to cross the Abyss. I was told that I must on no account veer, or even look, to the right or left, where there were all manner of threats, temptations, and distractions.

I embarked on the journey. At the place where the road crossed the path of the Strength card, I learned something new about the lion. I was required, at this point, to leave my second body — my astral body — behind, as I had left my physical body behind in the bed. This was the condition for crossing the Abyss and "shooting for Kether," the Crown.

I survived the whirling swords of attackers who may have been very fierce Gatekeepers. I came at last to a chamber with curving walls. The priestess reappeared, indicating that I had earned the right to knowledge of secret and essential things. She described the chamber as a "premonistory," a word unknown to me. Through an observation window, I looked out into an ocean in which people swam about in strange diving suits that resembled the skins of giant fish. Or perhaps they were fish people; some of the males were whiskered like catfish. It came to me that these might be the true people of Atlantis.

The priestess explained:

We came from the sea. The Source of Light determined to experiment with several species. Since most of the planet is covered with water, it was possible that the most propitious environment was the dominant one.

The early Masters came from the waters, in the literal as well as the cosmic sense. This is remembered in the Chaldean stories of Ea, known to the Greeks as Oannes, and in the myths of the Dogon and other African peoples. Our form was human only by adaptation: the equivalent, on the physical plane, of the contact pictures projected by archangels and ascended Masters to greet and educate humans who are journeying into the astral on the paths of initiation.

Hence the significance of the Hanged Man, in its reference to the element of Water, and of Nun and Tzaddi, associated with Death and the Star, in the Qabalistic tarot.

We remember the founding priesthood as Atlantean, in the exact sense of Plato's myth. It is recollected in a differing version in the Irish legends of Fomorians and invaders.

To this day, the sea is the guardian and repository of the deepest mysteries. It has absorbed and transformed the effluvium of human waste and veil; this is remembered in the story of the ten thousand sealed vessels Solomon had cast beneath the waves. Great entities live far beneath its depths, at levels no human has plumbed — or will ever plumb — in the corporeal body.

It is of the most urgent consequence that the sea should be appeased, its rulers propitiated. Never forget that the moon is ruler of the sea and its tides. The seas have been ravaged by mankind. The fish are dying. It is time for humans to give back, through sacrifice.

After recording the passage above, I picked up Dion Fortune's magical novel *The Sea Priestess* and soon found myself reading, for the first time, the chapter in which the narrator picks two cards from a gypsy's tarot deck: the High Priestess and the Hanged Man.

How to Escape a Fake Reality

We can hardly fail to notice, given the state of our world, that it is possible for a whole community to become ensnared in a fake reality, a constructed mind trap. Just as fertile minds from the world of visionary Islam have much to teach us about the imaginal realm, they inspire us to think about the conditions of artificial worlds of enchantment.

The maze constructed in the 2010 science fiction movie *Inception* to ensnare the mind of the target is far less sophisticated than ancient astral traps described, most memorably, in the vast Urdu fantasy cycle of Hoshruba.

In the form of the *dastangoi*, itinerant Urdu storytellers — eagerly sought from princely courts to humble markets — preserve an imaginal geography that includes constructed realities known as *tilisms*. The word *tilism*, related to the more familiar "talisman," describes a realm of enchantment created by sorcerers that becomes a prison for one who falls into it. Any world may prove to be a tilism, a mind trap constructed by jinns in defiance of the laws of God and of nature.

The vast tilism of Hoshruba, with its multiple layers of illusion and deception, is the realm of Afrasiyab, the Emperor of Enchantment. Its geography is more various and complex than that of the ordinary world. There are tilisms within tilisms, nested worlds created by magic and imagination. Humans live in such places but do not see where they are. It is much easier to fall into a tilism than to get out of one.

The only way to pierce the veils of illusion and overthrow a tilism is to find the tablet that holds its secrets, including the conditions for its destruction and the name of the person who will destroy it. The tablet could be concealed anywhere, often inside the tilism itself.

These traditions were largely unknown in the West until an Urdu scholar and novelist named Musharraf Ali Farooqi was stirred by a dream to embark on a fantastic enterprise. He dreamed he was visited by mythic creatures who came galloping right out of the great Urdu story cycle known as *The Adventures of Amir Hamza*. He made a tremendous contribution to world literature in giving us an elegant nine-hundred-page translation of this work, published by the Modern Library. But this was only the start of his labors. Farooqi has since produced the first volume of a translation of the oceanic *Tilism-e Hoshruba*.

To break out of a tilism — and to break others out — you must have been born to this task. Each tilism can be broken only by the person whose name is engraved as the Breaker of the Tilism on its guardian stone. These stones are like game boards in the great game of the multiverse. The game board holds the secrets of the tilism, including the conditions for its destruction and the name of the person who will destroy it.

My favorite bit involves a theme familiar from *The Arabian Nights*: we must tell stories in order to live, in order to stay human or recover our humanity.

The Emperor of Enchantment is about to look in the Book of Sameri, which contains the secrets of the past and the future. A queen who has already betrayed him to his greatest enemy cannot allow him to do this, because in the book he will read the details of her treachery. So she starts spinning a tale to divert him. The story she is telling is not just any story; it is *the* story, the one that contains them and their world. When he lets the queen become the storyteller of his own life, the Emperor of Enchantment forgets everything else — and fails to look in the book and detect her betrayal, until the breaker of his world arrives to fulfill his destiny.

We see again that to free our lives and our world we must find the right story and make sure that story is heard.

9

If You Can See Your Destination, You Are Halfway There

The secret law of manifestation has never been a secret to anyone who is fully alive and conscious. It can be summarized in three words: Desire. Believe. Feel.

1. **Desire:** Know what you truly, deeply want. Make sure your life vision is charged with desire. We get the word *desire* from the Latin *de sidere*, meaning "from the stars." Unless your vision is charged with desire, you have lost touch with your star and are bound to go astray. But if your desire is fully invested in your vision, then you cannot help stirring forces in the world to support you.

2. **Believe:** Know you have the power to fulfill your desires. Check in with your body. Call on the support of greater powers. Listen to your dreams and the many voices of the Speaking Land.

3. **Feel:** Sense yourself present, right now, in the place where you are enjoying the fulfillment of your desires. Taste it, touch it, feel it.

This is older than New Thought and very much older than the New Age. It is the secret of the ancient Polynesian art of navigation, called wayfinding or waymaking, the kind of navigation that can get you across thousands of miles of open sea in a voyaging canoe without maps or instruments. When you have a vision of your destination so strongly in your mind and your senses that you can taste it, touch it, smell it, you are better than halfway there. The voyage to the land of your heart's desires begins as soon as you are ready to turn in that direction.

Here is a beautiful example from the life of a creative dreamer.

When Books Made a Man

Singer-songwriter Kristin Sentman was in her late twenties, living in Prospect Park, Brooklyn, in an old Victorian brownstone. In the park across the street, she recalls, there was a music pagoda where she would go "to dance with ghosts and listen for the voice of my beloved who had yet to reveal himself in this life." One April, after heavy snow, she wandered through the drifts to the pagoda. As she sat there in stillness in the afternoon sun, she seemed to hear music from another world and felt the presence of her unseen lover. "I felt as though some meeting place had been assigned and that it was close to the time we had set to rendezvous and find each other again, but I didn't know where or when."

That night she snuggled down in bed with her books and journals. She had recently started writing songs. She had also developed literary passions that kept her up late — for Joseph Campbell and Carl Jung, for Greek mythology and quantum physics, for Buddhist and Native American traditions.

Immersed in her reading that night, she found herself too sleepy to move the books off the bed as sleep reached for her. Instead, she piled the books in a heap on one side of the bed. She was amazed to see that in the dark they made the shape of a man lying beside her. She rearranged the covers and snuggled closer, growing the illusion. She was gripped by a delicious fantasy. *What if I could make a man out of this pile of books?*

She grabbed pen and journal and recorded that question. Then her hand began to write a song that came streaming through her.

Once
A body of great works
Strewn upon my bed

You slept
Always beside me
Always ready to be read

Rise...
Hero, from the page
I'll make you from the Ancient, the wise
Rise and see
You're bound to love me

The verses flowed on and on, effortlessly and insistently, repetition giving the sense of a deep summoning. She poured love and longing and playfulness into this writing and pictured her pile of books rising to embrace her.

"Then," she recalls, "the deeper magic began to unfold in my life." Synchronicity got her on the road, moving from Prospect Park to Los Angeles without definite prospects but with a giddy sense of expanding possibility. She decided she needed to back her lovely voice with guitar. She dropped by a guitar store on Sunset Boulevard and told the clerk she wanted to take guitar lessons. Someone overheard her and gave her the number of their own guitar teacher, a guy with a PhD in jazz guitar. She went for a first lesson and felt deep joy and recognition. As she left his place on that first visit, she paused to look at his bookshelves. "He had every book I slept beside when I made the song to make them into a man." They came together, married, had beautiful children — and then Bryan helped Kristin birth her first record, as producer for her stunning album *River of Mist*, published under her married name, Kristin Sentman Clark. It is full of songs that call the soul. Truly, books can make a man.

Taking Young Composers to Their Premiere

Composer, music professor, and travel writer Gary White calls himself an "imaginaut" and defines the word like this: "An imaginaut is a person who frequently travels to the imaginal realms. This is not idle daydreaming. We imaginauts go there on business. We are business travelers."

He recalls composing music very young, spontaneously and without effort. Then, as an undergraduate at the University of Kansas, he read a small book on self-hypnosis and tried out the techniques. He would put himself into a self-induced trance for a few minutes and see whether fresh composition flowed. More often than not, it did. At this stage in his life he kept his method to himself.

Later, as a music professor, he developed techniques he could offer to his students that he hoped would not seem as far-out as self-hypnosis. "I would tell my students to imagine, as clearly as possible, the first performance of their work. The musicians would come onstage, and the audience would await the performance. The more vividly they could imagine this scene, the more successful they would be. The musicians would get ready and the performance would begin.

"I would emphasize that the students must listen carefully at this moment, because they would always hear music in their minds. They needed to get as much as possible of this music down on paper. For example, what was the tempo of the music? What melody, harmony, or rhythm did they hear? Typically, there was not much that could be captured at first, but I assured them that with practice they would get better at it. These fragments were the beginning of the composition they would create.

"Later they could determine if that was really where the piece should begin or if it needed an introduction. Was this the first movement of the piece or a later movement? These considerations could be thought through consciously, using what the student knew about the structure of music, and I could guide them through this process with discussion and suggestions. The visualization technique put the student into an altered state of consciousness, where the creative process could begin.

"The basic idea is the following: the original material comes from the realm beyond the conscious mind, and the student learns to draw on the imaginal realms as the source of ideas."

Gary was an inspiring and beloved teacher, and he has chalked up many, many frequent flyer miles as a business traveler to the imaginal world. He is also a certified teacher of Active Dreaming.

Counsel from a Medieval Mystic

"The outward work will never be puny if the inward work is great." The words are from Meister Eckhart, an extraordinary medieval mystic. Consider what he is saying. Work inside, work in your mind, work in your imagination, and then the world around you will shift and the effects on the outside world will become evident.

He also wrote this: "What we plant in the soil of contemplation we shall reap in the harvest of action." Once again, he is talking about the need to go deep within, to cultivate the imagination or what the medieval mind calls contemplation, in order to produce external effects.

Meister Eckhart also maintained that "there exists only the present instant, a now which always and without end is itself new. There is no yesterday nor any tomorrow but only now as it was a thousand years ago and as it will be a thousand years hence." It is amazing to hear this voice across the centuries, affirming what seems to me one of the most important insights into reality that we can achieve, the recognition that fundamentally the time is always now. When you grasp what that really means for you and your life, you have a freedom to imagine, to revision, and to change things beyond what the ordinary thoughts of the ordinary mind can possibly grasp.

Here is the counsel from Meister Eckhart that speaks most directly to the secret of manifestation we are exploring here: "When the soul wishes to experience something, she throws an image of the experience out before her and enters into her own image." We can reflect on this in many ways. We can think, for example, about how in dreams and dreamlike states we seem to visit the possible future and scout the ways ahead.

He invites us to think about more than seeing the future. He is nudging us to think about *choosing* our future by stepping into an energetic template we have already created. He suggests that energetically we travel ahead of ourselves. We don't do this simply as disembodied minds. Some part of ourselves that is not confined to the physical body — he calls it soul, and why not? — goes ahead of us. If we remember and apply what it has learned, then notice a possible future where things are working well, we can step into the place where we have already been.

Become a Waymaker

I was on Maui, driving by myself on the infamously dangerous road to Hana. It's a twisty road, much of it is one lane, and often you pass over narrow bridges where you can meet a truck coming at you down the middle of the road, fast. People wear T-shirts saying, "I survived the road to Hana."

I turned on the car radio to reduce the stress, and a story came on that seized my attention. While I was driving on that crazy road, they were talking about how you can navigate a wild ocean without maps or instruments. The story involved a group of sailors, boat builders, and visionaries who came together in the 1970s to build a replica of the big oceangoing canoes the ancient Polynesians used to cross the Pacific from Tahiti. This would be a catamaran with a nineteen-foot span that could carry a crew of ten. It would be constructed with the same primal materials used centuries ago, pandanus leaves for the sails, resin to caulk the boards.

The bold ambition of this team was to sail their canoe from Oahu back to Tahiti, where the first settlers of Hawaii came from. They wanted to replicate the achievement of the ancient sailors who crossed the Pacific without compass or charts, reading the wind and water and stars and doing whatever else they needed to do to survive the passage.

The narrator on the radio came to the crucial part of the story. The team went in search of a master navigator who still knows the old ways. Polynesians call this person a wayfinder or waymaker. They found the man they needed in Micronesia, on a small island. They brought him to Hawaii to train the crew of the boat. The navigator taught the crew to be at one with the water and the wind and to watch for the halo around the moon that tells you a storm is coming.

But there is a further level of knowing, and that is what the navigator reserved for his master class. I had to will myself to keep watching that twisty road to Hana as the radio show reached this part of the story.

As I recall the narrative, the wayfinder took the people who were going to sail to Tahiti up on a headland on the island of Oahu at night. He made them spin around with their eyes closed until they lost all sense of direction. Then he told them, "Turn in the direction of the island. Turn in the direction of your destination." When he was satisfied that the crew were more or less pointing their noses toward Tahiti, he said, "Now do this. Be there, go there. Be there with all of your senses. Be at the island that is your destination. Taste it, touch it, smell it, use all of your senses." This went on for a while. When he called them back, he said, "Now hold the island in your mind and in your senses so you do not become lost." I realized in that moment on the road to Hana that here is a remarkable key to manifesting what we most deeply desire.

That's how I first heard the story. I later did my research and talked to Hawaiian friends about it. I discovered that this tradition goes back thousands of years. It was by navigating in this way that Polynesians were able to go to Easter Island. They were in trouble at home, and some were desperate to locate a new place to live. A powerful dreamer, the royal tattooist, opened the sea road in a dream and got them there. They got to Hawaii in the same way and gave the islands a name derived from Hawaiki, the Polynesian name for paradise. Captain James Cook engaged a wayfinder to guide his voyages and relied on him when he sailed from Tahiti to New Zealand, a distance of more than 13,000 kilometers. Cook noted in his logbook that at every point during this immense journey the navigator never lost his sense of direction. He always knew exactly where to steer in order to reach their destination.

We have here an incredible key to finding and manifesting the life destinations we truly want. We are going to take elements from the master class in Polynesian navigation to find our way to the island where we can enjoy the fulfillment of our deepest desires. For the crew on the headland, the island destination was Tahiti. It could be Tahiti for you, too, if that's where your heart wants to take you. It's more likely to be an island in another sense, the I-land where you are going to find yourself living your life dreams.

Imaginal Adventure: Journey to the Island of Your Heart's Desires

Finding Your Place of Leaping

You are going to leap into this journey from a high place, like that headland on Oahu. I often start from the top of a special tree, a tree I know that also knows me, a tree I have used as a gateway for journeys in many directions. You may prefer to visualize a rooftop terrace or a mountaintop. You want a place in your inner landscape from which it is easy to imagine yourself seeing far across space, much further than you can see with ordinary eyes or the most powerful telescope. You not only see across space. From this vantage point, you can see across time. This voyage is going to take you to a possible and highly desirable future.

You need to set your intention. Your intention, I suggest, is to journey to a place in the possible future where you are enjoying the fulfillment of your deepest desires.

It is important that those desires come from deep in your being, not just from your head and your gut. Your body needs to believe you, and your higher self should be giving you the nod. The best way I know to make sure the winds of desire are blowing in the right direction is to open your heart center and let your heart be your pilot.

Take a moment. Place your hand on your physical heart and check how it is. This may be the moment to express some gratitude to this magnificent organ for getting you this far in life.

Now move your hand to the center of your chest. Find yourself coming into connection with your heart center. This is the place where you find courage. It is where you feel pain and joy most deeply. It is where you locate your personal truth. Sometimes we close off our heart center because we don't want to feel so deeply or be seen by others. We put a wall or a veil or a great stone in front of the heart. This is the time to open your heart and let it help to guide your way to the place of your deepest desires. Take your hand away from your heart and feel light from your heart — light of deep yearning — go before you, across the distance you will travel.

Instructions for the Voyage

You're going to go as far into the future as seems to be appropriate. You can choose how far out you want to go — one year, three years, five years, or further — but that is not required. You can simply tell yourself: *I am going to a place where I will find myself enjoying the fulfillment of my heart's desires.*

As the journey deepens for you, all your senses are going to come alive — taste, touch, smell, hearing, sight. Your vision might begin to rise through your sense of smell. The smell of saltwater, the smell of pine needles, of cedar, of a baby's breath or a lover's hair under sunlight. The vision might start to grow through the sound of music, or of waves, of a violin or a sigh.

The vision you grow may center on love. It may focus on partnership or family or community. It may center on creative work. It may focus on home or travel or peace or healing or all the above.

When a scene of fulfillment comes alive, you will enter it with all your senses. Don't waste a second telling yourself you can't have this, you're not young enough, you're not beautiful enough, you don't have the money, you don't have the health, or whatever. After the journey you can address possible problems, blocks, or challenges. Leave those issues aside for now. Ask that brilliant skeptic in your left brain to wait outside while you make this journey. Tell him, "We'll talk later." First the adventure, later the discussion.

Are you ready to embark? Make sure your intention is shining bright. You are going to grow a vision of a possible future in which you are enjoying the fulfillment of your heart's desires. If you find anything lacking in the scene, bring in what you need. You are going to enjoy the scene richly with all your senses. You are going to bring back specific sensory impressions you can embody in a physical object you will use as a talisman, something that will help you to hold and carry the power of your vision.

Get your body in a comfortable, relaxed position. Cover your eyes, if possible, with a bandanna or sleep shade. Follow the flow of your breath. As you inhale, breathe in a sense of adventure, expansion, bright possibility.

To power this voyage, you may want to use a recording of shamanic drumming or appropriate nature sounds. The sound of ocean waves may work particularly well.

Being There

A scene is coming alive around you, a scene in which you are enjoying the complete satisfaction of your heart's desires. Taste it, touch it, feel it. No judgment, no holding back.

Where are you? Who is with you? What do you most enjoy in this scene? Let your body show what it longs for — for health, for strength, for love, for a glass of champagne or a dance or an ice cream sundae. Indulge yourself richly.

You may want to let your vision expand, to show you a creative community, a loving family, a world at peace and in balance.

Is something missing? Bring it in, bring it *on*. Don't waste a second telling yourself why this is implausible or impossible. You are here to dream big.

As your vision grows stronger, breathe into the elements that most appeal to you, charging them with your energy and desire.

Holding the Vision

You are getting ready to return. But don't hurry back. You can linger for a while on your I-land, your place of bright vision. Is there more that you would like in the scene? Is someone or something still missing? Bring them in. Use the power of your imagination. Be shameless. Indulge yourself. You want that lover? Bring him or her in. You want that beach? Let's have it. You want that taste? Don't hold back. You want to enjoy the scene richly? Taste it, touch it, smell it. Let it come vividly alive.

Now, fully satisfied, you are returning to your physical body in the place where you parked it. Remember the secret of the Polynesian navigators: hold the vision in your mind and in your senses so you do not become lost.

Move your body. Stretch out, wiggle around. Relive sensations from your journey in your physical body. Notice the dominant taste of your vision, its smell, the soundtrack. Make a note of these things: the taste, the smell, the sound, the visuals, how it feels on your skin.

As you stay engaged with the play of your senses, search for a physical object you could use to hold and carry your vision. It might be a picture, one you choose or one you make. It could be a piece of music. It might be a fragrance or something you eat or drink. It might be a stone or a crystal or a piece of driftwood, a piece of jewelry or a scarf. You are looking for a talisman that will hold the energy and magic of your vision and help you to revive that. It may, of course, be a renewable talisman, like a mango or a Bellini. Ideally, you will find an object or an image you can carry and keep on your person as you seek to manifest your vision. Don't fret over this. Choose right now: an object, a taste, an image that you can appoint to be your vessel for manifestation, your focusing device, your welcoming beacon for forces that will come to assist you.

Facing the Three Big Steps

Now you are back in your regular space. Time to hear from the skeptic. You may need his help to identify the three major challenges or obstacles that lie between you and the manifestation of the life dream you have just grown. If you don't find any real challenges or obstacles, there is no need to invent them! We can simply think of steps you will need to take. Here is the question you now need to answer: What are the three big steps between you and the fulfillment of your vision? Write them down.

Picture yourself back on the high place from which you embarked on your journey to the land of your heart's desires. You are now going to scout forward on your possible life road and take a closer look at those steps or obstacles that came to mind. You might find a very realistic scenario playing out. Remember that you can play scriptwriter for this scenario. It might be that the steps or challenges that lie ahead come alive in a symbolic rather than literal manner. A huge boulder, a sealed door, a sheer cliff face might represent specific blocks or challenges on your way. *If you can picture your blocks, you can play with them or move beyond them.* Can that door be opened? Do you need to look for a different door? Can you climb that rock? Or do you need to go around?

More than likely, as you survey the life road before you, you will notice an important crossroads, a point at which you must make a vital decision. There may be many such crossroads in life. Often we speed through them without fully grasping the choices we just made. Choices lie ahead of you on your path of manifestation, and you want to recognize the nature of those choices. They might involve entering or leaving a partnership, or changing home or job or country, or taking a certain risk, or making a big shift in your personal habits and use of time and energy.

Maybe your three big steps involve new learning, acquiring new skills, making new connections, finding new ways to communicate, developing or deepening a daily practice, setting and fulfilling practical goals.

Look out from your high place. There in the distance, shining, is the I-land of your juicy life vision. Look more closely at the ways before you, at the choices and steps that might get you from where you are now to where your heart wants you to be.

Now look again at the three big steps before you. Are you inclined to define them differently? Has your list changed because you noticed things that weren't clear to you before? Revise your list if you need to.

Now come up with an action plan. Write down one specific, physical thing you can do and will do, as soon as possible, to move decisively in the direction of your heart's desires. Actually, you want to make three action plans, corresponding to those three big steps.

You can ask your dreams for guidance on a step that lies ahead of you. You can put your questions to the street, to the play of synchronicity in the world around you. You can call on your inner council. You can invite your magical child to help you practice the magic of making things up. In the place between sleep and awake, you can hold your vision in your mind and in your senses and let it grow stronger and richer, so rich and strong it wants to take root in your world.

Let's be real about all of this. There are going to be days when the gap between your vision and the disappointments and confusion of everyday life seems so enormous that you'll be inclined to give up hope.

But this is not about hope. It's about wayfinding and waymaking. It's about how to get across uncharted waters when you don't have a star to guide you or a compass. The teaching of those Polynesian master navigators is, once again: hold the vision in your mind, however dark the night, however rough the seas.

If you can dream it, you can do it. Take a break from the clutter and occasional despair. Clear your mind, open your heart. Let your heart's longing take you back inside the vision. Allow the vision to deepen and expand. If the scene involves your dream home, for example, explore the additions and renovations that may have been made since you last came here. Play with your ability to make further improvements.

Each time you revisit your vision, determine one more simple, specific action you will take to prove your resolve to move decisively toward manifestation.

Do this often enough, with feeling, engaging your inner senses — and taking physical actions to honor your vision — and the universe will start to believe you. People, resources, and opportunities may start to show up in your life in unexpected ways. Day by day, you bring your I-land closer to you.

10

You Can Grow a Dream
for Someone Who Needs a Dream

In Celtic tradition, you can sing the soul back home. Gwydyon, the shapeshifting shaman-poet of the Mabinogion, sings a lost soul down out of a tree by chanting a poem he composes in a complex form known as an *englyn*.

An oak grows between the lakes
Dark sky and glen
If I speak truly
This comes from Lleu's feathers

An oak grows upon a slope
The refuge of a passing prince
If I speak truly
Lleu will come to my hand

Guaraní shamans perform soul healing by giving you the right words. When a shaman is talking to you, they say, he or she is giving you soul. Their term *ayvu* means "word soul." This comes alive in you when your heart is touched, and the magic words enter you and change you.

We can learn to be soul singers and word doctors for each other. We can learn to grow a dream — a healing image, a soul story, a song that calls back soul — for someone who does not have a dream. In this chapter you will be invited to learn the arts of dream growing, story swapping, and poetic enchantment for the benefit of others. You'll learn my powerful and original vision transfer technique, which has brought fire and spirit to many. You'll rejoice when you see it working in the life of someone you've been concerned about through the brightness of returning soul shining in their eyes.

Word Doctors

When a stranger asks me what I do, as frequently has happened on plane trips, I often say, "I am a storyteller, and it is my pleasure to help others to find their bigger and braver stories, and live those stories, and embody them so well they want to take root in the world."

All my classes and trainings are courses in writing and naming, storytelling and communication, incitement to develop what in Celtic tradition is called the art of "goodly speech" — which is known to be the strongest weapon and the most powerful tool for healing, as well as for love and delight. The shamans who interest me are the ones who can heal the body and the experienced world by telling better stories about them. They call souls to where they belong with song and poetic enchantment.

In *Healing Fiction,* James Hillman explains how effective therapy is an exercise in storytelling. "Psychoanalysis is a work of imaginative tellings in the realm of poesis, which means simply 'making,' and which I take to mean the making of imagination into words," he writes. "Our work more specifically belongs to the rhetoric of poesis, by which I mean the persuasive power of imagining in words, an artfulness in in speaking and hearing, writing and reading."

True shamans have known this for millennia. Claude Lévi-Strauss wrote in "The Sorcerer and His Magic" that "the shaman provides a sick person with a language, by means of which unexpressed, and otherwise inexpressible, psychic states can be immediately expressed.

And it is the transition to this verbal expression — at the same time making it possible to undergo in an ordered and intelligible form a real experience that would otherwise be chaotic and inexpressible — which induces the release of the physiological process."

British anthropologist Graham Townsley has studied the word magic of Yaminahua shamans in Peruvian Amazonia. He reports that they use complex, opaque metaphorical language in their power songs, which are their most important tools for journeying and opening an interactive space with the spirits — and for bringing energy and healing through. This is called, literally, "twisting-twisting words." One shaman explains that with ordinary words, you'll "crash" in this deeper reality; "twisting words" let you circle around and see.

"When a shaman is talking to you, he or she is giving you soul," explains a Guaraní shaman. A word soul, or ayvu, brings harmony and healing. It is revealed in a sacred vision. Ava Tapa Miri, Little Seagull Man, dreamed that four deceased shamans came to him in a dream. They told him, "We have come from the Big God. We are here to carry you with us." They took him to a field full of birds beyond this world and taught him a sacred song. A very bright light appeared, and then came spirits with humanlike bodies he knew to be "the word souls of our culture." You cannot become a shaman without receiving a song in a sacred vision.

Doing It with a Song

Jung agreed to see a woman who had "incurable" insomnia that had resisted all previous treatment. In her presence, he found himself remembering a lullaby his mother had crooned to him in childhood. He started humming it aloud.

The song was about a girl on a little boat on a river full of gleaming fish. It evoked the rhythms of wind and water. Jung's patient was enchanted. From that night on, her insomnia was gone. Her regular doctor wanted to know Jung's secret.

"How was I to explain to him that I had simply listened to something within myself?" Jung reminisced, late in life, in the presence of his assistant Aniela Jaffé. "I had been quite at sea. How was I to tell him that I had sung her a lullaby with my mother's voice? Enchantment like that is the oldest form of medicine."

Ancient and indigenous peoples know that the right song is a way of transferring power and of raising and entertaining the spirits. In the Mohawk Indian language, the word for song, *ka'renna*, literally means, "I am putting forth my power." In the language of the Temiar Senoi of the Malaysian rain forest, a song of power, typically delivered by a dream, is a *norng*, which means a "roadway"; this may be a path for the soul between the worlds or a path for the traveler through the jungles of everyday life.

When Jung acted, spontaneously and intuitively, to bring healing with an old lullaby, he was following in the tradition of the spirit singers and word doctors all our ancestors knew and valued. We need to reclaim their way.

Dream Transfer

We can bring a dream — a healing image, a life vision, perhaps a pathway to the next world — to someone in need of a dream. Dreams give us fresh and powerful images for healing, and they open paths to sources of healing and guidance in a deeper reality. We can dream for others as well as ourselves and "transplant" healing and helpful images to them. Dream transfer or vision transfer (the terms are really interchangeable) is a powerful and innovative way of bringing a dream to someone in need of one (the depressed, the sick, the soul gone, the dying). This process has emerged from my teaching and practice over many years and is now a central element in my Active Dreaming workshops and advanced trainings in the areas of dream healing, soul recovery, and death and dying.

Once we have established sacred space and developed deep circle energy, we learn how to bring the gifts of dreaming to others. We find partners, sit quietly with them, and *dream for them*. We grow a dream for them with the help of gentle relaxation, meditation, and shamanic drumming.

The dream we receive for our partner may be one of our own life memories, the returning memory of a personal dream, an intuitive flash, or a series of images born fresh in our space. If the dream involves challenging or disturbing content, we always go through this and beyond it, opening paths to resolution and healing. We allow the dream to develop into a vivid scene and explore it with all our inner senses. Then we share the dream we have found and invite the other person to step inside it and explore its scenery. The dream beneficiary now tells the dream as his or her own dream and claims its landscapes and its energy.

This process has proven to be deeply healing and rewarding in many situations. It is easily learned and quickly brings our natural intuitive abilities richly alive. Dream transfer is especially powerful in helping the dying to move beyond fear and approach the last stages of life as an opportunity for personal growth and direct connection with sources of wisdom in a deeper reality. It is a method for helping those in our world who do not have a dream — a life dream or a dream of the night — to open their personal doorways to insight, healing, and a deeper life.

Getting Mom in the Pool

We can set the intention to dream for the benefit of another person. Since dreaming is transpersonal as well as personal, we may find that this facilitates healing inside the dream state itself, though we must not seek to intercede directly with another person without explicit permission. Better to put ourselves on one side and ask, as we might do in prayer, "I ask for healing for X." Or, to home in on the main theme of this chapter, "I ask for a dream to help X."

I was inspired to start practicing and teaching dream transfer as a formal technique after a friend asked if I could assist her mother. She told me her mother had been widowed two years earlier and was now in a dark and stuck place. She had never learned to drive or to balance a checkbook and now rarely left the house. She seemed to be scared of living and scared of dying.

"Why don't you ask for a dream for your mom?" I suggested.

My friend set the intention to dream for her mother. In the morning she called me with the dream she recalled. "I'm with Mom and we're shooting down the slide into a giant swimming pool. Mom's whooping it up, which is really strange because in regular life she's terrified of water and never learned to swim. But she splashes down, laughing. A barrier comes down so I can't follow, and a voice tells me, 'You may not enter at this time.' I manage to look over the barrier, and it gets weirder. Not only is Mom happy as an otter in the deep end, she's fooling around with a handsome young man in the pool."

We were both delighted by the dream. What better preparation for entering another life than a dream in which you are having fun entering a new element that used to scare you? It came to me in a flash: "We can make this Mom's dream."

I asked my friend whether she could call her mother, who lived a thousand miles away, and tell her the dream.

"I guess so," she responded. I suggested that she lay on the sensuous, sexy detail and see what happened.

My friend reported back that when she recounted the dream to her mother for the first time, there was silence on the other end of the line. Then Mom said, "Tell me again." After the second narration, Mom giggled and said, "Tell me about the guy in the pool."

This alone had started to lift the pall of gloom.

However, the effects of this simple dream transfer got better. A week later, my friend's mother called her to say, "I know who he is!"

"What are you talking about, Mom?"

"The guy in the pool!"

Mom proceeded to explain that at three in the morning she heard a knock on the door and opened it — despite her misgivings — to find a handsome stranger, a much younger man, on the porch. He swept her into his arms and kissed her passionately. Amazed, she looked at him more closely and recognized her deceased husband. "He looked about thirty years old, but honey, your father never looked as good as that!" Her husband told her, "I come from a country where it is always spring, and I'll take you there when the time is right."

After this, the mother lost her fear of living and of dying. She got out of the house and approached her own death, when it came two years later, with courage and grace.

This story lives with me as an example of how much may be accomplished with the simplest mode of dream transfer: to call up the right dream for another person and wrap it around them.

The Wind and the Book

Sometimes a very wonderful dream transfer is accomplished effortlessly. We find we have the right dream to give to another person, either the right dream *about* that person or a dream of power we can invite them to share.

When I was writing my book *Dreaming the Soul Back Home*, a European friend, visiting family in the United States, called me and asked how it was coming along. I replied that I had not done much focused writing of book drafts, but that I was relaxed because my whole life experience was feeding this book, and the deadline was still a few weeks away, which seemed like a very long way off to me. As a former journalist and student, I don't really believe in deadlines until they are so close I have to pull an all-nighter.

"I don't think you need to worry," my friend said. "I dreamed that you were in a magnificent grove of trees, holding a bunch of typed pages. You decided to take a nap.

"A magical wind whipped up, carried the pages out of your hands, and took them swirling round and round in the air. Finally the wind placed the pages on your belly. You woke up, examined the pages, and exclaimed with joy, 'That's it! My book is done!'"

I declared that I would make this dream my own and let it become my creative reality.

That is exactly what unfolded. When I sat down to work on my new book, the pages flew together. Some flew from my journals, some from my blog. Others seemed to come whirling down the chimney or through the skylight.

I felt that the wind from the dream was with me. I clasped the printouts of my book pages, said, "My book is done!," and hit the "send" button to get the digital version winging its way to my editor.

I decided that donated dream was a keeper. I would call on its magical wind whenever a new book deadline was looming.

Growing Your Bag of Stories

Nothing beats fresh creation, but if you are going to become a story healer you can also develop an inner library of tales that are worth telling twice.

In the Yoruba tradition, the high priest of Ifá divination, the babalawo, is supposed to carry thousands of stories in his head. When he throws a certain odu, or pattern, with his *opele* — a chain of bronze medallions — or with palm nuts, he will then dive into his mental calabash, sift through the stories relating to that cast, and deliver it to his client.

How is it possible to carry so many stories and then to intuit which one to bring forth? In the first place, all our ancestors prized the arts of memory and in particular the kind of bard or word doctor who could hold and transmit many, many stories. The stories might contain a whole cosmogony, the oral archives of a lineage of chiefs, the precedents for judicial action, spells of making and binding, the dicta of gods and spirits. The stories are easier to carry in cadenced form, with rhythm and rhyme and artful repetition. To know which story, or which version of it, to apply in divination would require long practice and perhaps a helpful spirit or orisha murmuring in the mind.

In our smartphone Instagram culture, we are unlikely to revive the ancient arts of memory and oral transmission. However, to become word doctors and dream growers for others, we do need to create and carry a story bag. As I write this, I see in my mind the Fool of tarot wandering with a bag hanging from a pole over his shoulder. Some of us feel that this is the central mystery of tarot: that all the major arcana, all the relevant patterns and archetypes of the world, are inside that humble sack.

Practice: Find a Dream of Power You Are Willing to Share

You have received abundant confirmation by now: there are dreams of power, dreams that make us fruitful. Sometimes we are inclined to hold these close, for fear of diluting that power or trivializing the dream by sharing it with someone who is not able to receive. However, you may find situations where the energy of a dream like this is so great that you can give it to others and receive gifts in return. I do this quite often with my own big dreams. Here's an example.

Your Next Big Step

The night before I got on Highway 1 in California after closing a weeklong workshop at the Esalen Institute, I dreamed that I was walking toward my rental car in the parking lot. I found a sheer cliff ahead of me and knew, in the dream, that I could not get around this or fly over it. These are options in some dreams, but I understood that the cliff represented a big next step in my life that I had to face on its own terms.

I am no rock climber, but I started looking for ways to scale the cliff. I found myself impeded by all the baggage I was carrying. I put down piece after piece, including my laptop, until I was holding just one piece of luggage, a white cardboard box. I had another go at climbing the cliff but found the assignment all but impossible, since it was nearly vertical and void of handholds or footholds. Suddenly, I received help. A lifeline was lowered to me by an unseen ally at the summit. The lifeline had an interesting design: it looked like an Iroquoian wampum belt, patterned with white and purple shell beads. I grabbed hold and was pulled up to the top instantly.

I was eager to see who had helped me. I was amazed to find my ally was a mountain lion. Communicating mind to mind, the lion instructed me to open the white box. I found it contained a beating heart. As the heartbeat sounded, I felt and saw positive waves of connection traveling to people and situations that lay along my road into the future, preparing me to be welcomed as I followed a path with heart.

I woke from this dream both elated and sobered, though that may sound wildly contradictory. Elated by the blessing of a spiritual ally opening the knowing of the heart. Sobered because I recognized I must now put down a lot of life baggage, including my tendency to spend too much time online, removing myself from the play of the natural world around me. The dream led me to make some very important life choices, including ending a certain relationship, and to dedicate myself more than ever to following the truth of the heart, beyond the head and the gut.

Over the years since this big dream, I have often used it as the substance for a vision transfer to help individuals and sometimes whole groups approach the next big step in their lives. I make the invitation like this: You are on your road into the possible future. You come to a near-vertical cliff, and you know there is no way to simply get around or get over this. You have come to your next big step, and you must find out what it involves.

You try to climb, but the cliff face is smooth, and besides, you now find yourself impeded by all kinds of luggage, including many things you did not know you were carrying. You drop your unneeded baggage, and you notice what it is, maybe that old attachment or self-limiting habit or attitude. You are left with just one small container.

You face the cliff again. You can find no way up. But now you discover you have a helper. A lifeline, maybe a rope ladder, is dropped to you by your unseen ally at the top. When you seize hold of it, you are immediately pulled up.

You are now going to meet your ally in your next life passage. It may be an animal. It may be an ancestor. It may be the face that your Greater Self has put on today.

You will now be asked to open the container you carried with you. When you do that, you are looking at an open heart.

As the heartbeat sounds out, you are able to see and reach out to people and situations at a distance across time and space, opening the ways for you to follow your path with heart into the future.

You are of course welcome to make this meditation your own, and to grow it, and to invite others to come inside and share its power.

Practice: Gift a Life Memory of a Moment of Power or Grace

Think back over your life and find a moment when you came into your power or freedom. Maybe it is a moment of grace when you felt the blessing of a greater power reaching into your life to help you through. Ask yourself whether you would be willing to make a gift of that memory to a person in need of a vision. To do that, you would need to ask them to take what they like and discard the rest, and then retell the story back to you their own way, making it their own.

I asked one group to reach back for life memories that could be gifted in this way, and we had lovely and sometimes astonishing responses. I found myself recalling a very cold morning when I was perhaps nine years old. My father had taken me to an Olympic-sized pool and told me, "Today you are going to swim a full mile. I know you can do it."

I was not enthusiastic. I had come out of hospital only a few days before and was so skinny my ribs stuck out. But I decided to give it a go and found that, when I got past the cramps that came after ten lengths, I could settle into an easy stroke — the Australian crawl, of course — and keep on and on. I decided to do five miles, not to please my father, not to show off, but to assure myself that my will was stronger than the many weaknesses of my body. By the time I finished the five miles, my legs were trailing, not kicking. I was neither fast nor graceful. But Aussies are generous people, and when I got out of the pool it seemed that everyone there joined in clapping their hands for the boy who had died and come back.

That was a moment I would love to bring to others, with the details changed to suit their lives and circumstances.

In that group exercise, Eva called up a very simple and powerful memory of a moment of grace that enabled her to overcome fear and fatigue. She was high up in the Andes, climbing endless steps and trekking along scary trails. Though fit and accustomed to hiking, she was having trouble breathing and felt her body was about to collapse. She begged the guide to let her walk back. He told her, "There is no way back."

Desperate, she prayed, "Mother Earth, please help me." And again, "Mother Earth, please help me."

As she struggled after the party, she felt energy rising up through

the soles of her feet, recharging her body. She reached the next ru-
ined temple along that trail laughing.

She offered us a version of her story we could make our own,
something like this: You are utterly exhausted. Your batteries are
drained. You can't go on. You are on the edge of despair. You can't go
back, and you can't go forward. You might even think it's time to check
out of your life. Then you feel your feet on the ground and the power
of the earth below you and around you. And you entrust yourself to
the Great Mother. "Mother Earth, please help me." And she does.

We were all thrilled to receive this gift and make it our own vision. You may want to make it your own too.

Practice: Gift a Power Animal

Vision transfer is especially easy when you have forged a close connection with a spirit animal and are willing to share some of that
energy. I think of a woman now who dreamed that she was with a
whole pride of lions. The pride seemed to be impossibly large. There
were hundreds of lion cubs in addition to the adults. The dreamer
wanted to know why she had so many lion cubs in her dreams. If
these were my dreams, I responded, they might be showing me that
I have plenty of lion energy to share. To awaken the lion energy in
another person is to give them the power of voice to speak their truth
and to be heard: when the lion speaks, everyone listens. And there is
the gift of courage, to become lionhearted.

In many indigenous traditions, you are thought to be less than
fully alive and ensouled if you lack a relationship with the animal
spirits. A shaman may try to assist you through a power animal retrieval. He or she will journey with the help of his or her own power
animals to find the right one for you, maybe one that has been avoiding you for most of your life because of your diet and lifestyle or
because you refused to brave up.

We can help each other restore our animal spirits by telling the
stories that bring them closer. After all, we humans are the animals

that tell stories about all the others. If I am seeking to bring in the Bear as a medicine animal or ally for another person, I will sing the Bear song with them, and I may offer one of the poems I have written to honor the Bear, like this:

> You are healing
> I have seen you open yourself
> as a medicine chest
> offering all you contain.
>
> You are protection
> I have seen you gather your kind
> to form an unbreakable circle
> of defense against the dark.
>
> Behind all your forms
> you are the mother.
> You made me find the right song
> to open a door in the roots
> of the life tree and receive your blessing
> in a world beneath the world.
>
> I bring others here to be nursed and healed
> in your generous lap
> and be joined to their dream souls
> their wonder children
> their powers of healing and creation
> that fled from them when they fled from you.

Practice: Ask for a Vision for Someone in Need of a Vision

If someone has asked you for help, or you have a particular beneficiary in mind, you may of course ask for a vision for that person. You can do this by dream incubation, like the woman who asked for a dream for her mother and received that wonderful scene of fun in the pool. You can do it in a relaxed state, like that of hypnagogia, which I find an ever-renewing field of fresh creation and inspiration. You may do it by calling on your spiritual allies and making a shamanic journey on behalf of a certain person. You can even make something up.

Here's an example of growing a healing image for someone in need of one in that fertile space between sleep and awake.

Healed under the Wings of the Blue Butterfly

A friend alerted me that she had been diagnosed with thyroid cancer and would like a healing image to supplement the medical treatments she had agreed to accept, something to make her an active player in her own healing. I lay down in a darkened room and asked for a healing story. A glowing blue light began to form, spreading out until it became the wings of a giant blue butterfly. What unfolded was so beautiful, it brought tears to my eyes.

I offered my friend this vision: "I see you lying on your back with your thyroid gland fluttering at your throat like a pink butterfly. Hovering over you is an immense benign figure. It looks like a giant blue Morpho butterfly, four times human size, with a lovely humanoid face and slender human body. It beams blue light down on you, around you, into you. You are bathed in lovely blue light.

"In the grace and beauty of this blue light, healing — whatever other modalities may be involved — comes easily and swiftly. Patterns of healing vibration join the motions of the great blue butterfly and the responses of the thyroid in a gentle energetic dance.

"I invite you to take any part of this vision that you like and make it your own."

She took all of it. I must add that the giant blue Morpho was no stranger. I had encountered it often in dreams and on paths and along the songlines of South American shamans, including the Makiritare of Venezuela. I knew it to be wholly good, a spiritual power of the highest quality.

Playing Death for the Golfer on the Plane

I had a date as Death in Cincinnati. I say "as," not "with," because I was going to lead my notorious workshop Making Death Your Ally, in which I play the Angel of Death while forcing participants through an interrogation on what they most regret doing or not doing in the life they are leaving. The purpose is to prepare them to leave the body with fewer regrets. As I boarded my plane, I was on the lookout, as usual, for how a chance encounter or other synchronicity might play to my theme.

An old boy was sitting in my aisle seat. When we compared boarding passes, he moved to the window seat. By now we had started a conversation. He had just turned ninety, he told me, and his name was Jack, which was my father's name. He seemed pleasant enough, but fairly soon he revealed himself to be one of those who, as the Irish say, puts the poor mouth on life. Never had any luck, never had any money, his women walked out on him, and more in the same vein.

I considered opening a book and pretending we had never met. However, I noticed that he was wearing a lot of golf club badges on his cap and his jacket. Golf was my father's passion, though never mine, and I saw a faint chance of rescuing the encounter.

"I see you like golf."

Jack gave me a big smile.

"Tell me about your greatest day on a golf course."

"I got a hole in one!" He became a poet as he described the sun burning the mist off the grass, the ball flying like a bird to land in the hole. Then his face fell. "I told you I never had any luck. No one saw me get my hole in one."

I might have given up at this point, but something kept me going. "Jeez. Is there anything you can do if you get a hole in one but don't have a witness?"

"Oh, yeah. You can send in a form, and they send in your name and spin it in a barrel down in the Carolinas. And if your name comes up, they fly you to Edinburgh to play golf at St. Andrews."

"Did you fill in the form?"

"Naw. Told you I never had any luck."

I was desperate now. If I was going to survive this flight, I had to shift the energy. A spirit of improv moved me to say to Jack, "I have a movie of your life playing in my head. Would you like to hear it?"

He was startled but said, "Sure."

"In your movie, Jack, you filled in that form, and they drew your name from that barrel down in the Carolinas. And now you're sitting in a silver jet in first class, sipping a single malt Scotch on your way to Edinburgh, and life is good."

Jack looked happy.

"And now you're out on the links at St. Andrews."

"How am I doing?"

"You get a birdie on the first hole and an eagle on the second."

I don't have much golf lingo and knew I would lose him the moment I used the wrong word. So I continued, "And a beautiful young woman is waiting for you at the third hole."

"What does she look like?"

I had Jack's fullest attention now. I did not know his taste in women, so I said, "She's slender…and curvy…"

"What color is her hair?"

"Reddish."

"Oh." His mouth turned down. "I never had any luck with red-heads."

Disaster. I sought to retrieve the situation. "Reddish highlights. Could be a trick of the morning light."

He stayed with me while I had them play a couple of holes

together, and of course he got a hole in one on that famous course in Scotland. Then I told Jack, "She takes you by the hand and leads you to a lovely old building."

He started breathing hard. The thought crossed my mind, *He could check out now. And that might not be so bad.*

"She brings you inside," I continued making up this script, "and sits you down at a table in the library of the University of Edinburgh."

Curiously, Jack did not seem disappointed.

"She places books in front of you."

"What subjects?"

"History, biology, philosophy," I extemporized.

"*How did you know?* Those are the subjects I wanted to study in college, but I never got there. I'm a high school dropout."

We stayed with the scene I had invented for quite a while. By the end of our conversation, Jack had told me he was going to deal with estate matters and write to the women who had left him to make all well. As the plane made its final descent, he asked me to describe again the scene in the university library.

We exchanged coordinates, and Jack wrote to me a week later to tell me this was the most important conversation of his life. "I am ready to live and to die."

Death was never mentioned on that plane, but it flew with us. In the thick of making a movie for Jack, I had no higher purpose than to get through that flight. Looking back, I saw that I had been inspired to perform an unpremeditated vision transfer. And that this stuff works.

Make It Up as You Go Along

Let's never underrate our power to make things up, the power of unfettered imagination. In my workshops, we often sing a song that nobody needs to memorize:

Make it up as you go along
Make it up as you go along
Make it up
Make it up
The way will show the way

As we repeat the verse, we fool around with it:

Fake it up
Shake it up
Bake it up

And we add to it:

The moon will light the way
The river is the way
The fox may know the way
The dream will show the way
The heart will find a way

Make it up!

11

You Don't Have to Drive Used Karma

On the drive into Cassadaga Spiritualist Camp in Florida, among porch rockers and hunchbacked palms and shingles for psychics and tarot readers, I saw a sign that announced a Used Karma Dealer. We could all do with one of those, and we don't need to look beyond our inner intuitive and imagineer. I am not saying that there is not a legitimate role for authentic mediums; there are many people living on the Other Side who are eager to communicate with the living, and too few among those living on the physical plane who are listening to their dreams or willing and able to engage in direct conversation. I moved beyond my personal resistance to channeled material to discover, in the Seth books, a wonderfully coherent and useful model of reality creation and the multidimensional self.

The heart of the matter is that you have the ability to release yourself from guilt and shame and regret incurred in this life, and from the burden of ancestral histories, and from the possible shadow of other lives in past, parallel, or future times that may be influencing your present story. This requires you to step out of your self-limiting stories into your big story, away from the beliefs and accommodations of the little self and toward the creative purposes of a Greater Self.

The kahunas of Hawaii teach that if we are going to manifest something worthy in this life, we must retrain the ordinary mind, the little self. This requires us to bring together the innate wisdom of the body with the purposes of a Greater Self, called aumakua or High Ancestral Soul. When the Greater Self gives its approval, energy, and perspective and the body consents, we can get the little mind working on the right lines.

This requires us, of course, to recognize that the time is always now, except when the time is *GO*.

Winged Soul in the Sky

In my dream, I have been a speaker at a conference attended by a group of dealers in art and antique jewelry. I was impressed by the beauty of jeweled belts that two of them have in their stock.

Now I am outside. The world around me is shimmering. I marvel as the landscape becomes a field of crimson, streaming like silk. High above, to the left, I see a golden winged figure. Is it a golden bee or a hummingbird?

"Ba." Clear as a bell, the one syllable is spoken in a beautiful feminine voice.

I remember Egypt and how the *ba* soul, seen as a human-headed bird, takes flight from the heart. The gods of Egypt, the *neteru*, have ba souls too. The sun god Ra, as I recall, has seven, and they take many forms. The *bennu* bird the Greeks called the phoenix is a ba of Ra.

I rise before the sun, thinking of the sun god, because of that vibrant field of red and that glorious golden winged soul.

I found this dream report dated March 31, 2012, when I opened an old journal at random while working on this chapter. It is one of hundreds of dreams of ancient Egypt and its mindset — *l'imaginaire égyptien* — that I have recorded from as far back as I can remember. In dreams, the ancestors are calling, calling. Ancestors of our bloodlines, and of the lands where we live or travel, and of traditions to which we are connected across space and time. Our dreams will show us where we need to clear ancestral karma and where we can claim an empowering connection with the wise ones. Go deep enough in dreaming, and you will understand that outside linear time — to which dreamers are not confined — all these connections are playing right now.

I am no longer surprised by the high proportion of people who find Egyptian connections when they open to dreams and learn more about their soul families, their counterparts, and possible reincarnational dramas in different times. Egypt did a lot of dreaming, and its soul craft fascinates every child who goes to the Egyptian room of a museum and sees the statues and paintings and mummy ware that reflect multiple aspects of soul and spirit and shadow operating in and out of the body in life and after physical death. Let's taste three Egyptian ways of releasing unwanted karma, from this life and any that weigh upon it.

Give It to Isis with Bread and Beer

If you are burdened with bad memories, from the night or the day, you take a thick hunk of bread, soak it in beer, and sprinkle it with herbs while praying to the goddess, as Great Mother, to lift the dark thoughts or dreams from your body and your mind. There are words of power — *heka* — suggested for that, as is always the case in Egypt. You tell your bad dream to Isis, addressed as the Mother. In the A. H. Gardiner translation, the goddess herself says to the sufferer: "Come out with what you have seen, in order that the afflictions you saw in your dreams may vanish." The ritual ends with a triumphal cry from the one who has performed the cleansing ceremony and is now ready to receive pleasant experiences: "Hail to thee, good dream that is seen by night or day!"

With the bread and beer, you are returning gifts of the goddess to the goddess. You mop your face with them, and then you get rid of what is left, ideally by breaking it up over a river and letting the water carry the mess, and what it has taken from you, away.

Rebirth with the Sacred Family

You have been stuck in a box. Oh, yes, you remember. You accepted a life situation that seemed comfortable or unavoidable at the time, and then it started to suffocate you. People who loved you helped you get out before you expired. But then events and your own tendency toward self-laceration tore you to pieces. Parts of your vital energy left you because of choices that you made and shame and pain that you suffered. You may have lost your center and your moorings altogether. The brightness went out of your world. Some mornings you could not drag yourself out of bed. Some days you wished yourself dead, and your wishes may even have been fulfilled when you went down into the underworld with no light to guide you, to lie broken and supine in a cold crypt.

But a saving power would not let you go. You feel it now, as the stirring of great shining wings. They are beating incessantly, fanning you with vital spirit. A gentle rain is falling around you, each drop shaped like an ankh, the symbol of life itself. You are drinking life itself. You may see above the beating wings the radiant face of Isis, with the crescent moon in her hair, the goddess come to play shaman in bringing together the pieces of your soul. You may understand that whatever her features, this saving power is no stranger but your own Greater Self. As she raises you from the cold, dead places, you feel a surge of new creative energy, of green fire rising in you. You are fertile, and you can procreate; you are father-mother, the potent and the receiving, at the same time. In the embrace of the Shining One, you can now give birth to the golden child, the next creative phase of your life.

Burn, Baby, Burn

In many of my gatherings we have a fire ritual for releasing baggage from this life and heavy attachments from other lives. The baggage may include dead people who may have been traveling with us in our energy fields and the ghosts of old relationships and former selves. To keep this really simple, in a form you can practice as a physical ritual by yourself or with a supportive partner in the safety of your own home, let me light the fire of releasing like this.

Practice: Fire Ritual of Releasing

Build a fire in a safe place. An outside fire pit is ideal, but an open hearth will also work. Anyone who is going to take part in the ritual should bring wood or kindling to help make the fire. At the start of the ceremony, you give thanks to the spirits of the fire and offer something to them (in North America we give tobacco).

Go deep within yourself, deep into the well of memory, and find what you most need to release from your life in order for you to be most alive and present now. Your dreams and journeys you have made in following this book will help you. You need your heart and gut to guide you. You may focus on a certain attitude or pattern of behavior, on your need to exorcise your ex, on casting off an addiction or a self-sabotaging belief.

Make a short list of the things you most need to release. In a large group, we limit this to three things. In a smaller group or in solitary practice, you may work with a longer list.

Make an image to burn that corresponds to each of the things you wish to release. The more imagination and craft you put into this, the greater the rewards. I think of women who made long paper chains to represent histories of bondage they were ready to let burn. I think of the people who brought snakeskins to demonstrate that they were ready to drop the old life as the serpent sheds its old skin. I think of the chain smoker who wrote a poem for his greatest love,

Lady Nicotina, on heavy art paper and then ate as much of it as he could before vomiting the mulch into the fire. I think of the lady who crafted a figure of her former partner, anatomically correct down to the last detail. (I wouldn't encourage others to go quite that far.)

Now you call in helping powers with the sacred songs and names that work for you. You thank the elemental spirits that will help you to release unwanted karma and baggage and convert it into neutral energy that will support the earth.

When you approach the fire, make a gesture or offering to acknowledge the helping spirits. You will announce each of the things you are releasing. If you are in the presence of others and some details are very personal, you can make a general statement, like "I release an old relationship."

After each statement, you place the corresponding paper or object into the fire. You make sure that the fire takes it. Each time you do this, blow into the flames. Spirit travels on the breath, and this may be the most important part of the ritual.

When you are done, you may picture yourself stepping through the fire and coming out different, cleansed, and shining, ready to receive an afflux of fresh spirit and vital energy in the space within you that you have opened.

This may not sound very Egyptian so far. Wait a moment. We can build this simple fire ritual into a plan for phoenix rebirthing. You can also approach the following exercise as an independent visualization, a potent act of imagination. I can assure you that it works.

Word Magic: Becoming the Phoenix

We are about to go full Egyptian by doing word magic. My friend Normandi Ellis dreams into the mind of ancient Egypt, and Egypt dreams through her. She has taken us deep into the codes of the *medju neter*, the words of the gods, and brought us inside the library of Seshat, goddess of scribes and writing. In her luminous early work, *Awakening Osiris*, she takes chapter 83 of the Papyrus of Ani, widely known as the Egyptian Book of the Dead, and gives us a passionate rendition in English of the spells for transfiguration that invite us to step into the fire, let our old life be turned to ashes, and rise again shining.

Normandi's poetry soars free from the text, evoking the Greek legend of the phoenix. The Egyptian name for the phoenix is *bennu*, and it is depicted as a great blue heron with the two mating plumes on its head. Normandi's version flies far from the literal translations of this chapter of the Book of the Dead. As she told me, "My work with the hieroglyphs stems from work with the sound, with the image, and with the symbolic or narrative content. So there can never be a literal translation. It becomes a poetic meditation." Normandi succeeds brilliantly in evoking the heart of this practice for transfiguration through fire. It is "a million million times" true, we are told, that the one who becomes the phoenix is strong and free in all worlds. Normandi has given me permission to quote the following excerpt from *Awakening Osiris*. Receive these words and let their magic work in your imagination:

> I flew straight out of heaven, a mad bird full of secrets....I am the seed of every god, beautiful as evening, hard as light. I am the last four days of yesterday, four screams from the edges of earth — beauty, terror, truth, madness — the phoenix on his pyre....
>
> I will live forever in the fire spun from my own wings. I'll suffer burns that burn to heal. I destroy and create myself like the sun that rises burning from the east and dies burning in the west. To know the fire, I become fire. I am power. I am light. I am forever. On earth and in heaven I am....
>
> Generation after generation, I create myself. It is never easy....I wage a battle against darkness, against my own ignorance, my resistance to change....I lose and find my

way over again....There is no end to becoming....I praise the moment I die in fire for the veils of illusion burn with me....I hold that fire as long as I can. My nose fills with the smell of seared flesh, the acrid smoke of death, so that years from now I might look on that scar and remember how it was to hold the light, how it was to die and come again radiant as light walking on sand.

I have entered fire. I have become invisible, yet I breathe in the flow of sun....I am the god of the world in everything, even in darkness. If you have not seen me there, you have not looked. I am the fire that burns you, that burns in you. To live is to die a thousand deaths, but there is only one fire.

Become the fire, rise as the phoenix, and leave your used karma behind in the ashes.

Encounters with a Greater Self

Ultimately we make peace between the many aspects of our selves by rising to a conscious connection with the Self on a higher level, a Self that is no stranger. There are many ways of perceiving and receiving the knowledge and power of a Greater Self. In practical terms, your most important life teacher may be the aspect of the Greater Self whose home base is the level of consciousness and reality immediately above the one where you spend most of your time.

This was the wisdom of the Neoplatonist philosopher Plotinus. He taught that every human soul is a spectrum of possible levels of consciousness. Each of us is a cosmos, and we choose the level on which we live. Whatever level we choose, our spiritual guardian or daimon is on the level just above. Live well and evolve, and you may rise to a higher level with a daimon on a higher level again.

"Our guardian is the power immediately superior to the one we exercise," he wrote, "for it presides over our life without itself being active.... Plato truly said that 'we choose our guardian'; for, by the kind of life that we prefer, we choose the guardian that presides over our life." Plotinus then explains that "our guardian helps us to fulfill the destiny we have chosen [before birth]." Reassuringly, "He does not permit us to descend very far below the condition we have chosen."

Then Plotinus hits us with one of the most rousing statements from the Platonic tradition: "The soul has the power to conform to her character the destiny allotted to her."

When I lay down for some horizontal meditation on the afternoon of October 14, 1993, I had mental contact with an intelligence that told me, "Dreams are the primary dimension of being." My inner voice added that the most important thing to teach people is, "Dreaming and waking are the same."

I felt within the larger presence — and its presence within me — throughout the day. I came to understand that it is with me, and has been with me, even in situations from which I have fancied that the higher self absents itself out of discretion or disgust.

Your life partner, the soul pal who will never leave you, is your higher self, the soul of your soul, on the level where you can engage with each other. To open fully to this engagement requires a surrender of ego agendas and what don Miguel Ruiz calls the Four Agreements, self-limiting beliefs and accommodations that bind the soul. It may take desperate circumstances to bring this about or a desperate state of mind. What follows the surrender is not a master-servant relationship but an active engagement, a blissful friendship in which you are never alone.

I like to call my slightly higher self, Plotinus's guardian, my Double on the Balcony. When I set out to meet him, I follow the road of dreams to a terrace above the world. Sometimes it is the rooftop of a tall building, twenty stories up or more. Often the terrace has the air of a civilized café, operating just for us. I find him seated at a table, perhaps with a glass of wine the color of moonlight. He is usually impeccably dressed in a perfectly tailored white suit or a dinner jacket. Occasionally I have the impression that he has a female companion; once she seemed to be an opera singer. But she is never part of our conversation.

He is impossibly beautiful. He looks like a man in the prime of life, maybe thirty years old, yet carrying the knowledge of millennia. He does not judge me. He is my witness. He knows all of my life. It is as open to him as the contents of a dollhouse when you remove the back and the roof. More than this, he remembers my other lives.

I should say, rather, *our* other lives. Something I have remembered, through our conversations, is that we have a twinning relationship across time. When I am in the body in a life on earth, he is up here, on his balcony above the world. He still enjoys pleasures and creature comforts, but he is not enmeshed in the confusion and clutter of the physical world. He can sample delights that we associate with a physical body without being confined to one. The babalawo in me, the African diviner he calls my witch doctor, says it has always been like this. While one of us is down in the marketplace of the world, the other observes as a "double in heaven."

I like that phrase, but his is a near heaven, rather than a remote one. He is a free self. He is not bound by the conditions of physical life. From his terrace, he can see the big picture. When I join him up there, I can see the crossroads and forking paths of my life from an aerial perspective.

He shows me some navigational challenges that lie ahead. There's a spaghetti junction with whirling strands of traffic going off in all directions like an exploding bowl of pasta. It's dizzying to look at. Inspecting this with his mildly humorous detachment, I see the scene lift to reveal a manageable locale, the Place de la Concorde in Paris. Now I can survey, one by one, the possible roads I can take from that place of decision. He reminds me that when life on the ground poses difficult choices — when I run into blockages or risk making a turn without reflecting on where that direction will take me — I should come up here, look at things from the higher perspective, and freeze the action while I observe myself traveling more than one of the possible roads in order to clarify and compare the probable outcomes.

From such encounters comes a daily practice, one I can share with others. I picture myself in the thick of a situation where I am facing a choice or conflict or dilemma. I see myself pausing from acting or worrying, placing myself in a quiet mental space, away from whatever is going on around me. I feel light coming down around me, until I am within a column or pillar of light. This brings the sense of blessing and protection. I sense benign energies and intelligence reaching down to me within the pillar of light. Then there is the sense of traction, of being carried up within the pillar. I could be carried up many levels, as if on an elevator. But it is sufficient, for everyday navigation, to go up just one level, to that terrace above the world.

Here I find again my Double on the Balcony. From his table, I can see a relief map of my current life and of other lives and situations that will concern me. When the traffic patterns are hard to read, I can have everything slow down or stop so I can study it at my leisure.

As we go through a process of spiritual evolution, we may grow to the point where we can fuse our current personality with that of a slightly higher self and progress to a relationship with a self on yet a higher level, and so on up the scale. Through successive transformations, we may reach a level where we are able to survey — on a continuing or even constant basis — our relations with many aspects of our multidimensional self, including personalities living in other places and times, without losing our ability to navigate in our present bodies.

You Stand at the Center of All Times

"You must read Jane Roberts!," the lively, voluble Latin woman shouted at me on my doorstep before she had even crossed the threshold, on August 5, 1988. I had met her in Brazil a couple of years before. We shared a taste for caipirinhas and spiritual adventures, and when she told me she was visiting a daughter who lived half an hour south of me, I naturally invited her to visit us at the farm.

I had heard of Jane Roberts and was aware that I was living in her neighborhood, since she came from Saratoga Springs and later lived in Elmira, New York, whose other familiar presences included my beloved Mark Twain. But I had never opened one of her books. I was wary of psychic mediums, maybe because one in the family had foreseen my death (accurately) when I was three years old. I was usually unimpressed by channeled material, which sometimes seemed to come through in overly pompous, foggy, or inelegant forms.

I could not resist the archetypal cameo of the messenger on the doorstep. I went to a bookshop and purchased everything by Jane Roberts that they had in stock. I started reading *Seth Speaks*, as my visitor suggested, and discovered a wonderfully clear model of our relations with other personalities and personality aspects within the multidimensional self.

Who is Seth? In describing himself, he prefers not to use the word "spirit." He jokes that he is a "ghost writer." He says, "I am an energy personality essence, no longer focused in physical matter....To write this book...I adopt from my own bank of past personalities those characteristics that seem most appropriate." He could communicate through Jane Roberts because she was a "window." Within her psyche is "what amounts to a transparent dimensional warp that serves almost like an open window through which other realities can be perceived."

Where is Seth based? Not in what we think of as the afterlife. "You must die many times before you enter into this particular plane of existence....In my work as a teacher I travel into many dimensions of existence, even as a traveling professor might give lectures in various states or countries.... When I enter your environment, I turn my consciousness in your direction. When I contact your reality... it is as if I were entering one of your dreams."

A multidimensional teacher is trained to monitor and engage with all "probable selves" of a subject in different times and dimensions. Seth adds, "When one has been born and died many times, expecting extinction with each death, and when this experience is followed by the realization that existence still continues, a sense of the divine comedy enters in."

As a former journalist, I am trained and disposed to check on the reliability of any source. But the true test for a source of this kind is the quality of the material that comes through. And the Seth material is extraordinary.

Seth affirms that we live in many times, and it is all happening now. We are connected to personalities living in the past and the future and in parallel realities. Their gifts and their dramas are relevant to us. And it is all happening now.

Reincarnation is for real but only one of many afterdeath options, and we mustn't get trapped in linear conceptions of karma and in past-life "passion plays," because any past or future is a probable reality that can be accessed and changed now.

As Seth points out, "Knowing your reincarnational background, but not knowing the true nature of your present self, is useless. You cannot justify or rationalize present circumstances by saying, 'This is because of something I did in a past life,' for within yourself now is the ability to change negative influences." Yes. And this can be applied to the lives we may lead within one single span of years. As a matter of fact, if we want to grasp the nature of reincarnation, we would do well to study how we can rebirth ourselves several times within our present lifetimes.

When you change your life utterly, you may find you have some karma to deal with, bequeathed by your former selves. You may be distracted by bleed-throughs from parallel versions of you who made different choices and are walking not far from you, on paths you abandoned.

Part of the secret logic of our lives is that we are all connected to counterpart personalities — Seth calls them "probable souls" — living in other times and other probable universes. Their gifts and challenges can become part of our current stories, not only through linear karma but through the interaction now across time and dimensions. The dramas of past, future, or parallel personalities can affect us now. We can help or hinder each other.

"You may draw upon knowledge that belongs to other independent selves." We can tune in to parallel selves by switching consciousness and above all by waking up to what is going on in our dreams. Great creativity is "multidimensional art," in which the creative mind is able to draw on the gifts and the energy of many selves. "Its origin is not from one reality, but from many, and it is tinged with the multiplicity of that origin." In ordinary life, we may be able to borrow physical strength and skills from other selves who developed differently from our present self by drawing on "latent layers" that are traveling close to us.

We are connected in a multidimensional drama, and this may generate events in the lives of both our parallel selves that will appear as chance to those who cannot find the transtemporal pattern. Such connections may be triggered by travel. You go to a new place, and you encounter the spirits of that land — including personalities that may be part of your own multidimensional story.

As I now understand these things, our family of counterpart souls is joined on a higher level by a sort of hub personality, an "oversoul," a higher self within a hierarchy of higher selves going up and up. The moves that you make can attract or repel other parts of your larger self.

Your power is now. You stand now at the center of all times and dimensions. Your challenge is to explore how much it is possible to influence for the good of all through the choices you now make.

Tracking Your Parallel Selves

Physics supports Seth and the evidence of the dreams in which we seem to be living continuous lives in other realities. It is an increasingly popular hypothesis that all of us are likely living, in this moment, in one of a possibly infinite number of parallel universes and that every move we make (or fail to make) causes our world to split, though we rarely, if ever, notice.

As a brilliant Princeton postgrad student, Hugh Everett dreamed up the many-worlds hypothesis. He aspired to reconcile quantum mechanics and classical physics. The basic question he posed was: If an atom can be two places at once, why can't we? In the quantum field, it seems that a particle can be any number of places at the same time — until the act of observation fixes one quantum event out of a multitude of probable events.

But our normal experience of physical reality, on the human or macro scale, is quite different. Hugh Everett's bold proposition was that quantum effects are at work in every part of the universe, on every scale, all the time. We don't notice this because our universe is constantly splitting. Any move we make and breath we take generates a new universe. In the moment we observe such things — in the quantum field or in a city street — we generate a parallel universe in which a parallel observer is either not looking or looking in a different way. "We live in an infinite number of continually interacting universes," Everett proposed. "All possible futures really happen."

While Everett's hypothesis was largely ignored in his own time, the many-worlds theory is approaching a consensus view among many leading-edge physicists today. We find confirmation for it in dreaming, when we wake up to the possibility that dreams in which we seem to be leading continuous lives in different realities may indeed be glimpses of parallel lives we are living in parallel worlds.

We can open doors between worlds without need of the subtle knife from Philip Pullman's novels. In one of my workshops, with the aid of shamanic drumming and focused intention, I helped a group to open a portal through which we could journey to explore the situation of parallel selves who made different life choices. I was able to observe parallel Roberts on five distinct event tracks. I returned from my journey feeling profoundly grateful that the choices I made have kept me off three of those roads in my present life. I recognized that I slip in and out of these lives, and many more, in dreams.

When we shared travel reports in that workshop, we found that nearly everyone had brought back important gifts. One of them was often a sense of closure, through the understanding that making a different life choice would not have resulted in a happier or more desirable outcome. Another gift was the understanding that we can reach out to our parallel selves and borrow their knowledge and their skill sets. Then there was the vivid awareness that we don't need to let ourselves be consumed by regrets over lives we might have lived when our parallel selves are leading all those lives, right now, on the countless roads of the multiverse.

Grateful for the Life She Has Now

A courageous dreamer in one of my classes chose to focus her journey on her regrets over people and possibilities that were no longer in her present life. As she told me, "I allowed myself to play out some of my lost dreams."

Her burning ambition at sixteen was to become a singer and actress on Broadway. A naysayer in her family wrecked any chance of her following that dream. When she journeyed to the self who had made it onstage, she saw an empty life, with a glamorous Manhattan apartment but a loveless, sterile marriage, no kids, and a stressful and exhausting schedule.

She looked in on another parallel self who had chosen to stay in a relationship that had broken up in her default reality. This alternate life story was also playing in New York City. She found that she and her partner had made plenty of money and were well respected in their careers but that the relationship was toxic behind closed doors, marred by mutual deceit and multiple infidelities.

Bravely, she chose to explore another alternate event track, in which the partner with whom she found deep love and fulfillment had not died three years before. She found herself with him and short of the heaven on earth she had wished for. They were troubled by losses and financial worries. He had insisted on moving to a mountain cabin, which made it impossible for her to continue the work she loved.

These glimpses of other possible lives brought pain but also closure and, beyond that, a deep sense of gratitude for the life she has now. She affirmed that this gave her confidence to rebirth her career, find joy and juice and abundance through new opportunities, and live the next chapter of life on her own terms.

Tea with the Writer Who Did Not Drop English

In midlife, Anna succeeded in publishing her first book. She wondered how her life would have unfolded had she started earlier. She decided to journey back to a moment of choice when her life diverged from that of a probable self who became a published author in her twenties.

She found that the critical moment came when she was in school in England, aged seventeen, and made a decision about her A levels.

"In this current life, I chose to do four A levels, including physics and English. My English teacher was so lovely and so encouraging. He loved my work and thought I had real talent as a writer. But there was a timetable clash between the physics and English lessons. I went to the headmaster and said, 'I can't do this anymore. There are too many timetable clashes. I am falling behind in both subjects. I want to drop one.'

"He told me I should drop English because it would be harder for me to get into university if I mixed arts and sciences. In this lifetime I took his advice, much to the sadness of my English teacher and of my own heart. I went on to do biochemistry at university.

"On this parallel event track I speak up for myself and insist that I love English and I will be able to do something good with it in my future. And he reluctantly agrees to let me drop physics instead.

"I track forward in this life and I get an A in my English exam. I go to the University of Bath and I do combined honors — biology and English. I love the city of Bath, and I stay there after university. I work for the city council. I work in a creative department for them. I still meet and house share with a good friend from my current life, and we go on many adventures together. I also write and write and write. I write fiction and poetry. I write about my adventures. I write about my spirituality. I become a published author at a much younger age.

"Strangely, there is not a massive difference in my personal life. I have a similar set of friends to this life. I meet the man who is my husband now, and we are married in both worlds. However, in the alternate life I don't move to London. We buy a house near Bath, and I just go to London to speak to my publisher. I do envy the creative success of that other Anna and the ease with which she can get her books published."

After this journey, Anna decided to do something very creative indeed. She would make another journey and see whether she could sit down with her other self — the one who did not drop English — and find ways in which they could join forces and help each other right now. She found the right place of rendezvous, a café in Bath. Over tea and scones, Anna floated her proposal. The other Anna, the successful author, told her, "I'd love to be part of your life. Your skills of journeying are amazing. I'd love to use some of your material in my writing, and I will help you with your writing contacts and help you to value all your creativity more."

Anna said, "That sounds like a fair exchange." In the scene, she experienced what felt like a fusion of energies. She imagines this flowering into new literary creation and publishing success in two possible futures. May it be so!

No Regrets

I dreamed once that I was with a former love with whom my relationship had turned sour, ending in pain. In the dream, we were friends again, relaxed but not romantic, talking about how both of us had actually gained from our separation, bitter though the circumstances were at the time. We had a drink or two, and then started belting out the famous song of Edith Piaf, the Little Sparrow: "Non, rien de rien / Non, je ne regrette rien." We were happy and laughing, and when I woke I was still laughing, with the sense that deep healing had been accomplished in the space of the dream. That sense stayed with me for years after.

Living and dying with as few regrets as possible seems like an excellent plan to me. It may require cleaning up, making amends for pain we caused others, forgiving or demanding justice for harm others have caused us, doing things that we regret having left undone, or finding courage that failed us before in order to make a decisive new leap in life. This is all part of ceasing to drive around in used karma.

Our road forward might involve finding our way back to a younger self and whispering in his or her mind, to offer course correction or encouragement or both. It might involve checking in on one or more of our parallel selves and following their paths into the possible future. In this way we may be able to release ourselves from regrets over a life we are not living now and even rise to the understanding that a path not taken in this world is a path that we did take in another of the many worlds, so that in a sense we can and do have it all.

As always, our dreams will show us how to approach these things if we catch them and learn that they are not merely texts for analysis but fields of action and interaction with other people in other realities.

As an imaginal workout, I want to invite you to go back in time to a moment when you made an important life choice.

Imaginal Exercise: Tracking Your Parallel Selves

Your starting point is a high place, a place of vision. As before, you could choose a high rooftop or a mountaintop. If you have succeeded in growing your Tree of Vision strong in your mind, as you were encouraged to do in chapter 2, this is a departure gate that will never fail you. Relax in a quiet, darkened space and picture yourself up in the high branches. You may find that you have bird allies up in the high branches that can lend you their keen sight and flying abilities.

If you look in one direction, you can see the road or river of your life running into your possible future. Turn the other way, and you can see the road or river of your life running from your past to where you are now. On either side, you may already have the sense of parallel life roads.

You are looking back over the course of your present life, searching for the moment when you made a critical choice and your world split. You chose to stay with that person or to leave them, to change or not change your job, your residence, your country. You may discover, with the perspective you can now attain, that the choice might have seemed a small thing at the time or that you may have rushed through a crossroads without noticing that you were making a choice.

Your assignment is to journey back to that moment of choice and track, initially as an observer, what happens to your parallel self who made a different choice and took the road not taken by you in your default reality. You will follow your double on that other life road all the way to your present time and, if you are willing, into the possible future.

Your impressions and feelings may be mixed. No doubt you will see things you regret missing in your present life — scuba diving in Fiji; that night of endless lovemaking in Split, Croatia; that book launch in Corte Madera, California. You may see things you are glad you did not go through in your present life — an illness, an infidelity, a disappointment, a betrayal.

At the end of the journey, you may simply have the satisfaction of knowing that, as in the Gwyneth Paltrow movie *Sliding Doors*, it's not necessary to give one life a higher rating than another. You may find you are very grateful for the life you are living now and don't need to waste any more time in regret over things you may be missing. You may notice that there are issues in a parallel life that shadow your present life, as if people in your default reality hold you accountable (for good or bad) for things you are doing in the other reality. You will surely recognize that you have been dreaming that other life and maybe many others.

You can now consider whether, like Anna, you might want to see if you can be more than an observer.

Here's a grand venture for an imagineer: Imagine you can sit down with a parallel self who has her own gifts and dramas and accomplishments and talk through what good you might be able to do for each other. Can you even imagine a future situation in which you might be able to join forces to bring something new and wonderful into your world?

If you are willing to try that, perhaps your imagination will let you see your road converging with those of more than one possible self. How about four? We might call them the Fabulous Four. Let's give them archetypal names derived from primary qualities of their differing lives. For a woman these might be Mother, Priestess, Artist, Queen (or CEO).

Back in your high tree or rooftop perch, you are looking now into the possible future. You see your present life road running before you into landscapes that may be indistinct or rather vivid since you did some waymaking. Four parallel roads are converging with yours. Four of your parallel selves whom we can now see as aspects of your multidimensional self are coming together.

When their energies converge, something extraordinary happens. There is an explosion of beautiful light. Something like a great flower forms ahead of you. It might be like a vast lotus of many petals and many colors.

In the heart of the lotus are four selves of you. They are distinct and different, but they're coming together with all their gifts.

You go ahead on the road of your life to the point where you can join forces with these fabulous four aspects of yourself. When they come together, they have a combined force and capacity for creative life that is far beyond what one person could do alone. In this moment you are joined by the radiance of a Greater Self, bringing shimmering possibilities for fresh manifestation.

12

The Stronger the Imagination,
the Less Imaginary the Results

Here's where this journey has brought you: to the place of creation. You know that the time is always now, except when it's GO. You can step outside linear time to heal your past and co-create your future in the shape of your heart's desires. You can stir the quantum soup of possibilities and select what will emerge into form and manifestation.

You are ready to test the truth of what Rabindranath Tagore, the poet of the land of the Bengal tiger, urged us to understand: "The stronger the imagination is, the less is it merely imaginary and the more is it in harmony with truth."

You are also prepared to draw confidence from this companion statement from Tagore's friend William Butler Yeats, poet and magus of the Celtic mist: "Everything we formulate in the imagination, if we formulate it strongly enough, realizes itself in the circumstances of our life, acting either through our own souls, or through the spirits of nature."

Let's have Emerson chime in: "Nothing great was ever achieved without enthusiasm. The way of life is wonderful: it is by abandonment. The great moments of history are the facilities of performance through the strength of ideas.... They ask the aid of wild passions... to ape in some manner these flames and generosities of the heart."

All of this becomes joyful when you find what you love and let the world support you. When you give your best to your calling, greater powers come to your aid.

Do Something before You're Ready

Napoleon said it, I read as a boy: "On s'engage et puis on voit." I have carried that counsel for most of my life. It escapes easy translation into English. "Engage and then you see" is the literal translation, but it might not capture many English speakers for whom getting engaged brings thoughts of buying a ring rather than of entering a field of action, although marriage is itself a field of action and marrying your chosen field, as we shall see, is central to the art of growing big dreams.

Napoleon was talking about that moment when battle lines are drawn up and the world is quivering with the prospect of action and the marshal waves his baton and the game is on. "On s'engage et puis on voit" does not imply an act of blind daring, of going in unprepared. Napoleon is not counseling us to go into the field of life without planning. He is reminding us that we can never prepare in advance for what awaits us and that until we get into the field, we may not understand what it contains.

I think of the Estonian saying, "The work will show you how to do it." I also think of the magic of beginning, of making a decisive start.

When we take on a creative project — and its associated element of risk — and step out of whatever box we have been in, we draw supporting powers, especially the power that the ancients called the genius or the daimon. Most people understand this intuitively, even though we may fumble for an agreed language to describe it.

When I am working on a new book or a new course, I think of Napoleon and remind myself that if you wait until you are fully prepared to do something, you may never get it done. Perfection is not available in our human condition. It's important to do things before we think we are ready.

Here is a case in point, mined from my own journals in the period when I was working on my book *The Secret History of Dreaming.*

I have spent the past few days reading and sketching my way into a chapter about Jung and Pauli. I have been prey to both the temptations and the performance anxiety associated with this theme.

One of the temptations is to wait until I have read or reread the 18 volumes of Jung's Collected Works (I own nine of these volumes, plus five volumes of selections from the others) and his memoirs and letters, and at least half a dozen of the biographies, and a dozen of the studies of his approach to synchronicity (all of which are also on my shelves or my desk).

There's also a strong temptation to wait until I have found someone to explain Pauli's Exclusion Principle, and Riemann Surfaces, and Violation of Parity and the Fine Structure Constant to me, and exactly where and why he differed with Einstein and (on another front) with Niels Bohr and the Copenhagen School, and the whole debate over symmetry — and until I have found someone else to disinter and translate Pauli's full correspondence with Aniela Jaffé and Marie-Louise von Franz. Oh yes, and of course to delay getting on with this chapter until I have hunted down the text of Schopenhauer's Essay on Spirit-Seeing, which turns out to have been a critical influence on Pauli's approach to dreams and reality and — after he pushed Jung to read or reread it — on Jung as well (but is almost completely unavailable in English today and which I have — so far — been unable to locate online).

At the very least, I realize, I want to go through the entire Jung-Pauli correspondence yet again (and the 400 Pauli dreams summarized and analyzed previously in Jung's

Psychology and Alchemy) page by page, checking every reference, grounding every allusion in the personal and general history of their lives and their time, making sure I have missed nothing and understood everything.

The performance anxiety centers on knowing that I understand Pauli's physics no better than Jung, and do not have the advantage of having Pauli around to give me personal tutorials. And on the fact that there are a thousand Jungians (maybe many more) around ready to howl at any misrepresentation of the master.

There is only one satisfactory response to such temptations and concerns.

The only recourse is to get on and write the chapter *now*, regardless.

Marry Your Field

"The poet marries the language, and out of this marriage the poem is born." This beautiful, passionate statement was made by W.H. Auden, and it takes us right inside the crucible in which all creative action is born. It's sexy, it's spiritual, it makes your heart beat faster, it puts a champagne fizz of excitement into the air. It suffuses everything around with incredible light, so you feel you are seeing the curve of a flower stem or the bubbles in a glass for the very first time.

Such depth, such passion, such *focused* rapture is not only the province of poets, though we may need poetic speech to suggest what and how it is. The essence of the creative act is to bring something new into the world. You may still not be sure about how exactly you can do that.

Let me offer some eminently practical guidance, based on what Auden said about the roots of creation. I said some of this in *Sidewalk Oracles*, but I need to say it here, even more strongly.

Start by marrying your field.

What is your field? It's not work in the ordinary sense, or what your diplomas say you are certified to do, or how you describe yourself in a job résumé — although it can encompass all those things. Your field is where you ache to be. Your field is what you will do, day or night, for the sheer joy of the doing, without counting the cost or the consequences. Your field is the territory within which you can do the work that your deeper life is calling you to do. Your field is not limitless. You can't bring anything into creative manifestation without accepting a certain form or channel, which requires you to set limits and boundaries. So your field is also the place within which the creative force that is in you will develop a form.

If you are going to bring something new into your world, find the field you will marry, as the poet marries language, as the artist marries color and texture, as the chef marries taste and aroma, as the swimmer marries the water.

Let's say you have a notion that your creative act may involve writing. Maybe you even think you have a book or a story or screenplay in you. For you, marrying the field will require you to marry words and be their constant lover. You'll engage in orgies of reading, have tantric sex with a first (or third) draft. You'll kiss your lover in the morning by writing before you venture into the world, and when you go out you'll gather bouquets for your sweetheart by collecting fresh material from the call of a bird, the rattle of a streetcar, the odd accent of that guy on the cell phone, that unexpected phrase in the subway car ad.

You'll work at all this, because marriages aren't always sweet. Some days you may hardly be on speaking terms. Some days you feel your partner hates you or is cheating on you with someone else, maybe the fellow who just got a piece in the *New Yorker* or is merely on the screen in a Facebook watch party or a Zoom poetry slam. But you carry on. You fetch the groceries or meet the delivery guy at the door. You tuck your partner up in bed at night and promise to dream together.

And out of this constancy, through tantrums and all, will come that blaze of creation when the sun shines at midnight, when time will stop or speed up for you as you will, when you are so deep in the zone that no move can be wrong. Depending on your choice of theme and direction, you may find you are joined by other creative intelligences reaching out to you from across time and dimensions in that blessed union that another poet, Yeats, defined as the "mingling of minds."

When the sun no longer shines at midnight, when you are back on clock time, you won't waste yourself regretting that today you're not in the zone. You are still married. You'll do the work that now belongs to the Work.

Entertain Your Genius

The Romans never described a person as a genius. They might say, "Marcus *has* a genius" — meaning a special relationship with a tutelary spirit. The word *genius* is related to the Latin *gignere*, which means "to engender" or "to beget." It implies reproductive energy, the power of inseminating new life. To choose and act creatively, we must be able to put our commonplace selves, with their reliance on structures and schedules, off to one side and make room for the source energy of the begetter.

We draw greater support the greater the challenges involved in our venture. Great spirits love great challenges. The genius lends its immense energy to our lives or withholds it, depending on whether we choose the big agenda or the little one. The daimon is bored by our everyday vacillations and compromises.

To follow the way of the imagineer, you need to trust your feelings as you walk the roads of this world, develop your personal science of shivers, and recognize that you know far more than you hold on the surface of consciousness. You want to take dreams more literally and the events of waking life more symbolically. You need to take care of your poetic health, reading what rhymes in a day or a season. You want to expect the unexpected, to make friends with surprises, and to never miss that special moment.

You have a poet hidden inside you who knows all about these things. In dreams, your poet makes worlds. Your poet is not hiding from you, but you may have been hiding from him or her. Let your inner poet walk with you in your world, and your world will change. You will smell colors. You will hear voices in stones. You will find a universe in a flower. You will meet a goddess at a traffic light.

Here is some of what I hear when I attend to my hidden poet.

Maxims of the Hidden Poet

Did you really say that your dreams have nothing to do with reality? Your real problems begin when your reality has nothing to do with dreams.

Dreaming, you can travel without leaving home.

You can meet your loved ones at any distance, including beyond the apparent barrier of death.

Dreaming, you are a time traveler. You visit past, future, and parallel times.

Your consciousness is never confined to your body and brain, except by your failures of courage and imagination.

Instead of trying to interpret dreams according to everyday assumptions, use dreams to interpret the confused messages of everyday life.

Coming events cast a shadow before them. You have felt this some mornings as you emerge from a dream you may or may not remember. The shadow of a mass event can fall like a mountain over many.

Most days the shadow is softer and more intimate. As you rub sleep from your eyes, the shadow that falls over you may be cast by your roving dream self, returning to your time with a sun at its back that has not yet risen in your world.

Dreams can be the revenge of the imagination. In ordinary life your imagination may be bound to old stories and crushed by your efforts to fulfill schedules and fit in with other people's expectations. You may have lost the power to visualize anything beyond the surface world and to find the extraordinary in the ordinary. You may have so lost contact with your great imagineer, your inner child, that you reject the magic of making things up.

Dreams can blow a hole in the hard carapace of your self-limiting assumptions through which the moreness of life comes shining through. That opening can be the portal to realms of true imagination where creators, shamans, and mystics have always wanted to go.

Everything is waiting for you to wake up. You thought you were dreaming in your sleep, but while your body slept your soul was awake. Right now, as you go about your day, your soul is dozing. Wake up and dream.

In the world you now inhabit, you need to chop wood, carry water, as dreamers do in their daily practice. Write in your journal every day. Wait like a trout fisherman in those waters between sleep and awake for the fish to arise. Light beacon fires by letting others know, at any distance, that you have dreams to share. Make a safe space to share your dreams with a friend or a circle. Help each other discern what your dreams reveal about the secret wishes of the soul, how they may show you ways to survive in the dark times and bring treasures back from darkness, and what action your dreams require of you. Let the beacon fires spread and lift up the dark.

You can heal your body and your life by dreaming a better story. Why not dream a better world? How about now?

Writing Practice: Define Your Personal Truth

Your personal truth is what you remember and act on. It is not something you can find through an internet search. In Greek, the word for truth is *aletheia*, which means "not succumbing to Lethe," the waters of forgetfulness.

In that cause, give yourself enough private time and space to respond to the following questions from deep inside, from your heart and your gut, not merely your head. Say them aloud, then repeat them silently until responses well up within you:

What do I love?

What makes me happy?

What does my heart long for?

What would I risk everything to defend?

If my life ended today, what would I most regret not having done?

Write down your responses. If you find you can't answer one of the questions, note that down. It will create a space in your mind and your life that will be filled when you have learned and grown more.

Writing Practice: State Your Life Intention

When you have answered the questions in the previous exercise, you are ready to respond to the query Mary Oliver expressed as follows: "Tell me, what is it you plan to do with your one wild and precious life?"

So much in life depends on intention. It's time to come up with a big one.

Quick — what is your life intention?

I heard these responses in one of my workshops:

I want to live every day as an adventure.

I want to love and be loved.

I want to be a healer.

I want to bring something new into the world.

I want to fulfill my sacred contract.

I want to find my soul mate.

I want to write children's books.

I want to live my bigger story.

Whatever words you choose, they should pass the tingle test: they should give you goosebumps.

However you state your life intention, the universe won't believe you until you come up with an action plan that supports it. Write down one simple physical action you can take right away. Then do it. Once again, your personal truth is what you remember and *act upon*.

Everyday Practice: Recruit Creative Friends

When you have defined your life purpose and an action plan that serves it, you have a story that can travel. You're ready to start recruiting creative friends. A creative friend is someone who recognizes your need to live your bigger story and is willing to support you as you change and grow. Sometimes those who are closest to us have a really hard time with this, because they want us to stay the same: the person they think they know.

We may need patience and cunning to bring along some old friends and loved ones who are scared of change. We may also want to recruit some new creative allies. In that cause, we need to be able to explain ourselves. The human is an animal that must define itself or be defined. So let's talk about self-definition.

Practice coming up with two simple statements that you can use to introduce yourself.

In the first statement, you'll say something about your regular life. For example, "I'm Jill, I'm a software designer, I live in Evanston, I'm a single mother, and I love to go dancing."

Second, make a statement that reflects your life intention and/or the action plan that flows from it. Make this statement in the present tense and let it be wholly affirmative. Say it so anyone hearing you might be inspired to help. "I'm writing children's stories, and I'm always looking for new ideas." Or "I'm redecorating a barn where I'm going to paint." Or "I'm trying to live my bigger story."

When you have your statements clear and crisp, try both of them out on new acquaintances. Try the second one out on friends who may not have caught up with where you have traveled in your life and what your current intentions are. You may be pleasantly surprised by how much helpful support you'll enlist when you present yourself and your life project this way. If your heart is in your words, you will send out powerful waves, and good things will return to you.

Intermezzo: A Walk around a Lake

"Perhaps the truth depends on a walk around a lake," wrote Wallace Stevens. When I need to get rid of the clutter of negative thoughts and everyday worries, there are few things better than a good, long walk around a lake in the woods near my home in upstate New York. As I get back in sync with the rhythms of the natural world, I both lose myself — that is to say, my little self — and return to my deeper self.

A walking meditation has several phases. I start by paying attention to my breathing. I try not to interfere with its flow, though the most immediate effect of this refocusing of awareness is to produce longer, more regular inhalations and exhalations. My breathing changes as I set off at a faster clip across open ground. After a time, I find I am following my breath without trying to regulate its autonomic flow. When I reach the awareness that my breath is breathing me, I have already released many of the burdens I brought with me.

Now I extend my awareness into my body's movements over the rough ground. The play of light across leaves and lake water is beguiling, but it is still outside of me. I am not yet at one with it. My efforts to find stillness in gentle motion are threatened by the return of troubles and calculations that were with me before I came here. They gesture and snicker, pressing for my attention.

My solution is to make a full confession. I tell the trees and the stones and the lake everything that ails me. I give up any grief or shame I may be carrying. I drop my negative mantras. I am performing what the First Peoples of this land call a Confession on the Road. I know I am heard by the Speaking Land.

I give thanks at the water's edge. I am humming, then toning, letting the vowel sounds soar to higher and higher pitch. A song bubbles up in me, and I smile when it bursts free. I sing aloud all the way to the beaver lodge at the eastern edge of the lake and for another mile more to the abandoned jetty on the far side. The effect of my off-key warbling is to open a space at the center of my consciousness. At its distant periphery, I can observe old images of fear and worry and confusion looming up, then falling away like blown leaves as I choose to deny them the energy of my attention and belief.

As my inner space continues to expand and deepen, I feel again, blessedly, in contact with that still, small voice you know you need never question.

I celebrate and join in the sparkling beauty of the natural world around me. I breathe with the swaying branches of the evergreens. I shrug off my clothes and splash and swim in the lake. I am at one with everything around me. I could stay here all day, but words come flocking, and I must go home and write.

If you can't get out to walk around a lake in your physical body, do it in your imagination. You may be lying down in horizontal meditation or walking a treadmill or swinging in a hammock in the backyard. Turn on all your inner senses. Be there. Hear the birdsong, smell the pine needles. Your body will believe you, and your heart will open.

Everyday Practice: Making It Firm

I am in favor of affirmations. At a certain period in my life, I did not think much of self-help gurus who were pushing them. I still have major reservations about affirmations that seem to be pitched from the head instead of the heart and either project ego-driven "gimme" agendas or, alternatively, are shackled by received notions of what is spiritually correct. But I am greatly in favor of starting the day with a statement to the universe that affirms the intention to live as fully and creatively as possible and to return thanks for the gifts of life, especially when life seems hard. To affirm is literally "to make firm," or strong. To make a conscious affirmation, on any given day, is to firm up our whole approach to life. Whether we know it or not, everything is listening in our conscious universe.

I like to come up with fresh affirmations as often as possible. As the Inuit say, we need fresh words to entertain the spirits. However, I also find it good to voice default affirmations on any day they feel right, including those days on which fresh words are lacking. Here's a simple affirmation that came to me long ago, when my dreams and visions drew me into the imaginal realm of the Onkwehonwe, or Iroquois, for whom returning thanks is part of what keeps the world turning:

> I return thanks for the gifts of this lifetime
> and for its challenges
> I seek to walk in balance between earth and sky
> Affirming

Creative Practice: Join an Active Dreaming Circle

One of the best ways to expand your network of creative friends is to join a circle of active dreamers. You will find practical guidance on how to form and maintain a dream-sharing circle in my book *Active Dreaming* and directions to dream teachers in many locations at my website (see Resources). For a taste of what becomes possible within an intentional family of active dreamers dedicated to supporting one another's soul odysseys, here is a glimpse of what happened in two hours on a weekday evening in a dream circle I have been privileged to lead for many years near my home.

To the Moon and Back and Other Things a Dream Group Can Do in Two Hours

There were ten of us that evening. In the space of two hours we made time for everyone to share a dream or life story and be guided by a different person through the Lightning Dreamwork process. This encourages us to give and receive helpful feedback in the "If it were my dream" mode and to come up with action plans to embody energy and insight from the dream worlds in regular life.

"They tell me the gate has closed, but I push through and get on the plane. And find I am in Africa, driving a Jeep with a friendly lion on the hood and who knows where we are going."

This report got us off to a lively start. Another dream carried us into the rain forest. A couple of dreams — of going back to the childhood home or elementary school — carried not only nostalgia but the sense that a much younger self had gifts to bring into adult life, gifts of energy and joy and imagination.

A doctor's dream suggested an Rx for illness. A wildly funny dream of wearing lingerie to a gym and being celebrated by everyone around helped a man to recognize it was now safe to open up to his feminine side and show it to others.

The action required by some dreams is to reenter the dream, do more inside that space, and return with gifts. In this gathering, we were able to make a group shamanic journey through the portal of a dream with the irresistible title "To the Moon." In her dream, a woman found herself among lively children in a writing workshop being held on the far side of a fast-flowing river "at the bottom of the moon." The kids were assigned roles and started improvising stories by acting them out. All of us were eager to join that writing group, and the dreamer gave us permission to travel with her with the aid of shamanic drumming.

We did not know what "the bottom of the moon" meant, but we all found our way and had adventures in a marvelous creative space. I flew through a great round moon face like the entrance of Luna Park, a theme park I visited in my Australian boyhood. I rode with kids in a flotilla of boats on an underground river. Kids led the way to the other side of the water as the boats became dormant crocodiles that let us use their backs as a bridge. Enormous theatrical curtains, opening just a crack, promised new entertainments. Characters from children's books fluttered around us. I heard the buzzing propeller of Karlsson on the Roof, Astrid Lindgren's delightful character.

Then I stepped through the curtains, and the children started playing the roles promised in the original dream, acting out fresh stories. Right after the drumming sounded the recall, I urged everyone to write a couple of lines from their writing class on the moon. It was delightful to hear them all read aloud. I wrote in the voice of a girl complaining about a wild boy who was showing off the lunar horns he had sprouted: "'He's doing it again,' said Emma. 'He's putting up horns, and he doesn't know what to do with them.'"

If it is not possible for you to convene a physical dream circle, you can create one online using a platform like Zoom or Skype.

Jump Time

In her deliciously good book *Big Magic,* Elizabeth Gilbert insists that ideas are out there looking for the right people to carry and create with them. This matches the ancient wisdom of Aboriginal Australians, who say that the big stories are hunting the right people to tell them. Gilbert describes how, when she put aside the idea for a Brazilian "jungle book," it jumped, with specific characters and plot themes, to another wonderful writer, the novelist Ann Patchett, who brought it through as her novel *State of Wonder.*

Then there is her story of the poet Ruth Stone, who wrote:

Poems came to me
As if from far away.
I would feel them coming,
I would rush into the house,
Looking for paper and pencil.
It had to be quick,
For they passed through me
And were gone forever.

Thanks to Elizabeth Gilbert, Stone's mode of chasing poems like runaway horses is now famous. It's well worth seeking out more of her poems and noticing, along the way, how she rose above a dark river of grief and pain, especially after her second husband (also a poet) hanged himself from a door in the family home.

I love the description of how Ruth Stone struggles to catch poems. When a poem gets away from her, she feels it galloping away, "searching for another poet." Sometimes she manages to grab an escaping poem by the tail and tries to haul it back. "In these instances, the poem would appear on the page from the last word to the first — backward, but otherwise intact."

Many of us dreamers know exactly how that works, as we pull back dreams by the tail when they run away. How many of the dreams that escape — dreams of the night and dreams of life — go looking for another dreamer? When inspiration comes in one form or another, it is jump time.

Creation time is jump time in a further sense. It will take us from our comfort zone, from the gated communities of the mind, to what J. R. R. Tolkien called the Perilous Realm, where the wild things are.

You need courage to bring something new into your world. Courage is not the absence of fear. If you are fearless, you may be drugged or brainwashed or psychotic. Courage is fear conquered by something stronger than fear. This may be love, or loyalty, or the big story that has finally grabbed you, or the creative energy that bursts forth when you open the sacred spring of your imagination. "Creation comes from an overflow," Anaïs Nin told a seventeen-year-old aspiring author.

> So you have to learn to intake, to imbibe, to nourish yourself and not be afraid of fullness. The fullness is like a tidal wave which then carries you, sweeps you into experience and into writing. Permit yourself to flow and overflow, allow for the rise in temperature, all the expansions and intensifications. Something is always born of excess: great art was born of great terrors, great loneliness, great inhibitions, instabilities, and it always balances them.

Go deep into yourself and ask: "What is something new that I want to bring into the world?"

When you have the answer to that, ask: "What definite action will I take to bring that new thing into the world?"

Now let your creative imagination take you deep inside the following scene: Your whole life has been preparing you to take a creative leap, bigger than any you have made before. You are at the edge of an abyss. You can't bear to look down. The drop is immense; you can't see how far it goes down, through the swirling mists.

It's your time to jump, but you're paralyzed with fear. You shrink back from the edge, grasping after something solid and familiar. But there's nothing worth holding on to. Everything smells stale behind you and crumbles away under your clutching hands.

So you jump...

And you find that the abyss is no more and no less terrifying than the drop from the nest of a baby bird before its first flight.

And you'll work. You'll work as you have never worked before. But this work is not the drudgery of offices and routines. This is *the* work — "the hardest among those not impossible" (as Yeats said) — that your creative spirit demands of you and your growing soul requires. If you give yourself to this work, you will not only find that it is the very best kind of play, you will know rapture. Truly.

When We Become a Dreaming Society

I have a dream: that we will again become a society of dreamers. In a dreaming culture, dreams are valued and celebrated. The first business of the day, for most people, is to share dreams and seek to harvest their guidance. The community joins in manifesting the energy and insight of dreams in waking life. In a dreaming culture, nobody says, "It's only a dream" or "In your dreams, mister." It is understood that dreams are both wishes ("I have a dream") and experiences of the soul.

If dreams are honored throughout our society, our world will be different, magical. Let me count the ways.

We will deepen our relationships. Personal relations will be richer, more intimate, and more creative. There will be less room for pretense and denial. Sharing dreams, we overcome the taboos that prevent us from expressing our real needs and feelings and open ourselves to those of others.

We will enrich family life and home entertainment. "What did you dream?" is the first question asked around the table in a family of dreamers. In our dreaming culture, families everywhere will share dreams and harvest their gifts of story, mutual understanding, and healing. Parents will listen to their children's dreams and help them to confront and overcome nightmare terrors. Best of all, they will learn from their children, because kids are wonderful dreamers. This might be bad for TV ratings, but it will bring back the precious art of storytelling, helping us learn to tell our own story (a gift with almost limitless applications) and to recognize the larger story of our lives.

We will use dreams for diagnosis and healing. In our dreaming culture, dream groups will be a vital part of every clinic, hospital, and treatment center, and doctors will begin their patient interviews by asking about dreams as well as physical symptoms. Health costs will plummet, because when we listen to our dreams, we receive keys to self-healing. Dreams often alert us to possible health problems long before physical symptoms develop; by heeding those messages, we can sometimes avoid manifesting those symptoms. Dreams give us an impeccable nightly readout on our physical, emotional, and spiritual health.

Dreams will help us care for souls. As a dreaming culture, we will remember that the causes of disease are spiritual as well as physical. We will use dreams to facilitate soul recovery. In dreams where we encounter a younger version of ourselves or are drawn back to a scene from childhood, we are brought to recognize a deeper kind of energy loss, which shamans call soul loss. Through trauma or abuse, through addiction or great sadness, we can lose a part of our vital soul energy. So long as it is missing, we are not whole, and the gap may be filled by sickness or substance abuse. Dreams show us what has become of our lost children and when it is timely to call them home.

We will practice dream incubation. In a dreaming culture, we will remember to "sleep on it," asking dreams for creative guidance on school assignments, work projects, relationships, and whatever challenges are looming in waking life. When we seek dream guidance, we must be ready for answers that go beyond our questions, because the dream source is infinitely deeper and wiser than what Yeats called the "daily trivial mind."

We will take advantage of dream radar. Dreaming, we routinely fold time and space and scout far into the future. As a dreaming culture, we will work with dream precognition on a daily basis and develop strategies to revise the possible futures foreseen in dreams for the benefit of ourselves and others.

Our dream sharing will build communities. When we share dreams with others, we recognize something of ourselves in their experiences. This helps us to move beyond prejudice and build heart-centered communities.

Dreams will help us hone the art of dying. The path of the soul after death, say the Lakota, is the same as the path of the soul in dreams — except that after physical death, we won't come back to the same body. Dreamwork is a vital tool in helping the dying to prepare for the conditions of the afterlife.

Dreaming will enable us to walk the path of soul. The greatest gift of dreaming is that it facilitates an encounter between the little self and the Greater Self. Active Dreaming is a vital form of soul remembering, of reclaiming knowledge that belonged to us, on the levels of soul and spirit, before we entered this life experience. So much of the harm we do to ourselves and others stems from the fact that we have forgotten who we are and what we are meant to become. In dreaming, we remember, and we encounter authentic spiritual guides who will help us on our paths.

On Cutting the Mustard

In her essay "On Power and Time," Mary Oliver writes about a Greater Self — she calls it a third self that is "out of love with the ordinary; it is out of love with time. It has a hunger for eternity." It seems very close to the creative spirit Yeats called the daimon, who loves us best when we choose to attempt "the hardest thing among those not impossible."

Oliver presents herself writing at 6 AM, leaving it vague whether she has been up all night, since after all she is describing a presence that does not care about the time. "I am absentminded, reckless, heedless of social obligations, etc. It is as it must be. The tire goes flat, the tooth falls out, there will be a hundred meals without mustard. The poem gets written. I have wrestled with the angel and I am stained with light and I have no shame. Neither do I have guilt. My responsibility is not to the ordinary, or the timely. It does not include mustard, or teeth."

I rejoice in this passage in no small part because I am a devotee of mustard, as I think Oliver must also have been. One time, teaching in Samogitia, or western Lithuania, I made my hosts drive me thirty kilometers through a crazy thunderstorm to the nearest market that sold Dijon mustard. The point is that if you are a mustard lover and are willing to sacrifice it to stay in flow when the muse is with you, then you have earned her favor.

Breathing fire, Oliver says, "There is no other way work of artistic worth can be done." And then she goes straight for the solar plexus. "The most regretful people on earth are those who felt the call to creative work, who felt their own creative power restive and uprising, and gave to it neither power nor time."

Growing Big Dreams in the Time of the Pandemic

One of the effects of the novel coronavirus pandemic, notable even in the first few weeks after it reached Europe and the United States, was an explosion of public interest in dreams. People who never gave much thought to dreams and were rarely known to talk about them were suddenly dreaming up a storm and wanting to share their dreams with anyone who would listen.

The dreams reported covered a wide spectrum. While some seemed to dramatize fear and anxiety, others offered entertainment, sanctuary, and destination travel. While many reported having "bad dreams" and nightmares, others were grateful for dreams of reassurance in which they found themselves in the presence of departed loved ones and mentors, angels and goddesses, talking animals and benign space aliens.

I lead an international community of active dreamers; some three hundred teachers of Active Dreaming who have graduated from my trainings lead circles and workshops of their own in more than two dozen countries. I am routinely presented with hundreds of dream reports every week, via email, social media, and dedicated online platforms, as well as from current members of my online courses. With the growth of the pandemic, I was struck by how many people were now dreaming of the departed and returning to waking life feeling blessed and comforted, with the confidence that life goes on in whatever world. I myself dreamed of people on the Other Side who were engaged in preparing pleasant lodgings or whole family compounds for loved ones who might be joining them soon, and I heard many similar reports from other dreamers. In the time of the pandemic, as the dreams came back to us, we were reminded that among all its other gifts, dreaming may be the best preparation for dying — because we become familiar with other worlds, including those where the dead are alive, and learn through firsthand experience that consciousness is not confined to the body and therefore survives death.

Remember that Turkish proverb, "One calamity is better than a thousand counsels"? It may be hard to swallow in the face of a global calamity as vast as the pandemic, yet that bit of wisdom may still nudge us to look for possible gifts in the wounding. By being put on pause, locked out of external routines, many of us went within and found ourselves on roads to deeper self-knowledge as well as greater empathy for others. We came to admire as heroes people who may previously have been faceless to us: the delivery guy, the person at the checkout, the janitor, and of course medical staff and first responders everywhere.

We were driven to ask, as humans have asked in the face of other plagues and killer viruses: Did this happen because we fell out of balance with the forces of earth and heaven? Around 1700 BCE, confronting a plague that ravaged his people for a whole generation, the Hittite king Muršili II asked for his god to reveal to him in a dream why the gods were angry and what could be done to appease them. He made this a group effort by commanding all the priests in his capital to pray to see the god in their dreams the same night.

Today, dreamers may not be inclined to seek a face-to-face encounter with an Anatolian storm god. However, many of us have been communing with the powers of nature, with the ancestors, and with our dream allies to try to understand our best way forward, as individuals, as families, and as a species that has been deeply out of balance with other sentient life on the planet.

Science fiction writer Kim Stanley Robinson observed in the *New Yorker*, "The virus is rewriting our imaginations. What felt impossible has become thinkable. We're getting a different sense of our place in history. We know we're entering a new world, a new era. We seem to be learning our way into a new structure of feeling."

Remember Viktor Frankl in Auschwitz, using his imagination to survive one of the darkest nightmares of humanity and finding that what he grew in his imagination manifested in the world? The story is for our times. It reminds us that when we feel most vulnerable and helpless and alone, we can still choose our attitude — and if we choose wisely, we can change our world.

This book was completed before the pandemic fell upon us, and I have made few edits since. You may not see the long shadow of the coming pandemic in the dreams collected in the section titled "Dreaming as Epiphany" in chapter 1, although in hindsight it is clear that in other dreams from that period many of us were being given previews of what was coming. I have left that section, with all its sense of burgeoning possibility, in its original form because I trust that its promise will be realized and that what does not flower in one season will come through in another.

In the time of the pandemic, dreamers found relief and comfort in the fact that they could travel without leaving home. Dreaming, we can be as social as we like. Dreaming — especially in the liminal space between sleep and awake — we have access to inner and transpersonal guides who can counsel us. Because dreams are personal myths and myths are collective dreams, as dreamers we put ourselves on a mythic edge where our big story can find us, giving us courage and the blessed wind of inspiration.

As I write these final lines, I am receiving many reports of encounters with the deceased in dreams and half-dream states. The dead appear as they are — that is to say, alive in another reality. A woman named Ava dreamed that her departed mother started up a conversation by saying, with a chuckle, "Remember when we both thought I was dead?" Often the deceased have adjusted their appearance to look much younger and healthier than when last seen by their survivors. Sometimes they come visiting; sometimes the dreamer finds herself traveling to their realms.

Many recent dream reports provide a glimpse of the living arrangements the departed have created for themselves on the Other Side. In some of these dreams, the departed seem to be engaged in arranging comfortable living quarters for friends or family members who will be joining them. One dreamer's deceased mother gave her a tour of a palatial residence she has constructed for herself. Another dreamer was delighted to find she has a place in a community of scholars — with gourmet tastes and a fine sense of humor — who have been growing a delightful village over many years of linear time. In a dream of my own in the first spring of the pandemic, I observed a departed friend renovating cottages and apartments on a country estate that is not on any map of this world; the shelters were meant for family members who are still living on the physical plane.

Instead of being scared by their dreams of the dead, most of those reporting emerged calm and confident, assured that life goes on in one world or another. Crossing to the Other Side was a prominent theme. One dreamer made a crossing by water under the care of a mysterious ferryman, an element very familiar in mythic geographies. I found it fascinating that people were dreaming in this ancient mode when so many in our world, unfortunately, were being pushed into death without preparation or rituals of farewell and were probably in need of a ferryman.

I was brought many reports in which dreamers found themselves exploring their lifestyle options on the Other Side and being shown possible exit ramps from physical life. This material was not exotic to me; I have recorded many personal experiences of this kind since I died and came back as a boy.

It was clear that dreams of this depth were coming through because they were needed and more and more people were ready to attend to them. Michel de Montaigne said that because we do not know where death is waiting for us, we must be ready to meet death everywhere. Few people who are conscious fail to understand that this has become an urgent imperative in the age of the pandemic. The matter of death and what follows is too important for us to rely on hand-me-down beliefs. We need firsthand experience. This requires us to become, in our own unique ways, shamans of consciousness. Our dreams will show us those ways.

This practice is not only about rehearsing for death. It is about remembering what life is all about, reclaiming the knowledge of the soul, and moving beyond fear and self-limiting beliefs.

Use the keys you have been offered in this book, and you will find you can grow big dreams in more than one world.

Envoi: Notes for the Road

To find yourself you must lose yourself.
The One you are seeking is not inside you.
You are inside the One.

To be present in every time
you must be here, now.
Now is the center of all times.

Here, now, you can step on and off
the trains to past and future
and travel on parallel lines.

To get to a place you do not know
you must go by a way you do not know.
Burn your maps to make beacons.

To wake up, you must dream.
Without dreams, you are a sleepwalker
who could join the ranks of the living dead.

There will be monsters, of course,
dark dwellers at every new threshold.
Without them, how could you be ready to pass?

In dealing with demons, you must learn
to choose the forms of your worst fears
and laugh at your creations.

If you wish to see marvels around you
you must carry marvels within.
A mirror can't show you what you don't bring.

The gates of the Otherworld open
from wherever you are. Don't think
you have to drink jungle juice with anacondas.

Put your blade away, dragon slayer.
You only conquer the dragon when you raise it
and ride it and turn its energy toward Light.

Turn out the lights if you want to find the Light.
The visible is the skin of the invisible.
In the dark, it is easier to see with inner eyes.

Don't list the trickster among your demons.
He is your friend if you expect the unexpected.
Everything interesting happens on the boundaries.

If you want to be fully alive, be ready to die.
How about now? You feel the cool breath
of Death on your neck. Give him some foreplay.

To find the One, don't spurn the many.
Name only one God, and you'll always end up with two.
Seek the nameless behind the forest of names.

Make your confessions on the road,
not from behind a curtain. The hawk will hear you
and the rabbit, the lily, and the stone.

Walk on the mythic edge. Let your life
become a stage for divine events.
Notice what never-ending story is playing through you.

Look after your poetic health.
Notice what rhymes in a day and a life.
Follow the logic of resemblances.

Practice real magic: follow the passions of your soul
and bring gifts from the Otherworld into this one.
You'll regret what you left undone —

the fence you wouldn't jump, the dream you didn't follow —
more than anything you did when your cool lover
stops licking your neck and takes you in his full embrace.

Blessing for the Road

As we part company, let me offer this blessing to you:

As you go forward on the roads of soul
May your doors and gates and paths be open
and may the doors and gates and paths of any who wish
to do you or those you love any harm be closed.
May it be so.

Appendix

The Lightning Dreamwork Game

I invented a fun way to share dreams, get some nonauthoritarian and nonintrusive feedback, and move toward creative action. I call this the Lightning Dreamwork game. It's like lightning in two senses: it's very quick (you can do it in five minutes), and it focuses and brings through terrific energy. It's a game you can play just about anywhere, with just about anyone — with the stranger in the line at the supermarket checkout or with the intimate stranger who shares your bed. The rules are simple, and they open a safe space to share even the most sensitive material. You can play this game with two or more people. We'll call the principal players the Dreamer and the Partner. There are four moves in the Lightning Dreamwork game.

First move: The Dreamer tells the dream as simply and clearly as possible, as a story. Just the facts of the dream, no background or autobiography. In telling a dream this way, the Dreamer claims the power of the story. The Partner should ask the Dreamer to give the dream report a title, like a story or a movie.

Second move: The Partner asks the Three Essential Questions:

1. "How did you feel?"
2. "Reality check: What do you recognize from this dream in

the rest of your life, and could any part of this dream be played out in the future?"

3. "What do you want to know about this now?"

The Dreamer answers all three questions.

Third Move: The Partner now shares whatever thoughts and associations the dream has triggered for him or her. The Partner begins by saying, "If it were my dream, I would think about such and such." The etiquette is very important. By saying, "If it were my dream," we make it clear that we are not setting out to tell the Dreamer what his or her dream — or life — means. We are not posing as experts of any kind. The Partner is just sharing whatever strikes him or her about the dream, which may include personal memories, other dreams, or things that simply pop up. (Those seemingly random pop-ups are often the best.)

Fourth Move: Following the discussion, the Partner asks the Dreamer: "What are you going to do now? What action will you take to honor this dream or work with its guidance?" If the Dreamer is clueless about what action to take, the Partner will offer his or her own suggestions, which may range from calling the guy up or buying the pink shoes to doing historical or linguistic research to decode odd references. Or the Dreamer may want to go back inside the dream (see "The Dream Reentry Technique" below) to get more information or move beyond a fear. One thing we can do with any dream is to write a personal motto derived from it, like a bumper sticker or something that could go on a refrigerator magnet.

After road-testing the Lightning Dreamwork game in some of my advanced groups, I introduced the process to general audiences in 2000. Since then I have noticed that 90 percent of the people who mention it in writing misspell the name, making it "Lightening."

I used to play spelling cop, but I have tired of that, and also I notice that something interesting is showing through the slip. Learning to tell our stories to each other by this method does "lighten" the day, and it sometimes brings enlightenment and encourages us to lighten up. One of our dream teachers reminds me that the term "lightening" also refers to a stage of delivery just before birth in which the fetus descends down the birth canal. So Lightning or Lightening, it's all good.

The Dream Reentry Technique

The best way to know what is going on in a dream is to revisit it, get your mind back into the scene, and gather more information. When you think about it, this shouldn't be hard. If you have been to a restaurant or apartment in ordinary reality, you can be pretty sure you can find your way there again. A dream is also a place; because you have been there, you can go there again.

Beyond clarifying dream content, you might want to try dream reentry for a number of interesting reasons. The best cure for nightmares and other scary dreams is to go back and confront the challenge — even the rank terror — on its own ground and do whatever needs to be done to bring resolution. You may want to talk to someone who appeared in a dream. You may have been enjoying romance and adventure in a dream, but then the alarm pulled you out, and you would like to go on with that adventure. You may want more of the movie. And so much more.

To do dream reentry, you need the following things:

1. A dream that has real energy for you and the ability to pull that scene up on your inner screen and let it become vivid.
2. Intentions for your journey. Ask yourself: "What do I need to know?" And: "What will I try to do when I am back inside the dream?"
3. Fuel and focus for the journey. In my workshops we use shamanic drumming. You could use a recording of drumming or nature sounds (see Resources). You will want to screen out external noise and light.

Bon voyage!

Notes

Introduction

p. 4   *"Phantasia was the organ"*: Robert A. Johnson, *Inner Work: Using Dreams and Active Imagination for Personal Growth* (New York: Harper & Row, 2001), 130.

p. 8   *"Myth, by design, makes it clear"*: P. L. Travers, *What the Bee Knows: Reflections on Myth, Symbol and History* (London: Thorsons, 1990), 86.

1. Dreams Show You the Secret Wishes of Your Soul

p. 17   *Father Ragueneau noted*: Robert Moss, *Dreamways of the Iroquois* (Rochester, VT: Destiny Books, 2005), 37.

p. 18   *"Sargon did not lay down"*: "Sargon and Ur-Zababa," quoted in Gil H. Renberg, *Where Dreams May Come: Incubation Sanctuaries in the Greco-Roman World* (Leiden: Brill, 2017), 45.

p. 18   *In ancient Egypt*: Kasia Maria Szpakowska, "The Perception of Dreams and Nightmare in Ancient Egypt: Old Kingdom to Third Intermediate Period" (PhD diss., University of California, Los Angeles, 2000), 43.

p. 21   *"The best songs are the ones"*: John Lennon, quoted in Robert Moss, *The Secret History of Dreaming* (Novato, CA: New World Library, 2009), 125.

p. 24   *Rumi evokes beautifully*: A. J. Arberry, *Tales from the Masnavi* (London: Routledge, 2002), 267–68.

p. 25   *She complains to her retinue*: "Né l'impetrare ispirazion mi valse, /

con le quali e in sogno e altrimenti / lo rivocai: sì poco a lui ne calse!" (Nor did it do me any good to summon / inspirations for him, with which I called him / in dreams or otherwise, so little he heeded them.) Dante Alighieri, *Purgatorio*, trans. W. S. Merwin (New York: Knopf, 2000), 300–1.

p. 29   *"I have not obstructed water"*: The Negative Confession is in spell 125 of the Papyrus of Ani. In Raymond O. Faulkner's translation of the Theban Recension, the relevant passage reads as follows: "I have not diverted water in its season, I have not built a dam on flowing water." Raymond O. Faulkner, trans., *The Egyptian Book of the Dead: The Book of Going Forth by Day* (San Francisco: Chronicle Books, 1998), 115.

p. 30   *Scientists like Dean Radin*: Dean Radin, *Entangled Minds: Extra- sensory Experiences in a Quantum Reality* (New York: Paraview Pocket Books, 2006), 3.

p. 30   *Physicist Brian Greene speculates*: Brian Greene, "Endless Doppel- gängers," chap. 2 in *The Hidden Reality: Parallel Universes and the Deep Laws of the Cosmos* (New York: Vintage, 2011), 11–42.

p. 33   *"My Brownies, God bless them!"*: Robert Louis Stevenson, "A Chapter on Dreams," in *The Works of Robert Louis Stevenson* (London: Chatto and Windus, 1912), 16:177–89.

p. 34   *It was a single powerful dream*: "Jeffrey Eugenides: How to Believe in Yourself — Even If You Sometimes Don't," Oprah.com, Septem- ber 6, 2012, http://www.oprah.com/spirit/jeffrey-eugenides-how-to -believe-in-yourself/all#ixzz6DvpHdg6nhttp://www.oprah.com/spirit /jeffrey-eugenides-how-to-believe-in-yourself/1#ixzz26vknk12n.

p. 34   *His novel* Middlesex *is*: Jeffrey Eugenides, *Middlesex* (New York: Picador, 2002).

p. 42   *as the poet W. B. Yeats observed*: William Butler Yeats stated, "Our service to the dead is not narrowed to our prayers, but may be as wide as our imagination." Quoted in Lady Gregory, "Swedenborg, Mediums, and Desolate Places," appendix to *Visions and Beliefs in the West of Ireland* (Gerrards Cross, UK: Colin Smythe, 1992), 335.

2. Your Great Imagineer Is Your Magical Child

p. 49   *Though his tale ends*: H. G. Wells, "The Door in the Wall," in Ursula K. Le Guin, ed., *Selected Stories of H. G. Wells* (New York: Modern Library, 2004).

p. 65   *"The reluctance to put away"*: Rebecca Pepper Sinkler, "Confessions of a Former Child," *New York Times*, March 22, 1998, https://archive .nytimes.com/www.nytimes.com/books/98/03/22/reviews/980322.22 sinklet.html.

p. 65   *"To be concerned about being grown up"*: C. S. Lewis, "On Three Ways of Writing for Children," in *Of Other Worlds* (New York: Harcourt, Brace & World, 1967), 25.

p. 66   *"A normal adult never stops"*: Albert Einstein, quoted in John D. Barrow, *Theories of Everything: The Quest for Ultimate Explanation* (Oxford and London: Clarendon Press, 1991), 68.

p. 66   *Famed psychic Eileen Garrett*: Eileen Garrett, *Telepathy: In Search of a Lost Faculty* (New York: Creative Age Press, 1941), 36–37, 143–44.

3. What Is in Your Way May Be Your Way

p. 70   *At about age eleven:* Moss, *Secret History*, 182–88.

p. 70   *"I would have gone on"*: Joe Simpson, *Touching the Void* (London: Vintage, 1997), 214.

p. 70   *"The compensations of calamity"*: Ralph Waldo Emerson, "Compensation," in *Essential Writings* (New York: Modern Library, 2000), 170–71.

p. 72   *"Our actions may be impeded"*: Marcus Aurelius, *Meditations*, trans. Gregory Hays (New York: Modern Library, 2003), 60.

p. 72   *"Don't let the force of an impression":* Epictetus, quoted in Ryan Holliday, *The Obstacle Is the Way: The Timeless Art of Turning Trials into Triumph* (New York: Portfolio/Penguin, 2014), 32.

p. 80   *"Ma tu perche vai?":* Dante, *Purgatorio*, 16–27.

p. 80   *"Per ch'io te sovra"*: Ibid., 270–71.

p. 90   *"A writer — and, I believe"*: Jorge Luis Borges, *Twenty-Four Conversations with Borges: Interviews by Roberto Alifano, 1981–1983* (New York: Grove Press, 1984), 15.

4. You Have Treasures in the Twilight Zone

p. 92   *Maury himself observed*: Albert Maury, "Des hallucinations hypnagogiques, ou des erreurs des sens dans l'état entre la veille et le sommeil," *Annales médico-psychologiques* I (1848): 26–40.

p. 93   *"Pictures consisting generally"*: F. W. H. Myers, *Human Personality and Its Survival of Bodily Death* (London: Longmans, Green, 1903), 1:125.

p. 94   *William James, the great American*: William James, *The Principles of Psychology* (1890), quoted in Andreas Mavromatis, *Hypnagogia: The Unique State of Consciousness between Wakefulness and Sleep* (London and New York: Routledge, 1987), 28.

p. 95   *One of the most exciting*: Nathalie Angier, "Modern Life Suppresses Ancient Body Rhythms," *New York Times*, March 14, 1995.

p. 97   *"I seemed almost to touch him"*: Aelius Aristides, *Sacred Tales*, in *Complete Works*, trans. Charles A. Behr (Leiden: E. J. Brill, 1981), 2:297–98.

p. 98   *"god-sent experiences"*: Iamblichus, *On the Mysteries of the Egyptians, Chaldeans, and Assyrians*, trans. Thomas Taylor (London: B. Dobell and Reeves & Taylor, 1895), 115–17.

p. 99   *"The fact is, I did wake up"*: Ruth Ozeki, "*A Tale for the Time Being* Reader's Guide," Penguin Random House (website), https://www .penguinrandomhouse.com/books/312488/a-tale-for-the-time-being -by-ruth-ozeki/9780143124870/readers-guide.

p. 100   *"hypnagogia is significantly conducive"*: Mavromatis, *Hypnagogia*, 131.

p. 102   *"Day by day, in every way"*: Émile Coué, *La méthode Coué: La maîtrise de soi-même par l'autosuggestion consciente* (1920; repr., Vanves, France: Marabout, 2013).

5. Your Body Believes in Images

p. 110   *He found that spiritual beliefs*: Harold G. Koenig, "Religion, Spirituality, and Health: The Research and Clinical Implications," *International Scholarly Research Network: Psychiatry* (2012), article ID 278730, doi:10.5402/2012/278730.

p. 110   *he saw how to perform*: Otto Loewi, "An Autobiographical Sketch," *Perspectives on Biology and Medicine* 4 (Autumn 1960): 3.

p. 111   *"psychosomatic communications network"*: Candace Pert, *Molecules of Emotion: The Science behind Mind-Body Medicine* (New York: Simon and Schuster, 1999), 183.

p. 111   *"the body responds to mental input"*: Conversation with Larry Dossey, April 21, 2015.

p. 112   *Stress is responsible*: Email interview with Dr. Herbert Benson, November 5, 2007.

p. 113   *The celebrated journalist and peace activist*: Norman Cousins, *Anatomy of an Illness as Perceived by the Patient: Reflections on Healing and Regeneration* (New York: W.W. Norton, 2005).

p. 126   *"I want to tell you"*: "Shamanism, Dreaming, and Healing," conversation with Bonnie Horrigan on *The Way of the Dreamer*, hosted by Robert Moss, HealthyLife.net Radio, April 10, 2012.

6. Your Big Story Is Hunting You

p. 132   *"A dream is a personal experience"*: Joseph Campbell with Bill Moyers, *The Power of Myth* (New York: Doubleday, 1988), 40.

p. 133   *In Greek theater, mythos*: David Wiles, *Greek Theatre Performance: An Introduction* (Cambridge: Cambridge University Press, 2000), 12.

p. 133   *"In the absence of"*: Joseph Campbell, *The Hero with a Thousand Faces* (Novato, CA: New World Library, 2008), 2.

p. 133   *Psychologist Betty Meador was called*: Betty De Shong Meador, *Inanna, Lady of Largest Heart: Poems of the Sumerian High Priestess Enheduanna* (Austin: University of Texas Press, 2000), 10–11.

p. 134   *The great scholar of religions*: Wendy Doniger, *Splitting the Difference: Gender and Myth in Ancient Greece and India* (Chicago: University of Chicago Press, 1999), ix.

p. 134   *"Myth, by design, makes it clear"*: Travers, *What the Bee Knows*, 86.

p. 135   *It is in the introduction*: H.O. Sommer, *The Vulgate Version of the Arthurian Romance*, quoted in Emma Jung and Marie-Louise von Franz, *The Grail Legend* (New York: Putnam, 1970), 319–20.

p. 138   *I am riffing on*: This is my free version of a passage from the Sumerian poem "Inanna and Ebih," translated by Meador in *Inanna*, 94.

p. 140   *She composed forty-six temple hymns*: For translation and discussion of the temple hymns, see Betty De Shong Meador, *Princess, Priestess, Poet: The Sumerian Temple Hymns of Enheduanna* (Austin: University of Texas Press, 2009).

p. 140   *"in Enheduanna's writing"*: Meador, *Inanna*, 76.

p. 142   *In Gaul and throughout*: Miranda Green, *Animals in Celtic Life and Myth* (London and New York: Routledge, 1998), 204–7.

p. 142   *"The horse is absolutely crucial"*: Ibid., 207.

p. 142   *At a burial ground*: Maurice Toussaint, *Metz à l'époque gallo-romaine* (Metz, France: Paul Even, 1948), 206–7.

p. 143   *It is native to at least*: Samten G. Karmay, *The Arrow and the Spindle: Studies in History, Myths, Ritual, and Beliefs in Tibet* (San Rafael, CA: Mandala Publishing, 1998), 40.

p. 145   *"I would encounter darkness"*: Travers, "Walking the Maze at Chartres," in *What the Bee Knows*, 136.

p. 147   *We see her like this*: Bonnie MacLachlan, "Kore as Nymph, Not Daughter: Persephone in a Locrian Cave," *Diotíma: Materials for the Study of Women and Gender in the Ancient World* (website), 2004.

p. 148   *"The Mysteries do not only"*: Carl Kerenyi, *Eleusis: Archetypal Image of the Mother and Daughter*, trans. Ralph Mannheim (Princeton, NJ: Princeton University Press, 1991), 15.

p. 149   *"he who dies before"*: Quoted in Roger Woolger, *Healing Your Past Lives: Exploring the Many Lives of the Soul* (Boulder, CO: Sounds True, 2010), 35.

p. 149   *In Persian mythology Isfandiyar eats*: V.S. Curtis, *Persian Myths* (London: British Museum Press, 1996), 54.

p. 149   *Herodotus states that golden pomegranates*: Herodotus, *The Histories*, trans. Aubrey de Selincourt (London: Penguin, 1996), 389.

p. 150   *"Mythology might work its will"*: Jane Ellen Harrison, *Prolegomena to the Study of Greek Religion* [1903] (London: Merlin Press, 1980), 274.

p. 151   *"It was Persephone who demanded"*: Carol Pearson, *Persephone Rising: Awakening the Heroine Within* (New York: HarperOne, 2018), 29.

p. 153   *"the true nature of the gods"*: "Although the form under which the god is represented is pure imagination, the force associated with it is both real and active." Dion Fortune, *The Mystical Qabalah* (York Beach, ME: Samuel Weiser, 1989), 224–25.

p. 153   *"Through their dream"*: Louis Bird, *The Spirit Lives in the Mind: Omushkego Stories, Lives, and Dreams* (Montreal, QC, and Kingston, ON: McGill-Queen's University Press, 2007), 85.

p. 154   *"The elements — the atmosphere"*: Ibid., 92.

7. You Are Magnetic

p. 159   *"All things which are similar"*: Heinrich Cornelius Agrippa of Nettesheim, *Three Books of Occult Philosophy*, ed. Donald Tyson, trans. James Freake (St. Paul, MN: Llewellyn, 1993).

p. 160   *"We are magnets in an iron globe"*: Ralph Waldo Emerson, "The Divinity School Address," Harvard University, Cambridge, MA, July 15, 1838.

p. 160   *"each of us is responsible"*: John O'Donohue, *Beauty: The Invisible Embrace* (New York: Harper Perennial, 2005), quoted in Maria Popova, "John O'Donohue on Beauty, Why We Fall in Love, and How the Life-Force of Desire Vitalizes Us," *Brain Pickings*, https://www.brainpickings.org/2015/09/21/john-odonohue-beauty-love-desire/.

p. 164   *"a child playing"*: On a stone cube at Bollingen, Jung chiseled words from Heraclitus in Greek, which he translated as follows: "Time is a child — playing like a child — playing a board game — the kingdom of the child." C. G. Jung, *Memories, Dreams, Reflections*, ed. Aniela Jaffé, trans. Richard Winston and Clara Winston (New York: Vintage, 1965), 227. A recent translation of the line from Heraclitus offers this: "Lifetime is a child at play, moving pieces on a board. Kingship belongs to the child." Charles H. Kahn, *The Art and Thought of Heraclitus: An Edition of the Fragments with Translation and Commentary* (Cambridge: Cambridge University Press, 1987), 71.

p. 165   *In his essay*: C. G. Jung, *Aion: Researches into the Phenomenology of the Self*, trans. R. F. C. Hull (Princeton, NJ: Princeton University Press, 1979), 167–68.

p. 165   *"True realism consists"*: Jean Cocteau, *My Contemporaries* (Ann Arbor: University of Michigan Press, 1967), 141.

p. 169   *"There is a Toyota dreaming"*: "Talking the Dreamtime and Understanding Country: Munya Andrews," *Rune Soup* (podcast), February 12, 2020, https://www.youtube.com/watch?v=Wd_kJi9FdJI&feature=youtu.be&fbclid=IwAR1Ta2nC-dZgOB7zvVora5gm76VLgadEgs9R5htbmku60BSNZKaFeONhoX8.

p. 169   *"our land is our knowledge"*: Karl-Erik Sveiby and Tex Skuthorpe, *Treading Lightly: The Hidden Wisdom of the World's Oldest People* (Crows Nest, NSW: Allen and Unwin, 2006), 3.

p. 170   *"I was the youngest"*: Carolyn Landon and Eileen Harrison, *Black Swan: A Koorie Woman's Life* (Crows Nest, NSW: Allen and Unwin, 2011), 30.

p. 170   *"to Aboriginal people"*: Philip Clarke, *Where the Ancestors Walked: Australia as an Aboriginal Landscape* (Crows Nest, NSW: Allen and Unwin, 2003), 23.

p. 175   *When Jung was immersed*: C. G. Jung, "On Synchronicity" (lecture,

1951 Eranos conference), in *The Structure and Dynamics of the Psyche* in *Collected Works*, trans. R. F. C. Hull (Princeton, NJ: Bollingen, 1976), CW8, para. 970.

p. 175 *In her discussion*: Marie-Louise von Franz, *Projection and Recollection in Jungian Psychology*, trans. William H. Kennedy (LaSalle, IL, and London: Open Court, 1990), 190.

p. 176 *"Precisely because the psychic"*: C. G. Jung, *Mysterium Coniunctionis: An Inquiry into the Separation and Synthesis of Psychic Opposites in Alchemy*, trans. R. F. C. Hull (Abingdon-on-Thames: Routledge, 1963), CW14, para. 765.

p. 177 *"my researches into the history"*: Jung, "On Synchronicity," CW8, para. 816.

p. 177 *"we all have certain"*: J. P. Eckermann, *Conversations with Goethe*, quoted in ibid., para. 860.

p. 180 *"I have found that"*: Alvin Schwartz, "After the Golden Age," World Famous Comics, August 1, 2005, vol. 2, no. 170, http://worldfamous comics.com/alvin/back20050801.shtml.

p. 182 *"whose voice was soon"*: Æ [George Russell], *The Candle of Vision* (Bridport, UK: Prism Press, 1990), 10.

p. 182 *"I feel I belong"*: Æ, quoted in Travers, "The Death of AE," in *What the Bee Knows*, 244–45.

p. 182 *"the sanguine, the spirits"*: W. B. Yeats, quoted in George Mills Harper et al., eds., *Yeats's "Vision" Papers, vol. 2, The Automatic Scripts* (Iowa City: University of Iowa Press, 1992), 342n.

p. 182 *"Then she thrust a hand"*: Travers, "On Forgiving Oneself," in *What the Bee Knows*, 199.

8. There Is a World of Imagination, and It Is Entirely Real

p. 188 *Corbin encouraged us*: Henry Corbin, "Mundus Imaginalis, or the Imaginary and the Imagined," in *Swedenborg and Esoteric Islam*, trans. Leonard Fox (West Chester, PA: Swedenborg Foundation, 1995), 9.

p. 189 *"a climate outside of climates"*: Ibid.

p. 189 *"the forms of all works"*: Henry Corbin, *Spiritual Body and Celestial Earth*, trans. Nancy Pearson (Princeton, NJ: Bollingen, 1989), 126–27.

p. 189 *It is an "isthmus" between*: Roxanne D. Marcotte, "Suhrawardi's Realm of the Imaginal," *Academia* (website), 2011, https://www .academia.edu/4248873/_2011_Suhrawardis_Realm_of_the_Imaginal.

p. 189 *"the world of the subtle bodies"*: Mulla Sadra Shirazi, quoted in Seyyed Hossein Nasr, "Mulla Sadra: His Teachings," in *History of Islamic Philosophy*, ed. Seyyed Hossein Nasr and Oliver Leaman (London and New York: Routledge, 1996), 652.

p. 189 *"pilgrims of the spirit"*: Shihab al-Din al-Suhrawardi, quoted in Corbin, *Spiritual Body*, 118.

p. 189 *"Your universe and all others"*: Jane Roberts, *Dreams, "Evolution," and Value Fulfillment: A Seth Book*, vol. 1 (New York: Prentice Hall Press, 1988), 216.

p. 193 *"If you have little memory"*: Jane Roberts, *Seth, Dreams, and Projections of Consciousness* (Walpole, NH: Stillpoint Publishing, 1986), 10.

p. 201 *"My heart flew up in joy"*: Rumi, *Diwan-i Shams-i Tabrizi* 2730, trans. William C. Chittick, in *The Sufi Path of Love: The Spiritual Teachings of Rumi* (Albany: State University of New York Press, 1984), 140.

p. 207 *"The doorways to the invisible"*: René Daumal, *Mount Analogue*, reprinted in *Parabola* 13, no. 4 (1988).

p. 208 *This is sometimes accomplished*: The magicians of the Order of the Golden Dawn and its offshoots practiced Qabala, as distinct from the Jewish Kabbalah. The attributions of the tarot trumps and the Hebrew letters to the paths between the sephirot on the Tree of Life are explained by Robert Wang in *Qabalistic Tarot: A Textbook of Mystical Philosophy* (York Beach, ME: Samuel Weiser, 1992).

p. 209 *"To use the Tarot properly"*: Dion Fortune, *Practical Occultism in Daily Life* (Wellingborough, UK: Aquarian Press, 1980).

9. If You Can See Your Destination, You Are Halfway There

p. 219 *"The outward work will never"*: Meister Eckhart, quoted in Matthew Fox, *Christian Mystics: 365 Readings and Meditations* (Novato, CA: New World Library, 2011), 144.

p. 219 *"What we plant in the soil"*: Meister Eckhart, "*In His Quae Patris*: Sermon on Luke 2:49," in *Meister Eckhart: A Modern Translation*, trans. Raymond Bernard Blakney (New York: Harper and Brothers, 1941), 111.

p. 219   *"there exists only the present"*: Meister Eckhart, *Selected Writings*. (New York: Penguin Books, 1994), 73.

10. You Can Grow a Dream for Someone Who Needs a Dream

p. 229   *"An oak grows between the lakes"*: Jeffrey Gantz, trans., *The Mabinogion* (London: Penguin, 1978), 115.

p. 229   *Guaraní shamans perform*: Ava Tapa Miri (Little Seagull Man), quoted in "Guarani: Shamans of the Forest," in Nancy Connor and Bradford P. Keeney, *Shamans of the World: Extraordinary First-Person Accounts of Healings, Mysteries, and Miracles* (Louisville, CO: Sounds True, 2008), 100.

p. 230   *"Psychoanalysis is a work"*: James Hillman, *Healing Fiction* (Putnam, CT: Spring Publications, 1994), 3–4.

p. 230   *"the shaman provides"*: Claude Lévi-Strauss, "The Sorcerer and His Magic," in *Structural Anthropology* (New York: Basic Books, 1963), 167–85.

p. 231   *He reports that they use*: Graham Townsley, "Song Paths: The Ways and Means of Yaminahua Shamanic Knowledge," *L'Homme* 33, no. 126–28 (1993): 449–68.

p. 231   *four deceased shamans*: Ava Tapa Miri (Little Seagull Man), quoted in Connor and Keeney, *Shamans of the World*, 100–101.

p. 232   *"How was I to explain"*: C. G. Jung, quoted in Aniela Jaffé, *Jung's Last Years* (Dallas: Spring Publications, 1984), 106–7.

p. 232   *In the language of the Temiar Senoi*: Marina Roseman, *Healing Sounds from the Malaysian Rainforest: Temiar Music and Medicine* (Berkeley: University of California Press, 1993), 52–53.

p. 244   *including the Makiritare*: In the legend of Medatia, a great shamanic origin story of the Makiritare, Mahewa, the Morpho butterfly, appears over a magical blue lake of healing and is described as "the master of heaven's water." Marc de Civrieux, "Medatia: A Makiritare Shaman's Tale," trans. David M. Guss, in *The Language of the Birds*, ed. David M. Guss (San Francisco: North Point Press, 1985), 68.

11. You Don't Have to Drive Used Karma

p. 251   *"Come out with what"*: A. H. Gardiner, *Hieratic Papyri in the British Museum, Third Series* (London: British Museum, 1935). Reprinted with commentary in Szpakowska, "The Perception of Dreams," 272–73, 358–62.

p. 254   *My friend Normandi Ellis*: Normandi Ellis, *Hieroglyphic Words of Power: Symbols for Magic, Divination, and Dreamwork* (New York: Simon and Schuster, 2020).

p. 255   *"I flew straight out of heaven"*: Normandi Ellis, *Awakening Osiris: The Egyptian Book of the Dead* (Rochester, VT: Red Wheel/Weiser, 2009), 172–73.

p. 256   *"our guardian is the power"*: Kenneth Sylvan Guthrie, trans. and ed., *Plotinus: The Enneads: In Chronological Order, Grouped in Four Periods*, 4 vols. (Alpine, NJ: Comparative Literature Press, 1918), 1:236.

p. 257   *"our guardian helps us"*: Ibid., 1:239.

p. 257   *"He does not permit us"*: Ibid.

p. 257   *"The soul has the power"*: Ibid., 1:238.

p. 260   *"I am an energy"*: Jane Roberts, *Seth Speaks: The Eternal Validity of the Soul* (New York: Prentice Hall, 1987), 5.

p. 260   *He could communicate*: Ibid., 16.

p. 260   *"You must die many times"*: Ibid., 18.

p. 261   *"When one has been born"*: Ibid., 35.

p. 261   *"Knowing your reincarnational background"*: Ibid., 214.

p. 262   *"You may draw upon knowledge"*: Ibid., 109.

p. 263   *Hugh Everett's bold proposition*: Robert Moss, "The Sadness of the Man of Many Worlds," *Robert Moss Blog*, January 6, 2014, https://mossdreams.blogspot.com/2014/01/the-sadness-of-man-who -gave-us-many.html.

12. The Stronger the Imagination, the Less Imaginary the Results

p. 271   *"The stronger the imagination"*: Rabindranath Tagore, *Sādhanā: The Realisation of Life* (London: Macmillan, 1914), 59.

p. 271   *"Everything we formulate"*: W. B. Yeats, *Is the Order of R. R. et A. C. to Remain a Magical Order?* (London: Mandrake Press, 1901).

p. 271   *"Nothing great was ever achieved"*: Ralph Waldo Emerson, "Circles" (1841).

p. 272   *"On s'engage et puis"*: The statement "On s'engage et puis on voit" first gained currency when Vladimir Lenin quoted it in an article, "On Revolution," in *Pravda* on May 30, 1923, giving the source as "Napoleon, I think." Quote detectives have been unable to find it in any document containing Napoleon's dicta, and some think that Lenin just made it up. Either way, it's good advice.

p. 274   *"The poet marries the language"*: W. H. Auden, quoted in Robert Moss, *Sidewalk Oracles* (Novato, CA: New World Library, 2015), 75–76.

p. 279   *"Tell me, what is it"*: Mary Oliver, "The Summer Day," in *House of Light* (Boston: Beacon Press, 1990), 60.

p. 281   *"Perhaps the truth depends"*: Wallace Stevens, "Notes toward a Supreme Fiction," in *The Collected Poems of Wallace Stevens* (New York: Knopf, 2011), 386.

p. 286   *"Poems came to me"*: Ruth Stone, "Fragrance," in *What Love Comes To: New and Selected Poems* (Port Townsend, WA: Copper Canyon Press, 2010), 45.

p. 286   *When a poem gets away*: Elizabeth Gilbert, *Big Magic: Creative Living beyond Fear* (New York: Riverhead Books, 2016), 64–65.

p. 286   *what J. R. R. Tolkien called*: J. R. R. Tolkien, "On Fairy-Stories" (1939).

p. 287   *"So you have to learn"*: Anaïs Nin, *The Diary of Anaïs Nin, vol. 4, 1944–1947*, ed. Gunther Stulmann (Boston: Mariner Books, 1972), 65.

p. 290   *"out of love with the ordinary"*: Mary Oliver, "Of Power and Time," in *Upstream: Selected Essays* (New York: Penguin, 2016), 27.

p. 290   *"the hardest thing"*: W. B. Yeats, *Mythologies* (New York: Macmillan, 1959), 336.

p. 290   *"I am absentminded, reckless"*: Oliver, "Of Power and Time," 30.

p. 291   *"There is no other way"*: Ibid.

p. 292   *Around 1700 BCE*: Alice Mouton, "Portent Dreams in Hittite Anatolia," in *Perchance to Dream: Dream Divination in the Bible and the Ancient Near East,* ed. Esther K. Hamori and Jonathan Stöckl (Atlanta: SBL Press, 2018), 31.

p. 293   *"The virus is rewriting"*: Kim Stanley Robinson, "The Coronavirus Is Rewriting Our Imaginations," *New Yorker*, May 1, 2020, https://www.newyorker.com/culture/annals-of-inquiry/the-coronavirus-and-our-future.

p. 295   *Michel de Montaigne said*: "Nous ne savons où la mort nous attend, attendons-la partout." Michel de Montaigne, *Essais* (Paris: Didot, 1907), 1:137.

Bibliography

Achterberg, Jeanne. *Imagery in Healing: Shamanism and Modern Medicine.* Boston: Shambhala, 1985.

Æ [George Russell]. *The Candle of Vision.* Bridport, UK: Prism Press, 1990.

Agrippa, Heinrich Cornelius. *Three Books of Occult Philosophy.* Edited by Donald Tyson, translated by James Freake. St. Paul, MN: Llewellyn, 1993.

Alighieri, Dante. *Purgatorio.* Translated by W. S. Merwin. New York: Knopf, 2000.

Amara, HeatherAsh, *The Warrior Heart Practice.* New York: St. Martin's, 2020.

Angier, Nathalie. "Modern Life Suppresses Ancient Body Rhythms." *New York Times*, March 14, 1995.

Arberry, A. J. *Tales from the Masnavi.* London: Routledge, 2002.

Aristides, P. Aelius. *Complete Works.* Translated by Charles A. Behr. 2 vols. Leiden: E. J. Brill, 1981.

Barrett, Deirdre. *The Committee of Sleep.* New York: Crown, 2001.

Barrow, John D. *Theories of Everything: The Quest for Ultimate Explanation.* Oxford and London: Clarendon Press, 1991.

Becker, Raymond de. *The Understanding of Dreams and Their Influence on the History of Man.* New York: Bell, 1968.

Berndt, Ronald M., and Catherine H. Berndt. *The Speaking Land: Myth and Story in Aboriginal Australia.* Rochester, VT: Inner Traditions, 1994.

Bird, Louis. *The Spirit Lives in the Mind: Omushkego Stories, Lives, and Dreams.* Montreal, QC, and Kingston, ON: McGill-Queen's University Press, 2007.

Blakney, Raymond Bernard, trans. *Meister Eckhart: A Modern Translation.* New York: Harper and Brothers, 1941.

Borges, Jorge Luis. *Selected Nonfictions*. Translated by Eliot Weinberger et al. New York: Penguin, 2000.

———. *Twenty-Four Conversations with Borges: Interviews by Roberto Alifano, 1981–1983*. New York: Grove Press, 1984.

Boyd, Brian. *On the Origin of Stories: Evolution, Cognition and Fiction*. Cambridge, MA: Belknap Press of Harvard University Press, 2009.

Burke, Janine. *The Gods of Freud: Sigmund Freud's Art Collection*. Sydney, Australia: Knopf, 2006.

Caillois, Roger, ed. *The Dream Adventure*. New York: Orion Press, 1963.

Campbell, Joseph. *The Hero with a Thousand Faces*. Novato, CA: New World Library, 2008.

Campbell, Joseph, with Bill Moyers. *The Power of Myth*. New York: Doubleday, 1988.

Care, James P. *Finite and Infinite Games*. New York: Ballantine Books, 1986.

Carlson, Kathie. *Life's Daughter/Death's Bride: Inner Transformation through the Goddess Demeter/Persephone*. Boston and London: Shambhala, 1997.

Clarke, Philip. *Where the Ancestors Walked: Australia as an Aboriginal Landscape*. Crows Nest, NSW: Allen and Unwin, 2003.

Connor, Nancy, and Bradford P. Keeney. *Shamans of the World: Extraordinary First-Person Accounts of Healings, Mysteries, and Miracles*. Louisville, CO: Sounds True, 2008.

Corbin, Henry. *Creative Imagination in the Sufism of Ibn 'Arabi*. Translated by Ralph Mannheim. Princeton, NJ: Bollingen, 1981.

———. *Spiritual Body and Celestial Earth*. Translated by Nancy Pearson. Princeton, NJ: Bollingen, 1989.

———. *Swedenborg and Esoteric Islam*. Translated by Leonard Fox. West Chester, PA: Swedenborg Foundation, 1995.

Coué, Émile. *La méthode Coué: La maîtrise de soi-même par l'autosuggestion consciente*. 1920; repr., Vanves, France: Marabout, 2013.

Cousins, Norman. *Anatomy of an Illness as Perceived by the Patient: Reflections on Healing and Regeneration*. New York: W. W. Norton, 2005.

Curtis, V. S. *Persian Myths*. London: British Museum Press, 1996.

Daumal, René. *Mount Analogue*. Reprinted in *Parabola* 13, no. 4 (1988).

Doniger, Wendy. *Splitting the Difference: Gender and Myth in Ancient Greece and India*. Chicago: University of Chicago Press, 1999.

Dossey, Larry. *Reinventing Medicine: Beyond Mind-Body to a New Era of Healing*. San Francisco: HarperSanFrancisco, 1999.

Edelstein, Emma J., and Ludwig Edelstein. *Asclepius: Collection and Interpretation of the Testimonies*. Baltimore: Johns Hopkins University Press, 1998.

Eliade, Mircea. *Shamanism: Archaic Techniques of Ecstasy*. Princeton, NJ: Princeton University Press, 1974.

Elkin, A. P. *Aboriginal Men of High Degree*. New York: St. Martin's, 1978.

Ellis, Normandi. *Awakening Osiris: The Egyptian Book of the Dead*. Rochester, VT: Red Wheel/Weiser, 2009.

———. *Dreams of Isis: A Woman's Spiritual Sojourn*. Wheaton, IL: Quest Books, 1995.

———. *Hieroglyphic Words of Power: Symbols for Magic, Divination, and Dreamwork*. New York: Simon and Schuster, 2020.

———. *Imagining the World into Existence: An Ancient Egyptian Manual of Consciousness*. Rochester, VT: Bear & Company, 2012.

Emerson, Ralph Waldo. "The Divinity School Address." Harvard University, Cambridge, MA, July 15, 1838.

———. *Essential Writings*. New York: Modern Library, 2000.

Eugenides, Jeffrey. *Middlesex*. New York: Picador, 2002.

Farooqi, Musharraf Ali. *The Adventures of Amir Hamza*. New York: Modern Library, 2008.

———. *Hoshruba: The Land and the Tilism*. Toronto: Urdu Project, 2009.

Faulkner, Raymond O., trans. *The Egyptian Book of the Dead: The Book of Going Forth by Day*. San Francisco: Chronicle Books, 1998.

Feinstein, David, and Stanley Krippner. *Personal Mythology*. Santa Rosa, CA: Energy Psychology Press, 2009.

Fortune, Dion. *The Mystical Qabalah*. York Beach, ME: Samuel Weiser, 1989.

———. *Practical Occultism in Daily Life*. Wellingborough, UK: Aquarian Press, 1980.

Fox, Matthew. *Christian Mystics: 365 Readings and Meditations*. Novato, CA: New World Library, 2011.

Frankl, Viktor E. *Man's Search for Meaning*. Boston: Beacon Press, 2006.

Gantz, Jeffrey, trans. *The Mabinogion*. London: Penguin, 1978.

Garnier Malet, Jean Pierre. *Le double comment ça marche?* Paris: Temps Présent Éditions, 2007.

Garrett, Eileen. *Telepathy: In Search of a Lost Faculty*. New York: Creative Age Press, 1941.

Gilbert, Elizabeth. *Big Magic: Creative Living beyond Fear*. New York: Riverhead Books, 2016.

Green, Miranda. *Animals in Celtic Life and Myth*. London and New York: Routledge, 1998.

Greene, Brian. *The Hidden Reality: Parallel Universes and the Deep Laws of the Cosmos*. New York: Vintage, 2011.

Grushin, Olga. *The Dream Life of Sukhanov*. New York: Penguin Books, 2005.

Guss, David M. *The Language of the Birds: Tales, Text, and Poems of Interspecies Communication*. San Francisco: North Point Press, 1985.

Guthrie, Kenneth Sylvan, trans. and ed. *Plotinus: The Enneads: In Chronological Order, Grouped in Four Periods*, 4 vols. Alpine, NJ: Comparative Literature Press, 1918.

Harrison, Jane Ellen. *Epilegomena to the Study of Greek Religion* [1921]. New Hyde Park, NY: University Books, 1966.

———. *Prolegomena to the Study of Greek Religion* [1903]. London: Merlin Press, 1980.

Herodotus. *The Histories.* Translated by Aubrey de Selincourt. London: Penguin, 1996.

Hewitt, J. N. B. "The Iroquoian Concept of the Soul." *Journal of American Folk-Lore* 8 (1895): 107–16.

Hillman, James. *Healing Fiction*. Putnam, CT: Spring Publications, 1994.

Holliday, Ryan. *The Obstacle Is the Way: The Timeless Art of Turning Trials into Triumph*. New York: Portfolio/Penguin, 2014.

Horowitz, Mitch. *The Miracle Club: How Thoughts Become Reality*. Rochester, VT: Inner Traditions, 2018.

Houston, Jean. *The Hero and the Goddess: "The Odyssey" as Pathway to Personal Transformation*. Wheaton, IL: Quest Books, 2006.

———. *A Mythic Life*. San Francisco: HarperSanFrancisco, 1996.

———. *The Search for the Beloved: Journeys in Mythology and Sacred Psychology*. San Francisco: Tarcher Perigee, 1997.

Hyde, Lewis. *Trickster Makes This World: Mischief, Myth, and Art*. New York: North Point Press, 1998.

Iamblichus. *On the Mysteries of the Egyptians, Chaldeans, and Assyrians.* Translated by Thomas Taylor. London: B. Dobell and Reeves & Taylor, 1895.

Ingerman, Sandra. *Medicine for the Earth*. New York: Three Rivers Press, 2000.

———. *Soul Retrieval: Mending the Fragmented Self.* San Francisco: HarperSanFrancisco, 1991.

Jaffé, Aniela. *Jung's Last Years.* Dallas: Spring Publications, 1984.

Johnson, Robert A. *Inner Work: Using Dreams and Active Imagination for Personal Growth.* New York: Harper & Row, 2001.

Jung, C. G. *Aion: Researches into the Phenomenology of the Self.* Translated by R. F. C. Hull. Princeton, NJ: Princeton University Press, 1979.

———. *Letters.* Vol. 2, edited by Gerhard Adler. Princeton, NJ: Princeton University Press, 1953.

———. *Man and His Symbols.* New York: Doubleday, 1964.

———. *Memories, Dreams, Reflections.* Edited by Aniela Jaffé, translated by Richard Winston and Clara Winston. New York: Vintage, 1985.

———. *Mysterium Coniunctionis: An Inquiry into the Separation and Synthesis of Psychic Opposites in Alchemy.* Translated by R. F. C. Hull. Abingdon-on-Thames: Routledge, 1963.

———. "On Synchronicity" (lecture, 1951 Eranos conference). In *The Structure and Dynamics of the Psyche* in *Collected Works*, vol. 8. Translated by R. F. C. Hull. Princeton, NJ: Bollingen, 1976.

———. *Psychology and Religion: West and East.* Translated by R. F. C. Hull. Princeton, NJ: Princeton University Press, 1969.

———. *The Red Book: Liber Novus.* Edited by Sonu Shamdasani. New York: Norton, 2009.

Jung, C. G., and Carl Kerenyi. *Essays on a Science of Mythology: The Myth of the Divine Child and the Divine Maiden.* New York: Harper Torchbooks, 1963.

Jung, Emma, and Marie-Louise von Franz. *The Grail Legend.* New York: Putnam, 1970.

Kahn, Charles H. *The Art and Thought of Heraclitus: An Edition of the Fragments with Translation and Commentary.* Cambridge: Cambridge University Press, 1987.

Karmay, Samten G. *The Arrow and the Spindle: Studies in History, Myths, Ritual, and Beliefs in Tibet.* San Rafael, CA: Mandala Publishing, 1998.

Kerenyi, Carl. *Eleusis: Archetypal Image of the Mother and Daughter.* Translated by Ralph Mannheim. Princeton, NJ: Princeton University Press, 1991.

Knight, Gareth. *Experience of the Inner Worlds.* York Beach, ME: Samuel Weiser, 1993.

Koenig, Harold G. "Religion, Spirituality, and Health: The Research and

Clinical Implications." *International Scholarly Research Network: Psychiatry* (2012), article ID 278730, doi:10.5402/2012/278730.

Lady Gregory. *Visions and Beliefs in the West of Ireland* (Gerrards Cross, UK: Colin Smythe, 1992).

Lafitau, Joseph-François. *Customs of the American Indians Compared with the Customs of Primitive Times*. Edited and translated by William N. Fenton and Elizabeth L. Moore. 2 vols. Toronto: Champlain Society, 1974, 1977.

Landon, Carolyn, and Eileen Harrison. *Black Swan: A Koorie Woman's Life*. Crows Nest, NSW: Allen and Unwin, 2011.

Le Goff, Jacques. *The Birth of Purgatory*. Translated by Arthur Goldhammer. Chicago: University of Chicago Press, 1984.

Le Guin, Ursula K. *Words Are My Matter*. New York: Houghton Mifflin Harcourt, 2016.

Lévi-Strauss, Claude. "The Sorcerer and His Magic." In *Structural Anthropology*. New York: Basic Books, 1963.

Lewis, C. S. "On Three Ways of Writing for Children." In *Of Other Worlds*. New York: Harcourt, Brace & World, 1967.

Loewi, Otto. "An Autobiographical Sketch." *Perspectives on Biology and Medicine* 4 (Autumn 1960).

Lohmann, Roger Ivar, ed. *Dream Travelers: Sleep Experiences and Culture in the Western Pacific*. New York: Palgrave Macmillan, 2003.

Long, Max Freedom. *The Secret Science behind Miracles*. Marina del Rey, CA: DeVorss, 1976.

MacLachlan, Bonnie. "Kore as Nymph, Not Daughter: Persephone in a Locrian Cave." *Diotíma: Materials for the Study of Women and Gender in the Ancient World* (website), 2004.

Marcotte, Roxanne D. "Suhrawardi's Realm of the Imaginal." *Academia* (website), 2011, https://www.academia.edu/4248873/_2011_Suhrawardis_Realm_of_the_Imaginal.

Marcus Aurelius. *Meditations*. Translated by Gregory Hays. New York: Modern Library, 2003.

Matthews, Caitlin, and John Matthews. *The Encyclopaedia of Celtic Wisdom*. Shaftesbury, UK, and Rockport, MA: Element, 1994.

Maury, Albert. "Des hallucinations hypnagogiques, ou des erreurs des sens dans l'état entre la veille et le sommeil." *Annales médico-psychologiques* I (1848): 26–40.

Mavromatis, Andreas. *Hypnagogia: The Unique State of Consciousness between Wakefulness and Sleep*. London and New York: Routledge, 1987.

Meade, Michael. *The World behind the World*. Seattle: Green Fire Press, 2008.

Meador, Betty De Shong. *Inanna, Lady of Largest Heart: Poems of the Sumerian High Priestess Enheduanna*. Austin: University of Texas Press, 2000.

———. *Princess, Priestess, Poet: The Sumerian Temple Hymns of Enheduanna*. Austin: University of Texas Press, 2009.

Metzner, Ralph. *The Well of Remembrance: Rediscovering the Earth Wisdom Myths of Northern Europe*. Boston: Shambhala, 1994.

Mills, Harper George, et al., eds. *Yeats's "Vision" Papers. Vol. 2, The Automatic Scripts*. Iowa City: University of Iowa Press, 1992.

Montaigne, Michel de. *Essais*, vol. 1. Paris: Didot, 1907.

Montgomery, Charles. *The Shark God: Encounters with Ghosts and Ancestors in the South Pacific*. New York: HarperCollins, 2004.

Moss, Robert. *Active Dreaming*. Novato, CA: New World Library, 2011.

———. *The Boy Who Died and Came Back*. Novato, CA: New World Library, 2014.

———. *Conscious Dreaming*. New York: Crown, 1996.

———. *The Dreamer's Book of the Dead*. Rochester, VT: Destiny Books, 2005.

———. *Dreamgates: Exploring the Worlds of Soul, Imagination, and Life beyond Death*. Novato, CA: New World Library, 2010.

———. *Dreaming the Soul Back Home*. Novato, CA: New World Library, 2012.

———. *Dreaming True*. New York: Pocket Books, 2000.

———. *Dreamways of the Iroquois*. Rochester, VT: Destiny Books, 2005.

———. *Here, Everything Is Dreaming: Poems and Stories*. Albany, NY: Excelsior Editions, 2013.

———. *Mysterious Realities: A Dream Traveler's Tales from the Imaginal Realm*. Novato, CA: New World Library, 2018.

———. *The Secret History of Dreaming*. Novato, CA: New World Library, 2009.

———. *Sidewalk Oracles: Playing with Signs, Symbols, and Synchronicity in Everyday Life*. Novato, CA: New World Library, 2015.

———. *The Three "Only" Things: Tapping the Power of Dreams, Coincidence, and Imagination*. Novato, CA: New World Library, 2007.

Mouton, Alice. "Portent Dreams in Hittite Anatolia." In *Perchance to Dream: Dream Divination in the Bible and the Ancient Near East*, edited by Esther K. Hamori and Jonathan Stöckl. Atlanta: SBL Press, 2018.

Myers, F. W. H. *Human Personality and its Survival of Bodily Death.* 2 vols. London: Longmans, Green, 1903.

Nachmanovitch, Stephen. *Free Play: Improvisation in Life and Art.* New York: Jeremy P. Tarcher/Putnam, 1990.

Nasr, Seyyed Hossein. "Mulla Sadra: His Teachings." In *History of Islamic Philosophy,* edited by Seyyed Hossein Nasr and Oliver Leaman. London and New York: Routledge, 1996.

Nin, Anaïs. *The Diary of Anaïs Nin. Vol. 4, 1944–1947,* edited by Gunther Stulmann. Boston: Mariner Books, 1972.

O'Donohue, John. *Beauty: The Invisible Embrace.* New York: Harper Perennial, 2005.

O'Flaherty, Wendy Doniger. *Dreams, Illusion, and Other Realities.* Chicago: University of Chicago Press, 1984.

Oliver, Mary. *House of Light.* Boston: Beacon Press, 1990.

———. *Upstream: Selected Essays.* New York: Penguin, 2016.

Oppenheim, A. Leo. *The Interpretation of Dreams in the Ancient Near East.* Philadelphia: American Philosophical Society, 1956.

Pandolfo, Stefania. *Impasse of the Angels: Scenes from a Moroccan Space of Memory.* Chicago: University of Chicago Press, 1997.

Pearson, Carol D. *Persephone Rising: Awakening the Heroine Within.* New York: HarperOne, 2018.

Pert, Candace B. *Molecules of Emotion: The Science behind Body-Mind Medicine.* New York: Simon and Schuster, 1999.

Plotinus. *Complete Works.* Translated by Kenneth Sylvan Guthrie. 4 vols. London: George Bell, 1918.

Plutarch. "Concerning the Face Which Appears in the Orb of the Moon." In *Moralia,* vol. 12, translated by Harold Cherniss and William Helmbold. Cambridge, MA: Harvard University Press, 1995.

———. "Isis and Osiris." In *Moralia,* vol. 5, translated by F. C. Babbitt. Cambridge, MA: Harvard University Press, 1993.

Poirier, Sylvie. "'This Is Good Country, We Are Good Dreamers': Dreams and Dreaming in the Australian Western Desert." In Lohmann, *Dream Travelers,* 107–26.

Radin, Dean. *Entangled Minds: Extrasensory Experiences in a Quantum Reality.* New York: Paraview Pocket Books, 2006.

Raine, Kathleen. *The Inner Journey of the Poet.* New York: George Braziller, 1982.

————. *W. B. Yeats and the Learning of the Imagination*. Dallas: Dallas Institute Publications, 1999.

Renberg, Gil H. *Where Dreams May Come: Incubation Sanctuaries in the Greco-Roman World*. Leiden: Brill, 2017.

Roberts, Jane. *Dreams, "Evolution," and Value Fulfillment: A Seth Book*. Vol. 1. New York: Prentice Hall Press, 1988.

————. *The Education of Oversoul 7*. New York: Pocket Books, 1976.

————. *The Nature of Personal Reality*. New York: Bantam Books, 1980.

————. *Seth, Dreams, and Projections of Consciousness*. Walpole, NH: Stillpoint Publishing, 1986.

————. *Seth Speaks: The Eternal Validity of the Soul*. New York: Prentice Hall Press, 1987.

Rockwell, David. *Giving Voice to Bear: North American Indian Myths, Rituals, and Images of the Bear*. Niwot, CO: Roberts Rinehart, 1991.

Roseman, Marina. *Healing Sounds from the Malaysian Rainforest: Temiar Music and Medicine*. Berkeley: University of California Press, 1993.

Shulman, David, and Guy G. Stroumsa, eds. *Dream Cultures: Explorations in the Comparative History of Dreaming*. New York: Oxford University Press, 1999.

Simpson, Joe. *Touching the Void*. London: Vintage, 1997.

Smith, C. Michael. *Jung and Shamanism in Dialogue: Retrieving the Soul / Retrieving the Sacred*. Bloomington, IN: Trafford, 2007.

Stevens, Wallace. "Notes toward a Supreme Fiction." In *The Collected Poems of Wallace Stevens*. New York: Knopf, 2011.

Stevenson, Robert Louis. "A Chapter on Dreams." In *The Works of Robert Louis Stevenson*. London: Chatto and Windus, 1912, 16:177–89.

Stone, Ruth. "Fragrance." In *What Love Comes To: New and Selected Poems*. Port Townsend, WA: Copper Canyon Press, 2010.

Sumegi, Angela. *Dreamworlds of Shamanism and Tibetan Buddhism: The Third Place*. Albany: State University of New York Press, 2008.

Sveiby, Karl-Erik, and Tex Skuthorpe. *Treading Lightly: The Hidden Wisdom of the World's Oldest People*. Crows Nest, NSW: Allen and Unwin, 2006.

Synesius of Cyrene. *Essays and Hymns*. Translated by Augustine Fitzgerald. Oxford: Oxford University Press, 1930.

Szpakowska, Kasia Maria. *Behind Closed Eyes: Dreams and Nightmares in Ancient Egypt*. Swansea, UK: Classical Press of Wales, 2003.

———. "The Perception of Dreams and Nightmare in Ancient Egypt: Old Kingdom to Third Intermediate Period." PhD diss., University of California, Los Angeles, 2000.

Tagore, Rabindranath. *Sādhanā: The Realisation of Life*. London: Macmillan, 1914.

Tedlock, Barbara. *The Woman in the Shaman's Body*. New York: Bantam, 2005.

Thwaites, Reuben Gold, ed. *Jesuit Relations and Allied Documents: Travels and Explorations of the Jesuit Missionaries in New France, 1610–1791*. 73 vols. Cleveland: Burrows Brothers, 1896–1901.

Tolkien, J. R. R. *"The Monsters and the Critics" and Other Essays*. New York: HarperCollins, 2007.

Tolle, Eckhart. *The Power of Now: A Guide to Spiritual Enlightenment*. Novato, CA: New World Library, 2004.

Tolstoy, Nikolai. *The Quest for Merlin*. Boston: Little, Brown, 1985.

Toussaint, Maurice. *Metz à l'époque gallo-romaine*. Metz, France: Paul Even, 1948.

Townsley, Graham. "Song Paths: The Ways and Means of Yaminahua Shamanic Knowledge." In *L'Homme* 33, no. 126–28 (1993): 449–68.

Travers, P. L. *What the Bee Knows: Reflections on Myth, Symbol and Story*. London: Thorson, 1990.

Turner, Toko-pa. *Belonging*. Salt Spring Island, BC: Her Own Room Press, 2017.

Vitebsky, Piers. *The Reindeer People: Living with Animals and Spirits in Siberia*. Boston: Houghton Mifflin, 2005.

von Franz, Marie-Louise. *The Golden Ass of Apuleius: The Liberation of the Feminine in Man*. Boston and London: Shambhala, 1992.

———. *Projection and Re-collection in Jungian Psychology*. Translated by William H. Kennedy. LaSalle, IL, and London: Open Court, 1990.

Wang, Robert. *Qabalistic Tarot: A Textbook of Mystical Philosophy*. York Beach, ME: Samuel Weiser, 1992.

Wells, H. G.. *Selected Stories of H. G. Wells*. Edited by Ursula K. Le Guin. New York: Modern Library, 2004.

Wiles, David. *Greek Theatre Performance: An Introduction*. Cambridge: Cambridge University Press, 2000.

Wolkstein, Diane, and Samuel Noah Kramer. *Inanna, Queen of Heaven: Her Stories and Hymns from Sumer*. New York: Harper & Row, 1983.

Woolger, Roger J. *Healing Your Past Lives: Exploring the Many Lives of the Soul*. Boulder, CO: Sounds True, 2010.

———. *Other Lives, Other Selves: A Jungian Psychotherapist Discovers Past Lives*. New York: Bantam Books, 1988.

Yeats, W. B. *Autobiography*. New York: Collier Books, 1965.

———. *Collected Poems*. London: Macmillan, 1958.

———. *Essays and Introductions*. New York: Collier Books, 1977.

———. *Is the Order of R. R. et A. C. to Remain a Magical Order?* London: Mandrake Press, 1901.

———. *Mythologies*. New York: Macmillan, 1959.

Resources

Robert Moss website: www.mossdreams.com
The Robert Moss Blog: www.mossdreams.blogspot.com
Robert Moss's radio show *Way of the Dreamer*: www.healthylife.net

Online Courses

Robert leads many popular online courses for the Shift Network, bringing together creative dreamers from all over the world map: https://theshiftnetwork.com.

Video Series on Active Dreaming

The Way of the Dreamer with Robert Moss is available for download from Psyche Productions: www.psycheproductions.net.

Shamanic Drumming Recording

The digital audio recording *Wings for the Journey: Shamanic Drumming for Dream Travelers* is available for download from Psyche Productions: www.psycheproductions.net.

Audio Course on Active Dreaming

Dream Gates: A Journey into Active Dreaming is available for download from Sounds True: https://www.soundstrue.com/products /dream-gates.

Please note: This audio series is an independent production with different content from the book *Dreamgates* (which was written afterward).

Facebook Pages

Robert Moss Books: www.facebook.com/RobertMossBooks
Active Dreaming community page: www.facebook.com/activedreaming

About the Author

Robert Moss has been a dream traveler since doctors pronounced him clinically dead in a hospital in Hobart, Tasmania, when he was three years old. From his experiences in many worlds, he created his School of Active Dreaming, his original synthesis of modern dreamwork and ancient shamanic and mystical practices for journeying to realms beyond the physical. He leads popular workshops all over the world, including a three-year training for teachers of Active Dreaming and online courses for the Shift Network. A former lecturer in ancient history at the Australian National University, he is a *New York Times* bestselling novelist, poet, journalist, and independent scholar. His many books on dreaming, shamanism, and imagination include *Conscious Dreaming, The Secret History of Dreaming, Dreaming the Soul Back Home, The Boy Who Died and Came Back, Sidewalk Oracles,* and *Mysterious Realities: A Dream Traveler's Tales from the Imaginal Realm*. He has lived in upstate New York since he received a message from a red-tailed hawk under an old white oak.

www.mossdreams.com